Chuck Klosterman
and Philosophy

Popular Culture and Philosophy® Series Editor: George A. Reisch

For full details of all Popular Culture and Philosophy® books, visit www.opencourtbooks.com.

Popular Culture and Philosophy®

Chuck Klosterman and Philosophy

The Real and the Cereal

Edited by
SETH VANNATTA

OPEN COURT
Chicago and La Salle, Illinois

Volume 65 in the series, Popular Culture and Philosophy ®, edited by George A. Reisch

To order books from Open Court, call toll-free 1-800-815-2280, or visit our website at www.opencourtbooks.com.

Open Court Publishing Company is a division of Carus Publishing Company.

Copyright © 2012 by Carus Publishing Company

First printing 2012

Printed and bound in the United States of America.

Library of Congress Cataloging-in-Publication Data

Chuck Klosterman and philosophy : the real and the cereal / edited by Seth Vannatta.
     p. cm. — (Popular culture and philosophy ; v. 65)
   Includes bibliographical references (p.   ) and index.
   ISBN 978-0-8126-9762-9 (trade paper : alk. paper)
   1. Klosterman, Chuck, 1972—-Philosophy. 2. Klosterman, Chuck, 1972—-Criticism and interpretation. 3. Popular culture—Philosophy. 4. Culture—Philosophy. I. Vannatta, Seth, 1973-
  CB19.C474 2012
  781.66—dc23

                          2012000622

Contents

Chuck at the Crossroads of Low and High Culture

SETH VANNATTA

We all have guilty pleasures, don't we? During the summer of 1993, my guilty pleasure was watching *Saved by the Bell* reruns. That summer I bussed tables in Vail, Colorado. After the lunch shift I would swing by the video store, pick up a classic movie, a Hitchcock or an Academy award winner from long ago, get in a quick jog, and then veg on the couch for an hour and a half watching four episodes featuring Samuel Powers and Zack Morris. (The middle thirty minutes covered two episodes on different channels).

Somewhere in North Dakota, Chuck Klosterman (the first syllable rhymes with 'coast') was doing the same thing. But for Chuck, this was no guilty pleasure. Nothing more lofty or altruistic was being postponed by this ninety-minute routine. He wasn't even postponing his consumption of high art, watching *Citizen Kane*, for instance. I know this because Klosterman wants to rid the phrase "guilty pleasure" from English diction. He thinks it's a phony category of entertainment.

The contributors to this book do not agree as to whether Chuck is right that "guilty pleasure" is an empty expression. But I don't think they view reading Klosterman as a guilty pleasure, even if we think that concept is one worth keeping—or even if we think Chuck is lying to himself about the status of guilty pleasures.

Chuck's distaste for the phrase "guilty pleasure" is really just a suspicion that either the distinction between the street paved for "serious" work in philosophy and the one for spontaneous riffing on pop culture is bogus or the paint used to mark the direction of traffic has so faded as to be indiscernible.

Some serious-minded people have tried to issue philosophical traffic tickets to Klosterman. He's been accused of misinterpreting Jacques Derrida, of all violations! In the face of this accusation, Chuck pled guilty, telling his self-proclaimed high-culture copper that he had never read Derrida. When Klosterman did peruse the French philosopher's work, he was doubtful that his accuser had ever read Derrida either.

Klosterman wanders the streets without paying any attention to the rules commanded by high culture sovereigns. He follows his interests and inspirations, come what may. The contributors to this book have read some Derrida and lots of Klosterman, and they've consumed their fair share of *Saved by the Bell* reruns. (At least I have). In doing so we find ourselves at a strange intersection where high meets low—Kierkegaard meets KISS or Baudrillard meets Britney Spears.

Confronting the work of Chuck Klosterman at this entertaining intersection forces us to ask whether the roads that constitute two forms of culture, the high and the low, are real or imaginary. If these one-way thoroughfares are real, then they only intersect once if at all, and their crossing each other is potentially dangerous. Violent accidents await, and we need some traffic rules to prevent disaster. But if these roads are fake, then the intersection is really infinitely inflated, allowing a continuous flow of traffic, spontaneously producing new travel patterns and rules of engagement.

The contributors to this book bring some philosophical lens to Klosterman's project, as if to highlight what is already there, or to reflect on the same subject matter as Klosterman in a more consciously philosophical manner. This book is a celebration of the idea of engaging in culture in a thoughtful, reflective way. We are amenable to violating the supposed traffic rules maintaining the one-way streets of high and low culture. We are hopeful that such violations will produce new ideas about the meaning of pop culture and more.

The intersection of pop culture and philosophy is fortunate to have Klosterman as one of its libertarian traffic cops. But Chuck's a traveler too, and in reading his reflections on the meaning of music, movies, celebrity status, TV, and video games, we ask a lot of questions. How are our relationships affected by our inundation in pop culture and the multiplication of media? What do pop-culture trends say about our values? How do we rank our pleasures, goods, and interests if we're willing to break down the distinctions between high and low art? What's good, what's beautiful, and what's true?

Most importantly, how is our access to the good, the beautiful, and the true a refraction of our relationship to pop culture? If we can't glimpse behind the veils of irony, appearance, persona, and inauthenticity, what are we left with? Are we left only with phoniness, cynicism, and disenchantment, or can we recover a modicum of earnestness, reality, self-understanding, and authenticity in and through our favorite bands, sports teams, video games, movies, and TV programs?

Chuck tells us: "In and of itself, nothing really matters. What matters is that nothing is ever 'in and of itself'" (*Sex, Drugs, and Cocoa Puffs,* Preface). With or without Immanuel Kant's *noumena-phenomena* distinction in mind, Chuck reminds us that we seek access to the in-itself, to the real and the true, but we cannot escape our own perspectives. We are always unconsciously applying the categories of our understanding to the objects we engage with, and those objects include rock bands, video games, cultural icons, and sports teams. Nothing Klosterman writes pretends to be in-and-of-itself. Chuck doesn't pretend to write from a privileged perspective or from a foundational one. He writes in the middle of things and lets his interaction with the pop culture generate its own concepts. Then he uses those as formalized conceptual schemes to organize his pop culture realm. In doing so, he uses pop culture as a prism to do a philosophical biography.

In *Sex, Drugs, and Cocoa Puffs*, Chuck writes about a Guns N' Roses Tribute band, Paradise City, reflecting on the meaning of a band whose sole purpose is to efface their own identities in order to imitate the equally constructed identities of another band. In doing so, he shows us the layers of self, persona, and constructed identity not only in performing rock bands, but in ourselves as well. In *Killing Yourself to Live*, he travels across the country visiting the places where famous rock musicians died, and the story turns into a long reflection about the meaning of dying and its relationship to the meaning of rock stars' careers and memories, its relationship to love and sex, and ultimately its relationship to our own lives.

Klosterman writes in the space between inauthentically following the crowd, disingenuously attempting not to be a crowd follower by some self-stylized, already co-opted way of rejecting the mainstream, and the existential project of recovering a sense of self in and through our involvement with the stuff of pop culture. That space and that project of self-understanding is one strand of thematic unity in his writing. This is a more meaningful theme because he's so obsessed with death and dying. Living with the possibility of our own deaths is more authentic than the retreat from that possibility. Seeing the dying in the living is one of the ways I think Klosterman is recovering himself and helping his readers do the same.

Klosterman produces literature that challenges the traditional road rules of culture criticism. Klosterman champions the low culture of women's love of John Cusack and Coldplay and my generation's fondness for Kelly Kapowski. Chuck subversively undermines the travel tenets of culture criticism by suspending the distance and hierarchies between those who travel the supposed paths of high and low culture.

We find this liberating.

The varied contributors to this book follow Chuck's lead, navigating the intersection between Socrates and *Saved by the Bell* in a way that breaks down the strict distinction between supposedly high and low culture. The authors are fans and critics, devotees and doubters, but we're all inspired by Chuck's come-what-may mantra. We celebrate the logic of Klosterman's writing, his endless string of resemblances that compose his thinking about the soundtrack of his and our lives.

Chuck has reflected on our musings in the book, as he has written the epilogue. Of course this just adds another dimension to the meta-character of the book. Chuck writes on pop culture. We write on Chuck writing on pop culture. Chuck writes on us writing on him writing on pop culture.

As you read what follows, know that you are at a crossroads. The supposed high road traveled by the Immanuel Kants of the distant past and the supposed low road traveled by the Pamela Andersons of the recent past have intersected, and we only have Chuck Klosterman, the western canon of philosophy, and the stuff of pop culture to help us navigate them. We'll break a few rules along the way because we're not sure if the roads are real or not.

We're also not sure whether or not our libertine attitude is a guilty pleasure. Read on, and decide for yourselves.

BOOK I

Rock City
Reflections

1

In the Fly's Eye

RANDALL E. AUXIER

There's a spectacular moment in Chuck Klosterman's novel *Downtown Owl* in which he lists the simultaneous, individual thoughts of twenty-two teenagers who are stuck in a boring English class. The teacher has just asked them what it is like to live in a society like Orwell's *Nineteen Eighty-Four*. The students were thinking, and I quote:

1) How awesome it would feel to be sleeping.

2) Unaffordable denim skirts. Fuck.

3) What it would feel like to be asleep.

4) Sleeping.

5) The lack of cool guys living in Owl, at least when compared to how the guys in Oakes were described by a cousin in a recent telephone conversation.

6) An empty room, filled only with white light and silence. . . .

7) The iconography of Teresa Cumberland, chiefly the paradox of why no one else seems to realize that she is a total backstabbing bitch who talks shit about everybody in school and then acts as if she is somehow the victim whenever anyone calls her on it.

8) The potential upside of being comatose.

9) Theoretical ways to make a Pontiac Grand Prix more boss, such as painting a panther on the hood or moving the entire steering column and floor pedals to the passenger side, which would likely

3

be impossible without a cherry picker and extremely expensive tools.

10) The meaning (and linguistic derivation) of the phrase "Gunter glieben glauchen globen," as heard during the preface to Def Leppard's "Rock of Ages."

11) Being asleep, possibly inside a ski lodge.

12) Robot cows.

13) That one eighth grader with the insane tits, and the degree to which it would be life-changing to tickle her when she was naked. Was her name Judy? That seemed about right.

14) Sleeping.

15) My boyfriend has amazing hair.

16) I wish Grandma would just hurry up and die.

17) Nobody knows I have a warm can of Pepsi in my locker.

18) The carpeting in Jordan Brewer's semi-unfinished basement that smells like popcorn and would provide an excellent surface for sleeping.

19) The moral ramifications of stealing beer from a church rectory, which—while probably sinful—would just be so fucking easy. I mean, it's almost like they *want* you to steal it.

20) Being gay.

21) The prospect of a person being able to ride on the back of a grizzly bear, assuming the bear was properly muzzled. . . .

22) Firing a crossbow into the neck of John Laidlaw [the teacher] while he received fellatio from Tina McAndrew . . . (*Downtown Owl*, pp. 70–71)

It seems simple when it's finished, but I find this list very impressive. I'm pretty sure that not many people could really pull this off (and I know I couldn't). It's not only the wide variety of perspectives here; it's also their amazingly realistic infantility. (That's not a word, but I like it.) There is a complexity to Chuck's immaturity that is, in itself, a sort of maturity. It's like what would happen to a playful, fruity wine after twenty years in the bottle. No, never mind, bad analogy. Let's see . . . It's sort of like why *The Big Lebowski* is still funny. But that doesn't explain anything, it's the *same* thing. My point is: How can someone who is thirty-six even *remember* so many semi-mindless states of consciousness from so long ago? In a sense, he must still *be* there, or in this case, be *then*.

Maybe you're like me: if you really work at remembering some of the kids you went to school with—you'll probably need your yearbook, and your Facebook—it might be possible, with extreme effort, to come up with a list fifteen percent as good as this one. It just has an elegance, an economy, and—dare I say it?—even a sort of perfection. But then again, a housefly is also perfect in its own way, and this list is more like looking through the eye of a fly than your standard binocular literary demi-god. And I think that's part of what we like about the Dude (Chuck, not Jeff Bridges). This list of future Darwin Award winners (keep reading their story; it ends rather badly) is low culture at its, well, I was going to say "pinnacle," but that seems wrong. A pinnacle of the low? I think not. Klosterman's achievement is sloshy and smelly. This is a veritable octojohn of low culture.

An "octojohn" is an octagonal outhouse with eight holes back-to back, all excrement being deposited in a single underground concrete tank. This disgusting idea was realized on the campground of the Quiet Valley Ranch in Texas, where the Kerrville Folk Festival is held. Two double-octojohns (eight holes for women, eight for men) were constructed in 2001. This is an idea worthy of anyone who doesn't take any shit and certainly freely gives others shit. These architectural marvels are slated for demolition. When destroyed, there will no longer be a job for the hippie volunteer who "stirs the tanks," an unanticipated necessity to prevent massive "backsplash" due to the shape of the tanks and the way that shit doesn't always flow downhill unless the hill is pretty damn steep or the shit is pretty thin.

Example of a
Kerrville Octojohn

Since you're a Klosterman fan, you already know that he uses lists all the time. It's a serious part of his writing style. He not only uses lists to economize in communicating information. He sorts and orders possibilities, he sequences events, he ranks things for their quality (or lack of it), and most of all, he plays with our minds by displaying the baroque and twisted order of his own, his own . . . peculiar idiom. I gotta be honest here. I don't know Chuck, but I know he was raised Catholic, and reading almost anything he writes I imagine myself as the young priest in the booth and this special sinner has made a bet with his pals that he can suck me in with his bullshit until I'm actually laughing, and even get me to ask him for further elaboration on the details of these sins. "And how did you do that to a fish on Friday . . . er, ummm . . . my son?"

Making Shit Up

It might surprise you to learn that philosophers have always, always used lists to great effect. Most of the greatest works in the history of Western philosophy contain lists, and the lists aren't just sitting there innocently recording the existence of things. When you make a list, there is almost always an "immanent order," meaning that something you value highly lies under the list. Let's say you want to rank the five greatest rock bands of all time. That's easy. It goes like this:

1. **Stones**

2. **Beatles**

3. **Who**

4. **Pink Floyd**

5. **Zeppelin**

In that order. There is no doubt about this list (even though Chuck puts Zeppelin third on such a list, but that's objectively false; anyone can see Zeppelin is fifth). This is not my opinion, it's the way the universe actually *is*. But the word "greatest"— what does that mean? In this case it means lots of things. Since you're an intelligent person, I know you won't argue with the bands I included on the list, or even with my ranking. But so many stories can be told about why it is right. Let us celebrate the list.

The Stones have to be first because, as Chuck points out in *Downtown Owl*, it's the only band that provides a complete and nutritious aural diet (Chuck's character Vance Druid only listens to the Stones, and Vance is a hero, or as close to a hero as anyone can be in a book by the depressed for the depressed). Ah, now it comes clear. The operative factor in the order of this list is "completeness" of the music. This not only involves variety in sounds, but also variety in forms. There has to be blues, folk, country, and pop, even a bit of disco (for the same reason you put horseradish on a reuben—it's not that you like it, it's just that you need some pain with the pleasure), and it all needs to be cool.

My list also requires that the musicians resist the urge to indulge themselves, to the greatest extent they can manage (I mean, they *are* musicians, so you have to be realistic about this), and instead give the audience what *it* is hungry for. Completeness is measured from the side of the listener, not the high-end critic, not other musicians and producers; it's about the guy on the street who's smart enough to know the difference between what's cool and what sucks. So coolness is immanent in the list, recognizing that coolness has infinitely many forms and expressions, but is easily spoiled by any hint of self-reflexiveness. A person who is *trying* to be cool merely for the sake of being perceived as cool, is automatically not only not cool, but actually uncool. But it's okay to try to be cool because it's cool to be cool. That's a sort of piety to coolness itself. I mean, Elvis and Dylan and Springsteen are all cool, and they care about being cool, but they never cared whether *you* think they're cool because that would be petty and silly and small, and who the fuck are you anyway? And that's cool. Like my list.

I could go on, but maybe this is enough to make my point. Musical Completeness is really the factor in the universe that determines greatness, or should I say, the "magnitude" of a rock'n'roll band. It consists of:

A. Factors Determined Relative to Ordinary Listeners

1. Variety in rocking sounds

2. Variety in rocking forms

3. Low on the Register of Musical and Lyrical Self-indulgence

4. Coolness to Suckiness Ratio

B. Factors Determined by High-end Rock Critics and Musicians = 0

C. The up-chuck's factor, which is a certain unexpected capacity to resist cynicism while remaining thoroughly and totally snide. (This's why the Beatles come in second. John Lenon passes this test, but Paul McCartney does not.)

Now, I'm totally making up this shit, but that doesn't mean it's just shit that I made up. We could have, like, a pretty serious discussion about all this. It wouldn't lead anywhere, but who says we're trying to *get* somewhere? And so I'll confess, and you be my priest: I really don't know how I know that's the right order for greatest rock bands, but I do know it, and I will try my best, within the bounds of civility to make up a story that may not convince you of the truth, but will at least make you see why I can't really make this list in any other way. And that brings us to a surprising point.

A Firm Right Hand

I gave that example to try to show that there is "immanent order" in lists—usually it's a kind of value judgment, that something is *better* than something else. It's the immanent order that enables us to *make sense* of the list as a list of things that belong together. There can be lots of different ways to tell the story of a list and what kind of sense it makes, but every story you tell will only be partial. Some people call this "intensive order," which is just a way of saying that you can't ever place the parts side by side well enough to analyze them fully. So I could write a book on the Stones, Beatles, Who, Floyd and Zeppelin, five chapters, and it could be like the best book ever written on rock music, and there would still be plenty more to say, and other ways to understand that list.

So when you look at a list, you sort of "get" something, and the something you "get," the sense it makes, may be a very precise (or even very vague) sense of order. That order is based on some kind of value. If I give you a list like this:

eggs, milk, potatoe chips, soda, pretzels, dog food, card for mom's birthday

You know a shopping list when you see one, but if you're the right age, you also know it might be Dan Quayle's shopping list, and if so, you learned some things that weren't necessarily intended but that are immanent in the list (like, that Dan has a dog and is the spawn of a human mother, probably). The value judgments in the list are even more telling, which is that Dan probably likes junk food. No one in this day and age can look at such a list and fail to think "that man should eat better." In this case, the value placed on an item is expressed by its inclusion on the list in light of the obvious alternatives:

sprouts, chard, free trade coffee, cage free organic eggs, whole grain crackers, local cheese

This is not Dan Quayle's grocery list, or indeed a list made by any Republican. Republicans do not eat or value these items. But I can tell you a lot about the person who does make that list. That person feels guilty about eating animal products and is trying to minimize her environmental footprint, and believes she really ought to be a vegan but just can't quite get there and is tortured by her failure to live more simply. See how it works?

Even when you're just setting things in a time sequence, like Beatles, Stones, Who, Zeppelin, Floyd, you still choose one value over another. My list of bands records the sequence of the greatest impact on culture by each group. If I valued the sequence of their founding over that of their impact, the list would have been Beatles, Stones, Who, Floyd, and Zeppelin. Both lists make sense, and one could be mistaken for the other. If I just put that first list out there and asked you what was the immanent order, you might say "Date they were founded." You might say "That's a ranking of your favorite bands." You might say "Oh, that's just a list of famous English rock bands from the Sixties."

All of these would be sort of true, but not "necessary." And all I mean by that is you can feel in your bowels that even though what you have said may be *accurate*, as far as it goes, it isn't really "true." Sure, those are my favorite bands, but why *that* order and why am I listing my favorite bands? You're just guessing. And those guesses aren't really compelling, they don't seem to fit the list the way a key fits a lock. But when I say "that is the sequence in which they became famous," you'll feel something a little different, a little tug on your brain that stretches down into your gut, and says "that's *it*," or at least, "that feels complete; it would explain everything I see here." That tug is an experience of "necessity," and I am here to tell you, friends and enemies, that philosophers like to be tugged in just that way, and they are pretty frustrated when they can't get any of that necessity action tugging on them. No tug = unhappy philosophers. They are more pitiful than Chuck when he's whining about being dumped again. Yes, what philosophers like is the firm right hand of necessity, tugging on their fleshy cortices 'til the pudding congeals.

We will get back to lists and how they do what they do, but I need to make a little detour through your gonads first. (Yes, women have gonads, too, but I do not claim any of them will enjoy this essay. If they do, they could give me a call.)

TMI

I like Chuck's writing in spite of his narcissistic whining. It's not the narcissism—I mean, I like Hunter S. Thompson. And I don't mind whining, as such, because I like my own writing. But what if Hunter S. Thompson was from North Dakota and actually never did anything truly stupid? He would have an exaggerated idea of how interesting his love life is and would have nothing better to do than to spread it embarrassingly all over the pages of his books, which is what I am talking about.

I can't possibly be the only fan of the Chuckster who has regularly felt that he has a TMI problem. I know so many things about Chuck that I didn't need to know, didn't want to know, and wish I could forget. I'm also suspicious. I have a feeling that much of his narrative has been exaggerated and otherwise fictionalized for literary effect, and sometimes he says as much. He encourages me to think this in the first part of *Eating the Dinosaur*, where he basically confesses to lying about things he doesn't even need to lie about. So in any given instance, I don't know whether to be pissed that he told me something he really did that disgusts me, or whether his twisted imagination created it from tamer or less offensive images, and goddammit I hate being treated as a fool. I do not thrive on this aspect of the Klosterman literary legacy. I put up with it. Why? Well, I am sitting here with dozens of images in my memory that I wish had never appeared before my mind, but I kept reading, didn't I?

Plato actually talks about this problem. In the *Republic* he has Socrates tell this story:

> Leontius, the son of Aglaion, was going up from the Piraeus under the outside of the North Wall when he noticed corpses lying by the public executioner. He desired to look, but at the same time he was disgusted and made himself turn away; and for a while he struggled and covered his face. But finally, overpowered by the desire, he opened his eyes wide, ran toward the corpses and said: "Look you damned wretches, take your fill of the fair sight." (439e–440a)

Chuck teaches us the lessons of Leontius a little more gently, although he depends on our willingness to rubberneck. It is hard not to see the same basic story in Chuck's journey to the death sites of so many great rockers in *Killing Yourself to Live*. And his conclusion that he thought he might learn something from this, but really didn't, seems also like a gentle reproach to himself for thinking that some wisdom might be hidden in having a look. Part of us knows going to those sites is just TMI, and part of us just craves a peek anyway.

Socrates brings us back around to our story when he adds: "And in many other places don't we notice that, when desires force someone contrary to calculation, he reproaches himself and his spirit against that in him which is doing the forcing, and, just as though there were two parties at faction, such a man's spirit becomes the ally of speech" (440a–b)? This is the tug of necessity working with both the right hand of reason, and getting a little strange from the left hand of desire. But the right hand doesn't know what the left hand is doing, and the result is that one utters "WTF?"

That little feeling that you just have to say something, or write something, is what happens when that nice little tug on the brain arrives in your gonads and then chucks itself up. You sit there spilling your guts to anyone who will listen and before you know it, you've written or spoken your own little version of *Sex, Drugs, and Cocoa-Puffs,* and now the world knows and you can't take it back. You've tipped your hand, revealed your unconscious crap; in fact, you've become a living breathing shit-canon.

The Recoil of the Shit-Canon

So what? Nothing to be ashamed of. We're all as twisted up and out of control as Chuck, right? Sometimes, at least? Come on, be honest for once. Reminds me of a story from Steven Tyler's recent autobiography. He says:

> Early on in the band [Aerosmith] when I was still Jung and Freudened, I'd blurt out my sexual fantasies. I thought I was just being honest and saying what was on everybody's mind, but I made the mistake of talking this stuff in front of the band's wives. You know, stuff like how I liked doing it with two girls—twins preferably. "You're disgusting Steve" one of the band wives blurted out. . . . I'd say "What? Boys don't like threesomes? Don't all boys dream about that?" And I didn't expect my band mate to say, "Oh, yeah, I'm sorry, baby, that is my fantasy. And, honey, while Steven's brought up the subject of sexual fantasies . . ." What was I thinking? No man is going to tell his wife what he really likes. Because when he gets home, she'll Lorena Bobbitt his ass and he'll never find his licorice nib again. (*Does the Noise in My Head Bother You?*, p. 141)

Tyler was over sixty when he wrote this, and even he has learned a few things with age. One thing is, well, the nads never lie, but the truth is a damn poor guide to life in our lousy world. Desire is at the bottom of every list, and you'll never have the key to the list until you understand which desires are driving it, but the key that fits the door is never as simple as saying what you want. But young men don't get this, and old men learn it only from the recoil of the shit canon. Say what you want and see what happens. In Tyler's case . . . well never mind what all happened to him, but in Chuck's case, it's TMI and the effect is pathetic, and the recoil is that he eventually grew up. Sort of.

And what does it mean to outgrow the urge to say whatever wells up from your nads? It means you internalize the struggle

Plato describes in the anecdote of Leontius and his rubber-necking. We learn, eventually, to sublimate our urges, to schematize those images and sort them into complex forms of order, to grade and evaluate them according to their propriety, their attainability, their consistency with our previous choices and promises, and most of all, with respect to what others will think of us for valuing this rather than that, or that above this. When you're pondering a mate for life, as Chuck does throughout *Killing Yourself to Live*, one thing you do ponder is what does the choice of this person rather than that one say to the world about *me*, about what *I* value? There's no hiding it. Choose a pretty one and we know something about you. Choose a funny one and we know something else. Choose a cold one and we know a third thing. The recoil of the shit canon works thus: we will know what is really on your list by looking at the shit you kept and the shit you threw away (or that threw *you* away).

Intensive Magnitudes

A philosopher named Immanuel Kant (1724–1804) has something to say here. Most people think he's the third best philosopher in Western history, so if Plato is the Stones and Aristotle is the Beatles, Kant would be the Who. (If you're curious, G.W.F. Hegel is Pink Floyd and Friedrich Nietzsche is Led Zeppelin.) You can map lists onto one another, by the way, using some aspect of the immanent order in one list to clarify (or confuse) another list. And if you ever figure out the meaning of the sequence of numbers and letters in the first chapter of *Eating the Dinosaur*, please tell me what the hell it is. Anyway, I was going to talk about Kant for a minute. But that reminds me that I wanted to say something about how annoying Chuck's digressions are. So now I said it and can get back to Kant. Except when the digression is in the middle of something I'm bored with. In that case, it may be welcome. But I'm not bored with Kant, so I'll talk about that if I can remember what I was going to say.

Oh, right. Kant explained the difference between extensive and intensive magnitudes. You have probably heard this idea before, or even thought of it yourself, but here's the skinny. An extensive magnitude is a way of relating the parts of something to the whole, where the whole can be divided so that the parts perfectly add up to the whole, without remainder, and the whole can be broken down into those parts while still remaining the same whole. For example, there are a hundred cents in a dollar. Take a hundred pennies and that just *is* a dollar, or change a dollar for two rolls of pennies and you *still* have a dollar (even if nobody wants it now). Extensive magnitudes allow us to substitute the whole for the collection of its parts or vice-versa. If you have all the parts necessary for building a replica of the plane that went down with Buddy Holly aboard, you functionally have the plane, in the extensive sense. The fact that you'll have to put it together to start your museum of rock deaths is beside the point.

But there's another way of looking at the magnitude of things in the world. Some things have parts and are made of their parts, but somehow the parts taken alone don't add up to the whole. If I take that same dollar and I ask what it will buy, you could give me an extensive answer—a list of everything in the world that is priced at a dollar or less. Or you could give me an intensive answer: "Hey bud, you can get whatever someone will give you for it." That is an indefinite list, and highly contextual. In some situations, like when you're lost in the woods in Mississippi, a dollar isn't worth anything at all. In other cases, the guy with a dollar might be able to save the day, say, when the cute girl in line for Lady Gaga tickets is a dollar short and her credit card just got declined, and a dollar gets you her phone number as well as an appreciative flutter of the lashes. And what is *that* worth? Well, easily it's worth a dollar, but not in the sense of a hundred pennies. It's almost like there are two different dollars, the one that consists of a hundred pennies and the one that's worth whatever you can get for it, and they're the same dollar, but considered differently.

Now Kant says that not everything in the world has an extensive magnitude, but everything that truly exists does have an intensive magnitude. So there are some real things that you just can't break into their parts and still have the same whole, but everything real has an intensive magnitude nevertheless. This is a big idea. I have a hard time getting my head around it, but to give an example of something that has an intensive magnitude but no extensive magnitude: an idea. There are infinitely many perspectives on an idea, but no collection of these will tell you everything about that idea. An idea has potentially infinite effects in the world. It doesn't exist at just one place or at one time. Ideas show up when they show up, and they spread in mysterious ways, and you cannot measure it with surveys or tools or even with other ideas.

A Rare Moment of Sobriety

I want to remind you of two of Chuck's lists from *Downtown Owl*, one primarily intensive, one mainly extensive and both are very effective. There is no reason to get all happy and punchy over intensive magnitudes. They are rich and suggestive and they bear most of the deeper meanings in life, but they are also ambiguous and frustrating. And extensive magnitudes, while they feel cold and mechanical, have the sweet finality of fact. A good map gets you where you're going because of its extensive fidelity. The last thing you would want for navigation is a road map with an intensive order.

In the first list, one of our three main characters, Julia, a twenty-two-year-old schoolteacher, now in her first year in Owl, North Dakota, is having a conversation with Vance Druid (the guy who only listens to the Stones). It's the first conversation they have had when both were sober. She's pretty sure she has a crush on him, and here is how Chuck reports, no, *lists* the conversation:

> WHAT SHE SAID: So . . . tell me . . . how do you spend your non-drinking hours? Are you a farmer too? Everyone I meet is a farmer.
>
> *What she meant:* I don't know anything about you. You look like every other guy in town, you don't talk very much, and you don't seem to do anything except drink. *But I suspect you are different.* Somehow you seem unlike everyone else I've met in this community, even though there is no tangible evidence that would suggest my theory is valid. This is my gamble. So here is an opportunity for you to describe yourself in a manner that will confirm my suspicion and possibly make me love you forever, mostly because I am searching for any reason to increase the likelihood of that possibility.

WHAT HE SAID: Yeah, I farm with my two brothers. It's their operation really. I'm basically just a hired hand. It's not bad, though. It's fine. I enjoy it.

What he meant: I was my father's third son. When my father died, the ownership of the farm went to my oldest brother, because that's how it always works. I own nothing in this world.

WHAT SHE SAID: What kind of farm is it? Do you raise any animals?

What she hoped to imply: I will talk to you about things that don't interest me at all. Just be different from everyone else I've met in this town. It doesn't matter how you're different. I'm flexible.

WHAT HE SAID: We raise bison. (pp. 112–13)

Following this, the entire remainder of the chapter reports a three-minute conversation (requiring seventeen pages) with the long subtext of each remark made explicit. It gives three perspectives on the same conversation at once. The first is what you would hear if you were a fly on the wall—the extensive conversation, in which the conversation is equal to the words exchanged in the order they were said. But the second and third perspectives, no less real, belong to a larger intensive whole. When we are given what each person is thinking that the other person doesn't know, we begin to see the same conversation in wider horizon. And there are at least three more perspectives to consider:

1. **Chuck's perspective as the writer of the dialogue— why he chooses the words he does and not some others**

2. **Chuck's intentions as the author—what he is trying to communicate, or what he wants the reader to understand as a result of reading these words and not others**

3. **The reader's perspective on these words, which includes attitudes, thoughts, and a whole complex of responses, like, why is Klosterman reporting the conversation this way?**

Well, this chapter of that book was an idea Chuck had for conveying a few moments, and maybe he thought a lot about the idea or maybe he just tossed it off one night when he was stoned, but either way, it was an idea. It was a possibility for taking an extensive conversation and pushing forward some of its intensive values, those that are immanent in the list itself. You wouldn't read a book that didn't do this in some way or another. But there are lots of ways to do it. Chuck's idea was just a little more stripped down and quirky.

Note that Julia started out looking for the very thing I explained from the start of this chapter. She had a suspicion that Vance was different and she wanted to feel that tug of necessity, that feeling of confirmation that her theory was right. But intensive relations *never satisfy that desire.* That is why philosophers like extensive relations better. Intensive relations open out on the wide world, and they don't deliver finished concepts and certainties. They keep our imaginations reaching into the realm of possibilities. As this chapter proceeds, we're frustrated that Julia and Vance are so close to really connecting with each other, but in the end, they mainly just miss why the other person was saying what was actually said. So, the conversation didn't quite unfold the way Julia had hoped, but the ambiguities remaining were due to the fact that the extensive aspect of the conversation didn't reveal much of the intensive order.

It's worth pausing over the idea that when you think you want something, you should consider whether you want it extensive or intensive. If it's the first, that isn't hard to get in the world. But it doesn't satisfy anyone for very long. The having of an extensive value is less fulfilling than the wanting of it. The longing for an intensive relation to something is intangible but probably deeper and more real. I have thought that Chuck's constant waffling over his relationships seem to say something about a confusion he may have had when he was younger about the extensive characteristics of his lady friends. He sat around making lists and over-thinking his connections, but the gals who put up with him always seem to have understood what he didn't get. Love has extensive characteristics, signs of its existence, but it isn't something we can commit to a list: How do I love thee? Let me not endeavor to count the ways.

Cold Comfort

Chuck comes from a cold place and he can be a downright cold-blooded creature. The second list is about Julia and how she was not prepared for a sudden North Dakota blizzard (even though she was from Wisconsin, she is a city girl and clueless about the great prairie). This is what Chuck writes:

> Here are the things you need to do when trapped in a blizzard:
>
> 1) Stay inside the vehicle.
> 2) Remain calm.
> 3) Periodically examine your exhaust pipe, making sure that it is not blocked by snow.
> 4) Roll down the window (that is not directly facing the wind) one to two inches.
>
> Here are the things Julia did when trapped inside her car during this blizzard:
>
> 1) She stayed inside the vehicle.
> 2) She remained calm (p. 264).

That's it. He finishes this short chapter with a list of the seven stages of carbon monoxide poisoning, followed by a list of the six things Julia was thinking as she experienced the first six stages. (The seventh stage is death, which Chuck reports: "7—.") The chapter is wholly extensive and entirely lists. That is how he finishes off a character we have grown very fond of. Shit happens.

Killing Yourself to Live

I have thought about this a lot. One thing that drew me to Klosterman's writing was his amazing ability to multiply perspectives. But I really only came to respect him as a writer when I read *Downtown Owl*, and the reason was that there was finally some balance between the intensive disorder of his thinking and the extensive desperation of his habits of endlessly organizing and re-organizing all that stuff into lists. I wanted to see that the immanent values in the lists jibed with both the inner and outer realities of life as we all have to live it. He achieves this with his characters in that novel. He created the character of Julia just to kill her off. Why? There is no satisfactory reason, if you are asking for the intensive magnitude. And if you want the extensive answer, the one really tugging on your mind with necessity, well he gave you that list, didn't he? She didn't do what had to be done to save herself.

I had a cousin who died in exactly the way the character of Julia died, and at about the same age. I didn't know her well, but I remember when I heard what happened to her I experienced dissonance because she was beautiful, young, full of life, and deserved to live. And there you have a list, don't you?

A. Beautiful

B. Young

C. Full of Life

D. Deserved to Live

So here's your pop quiz. Is this list an extensive list of someone who is alive, or an intensive list of someone now dead? Or both. The fly's eye multiplies things intensively, uses intensive relations to broaden the perspectives on the possibilities of the world. But when the world acts, it tends to squash such flies by converting those intensive values into extensive necessities. Chuck gets this. He's a sort of fly on holiday with an indefinite amount of time to get the priest to laugh, or at least chuckle under his breath.

Oh, and my list of rock bands is the one and only example of an intensive magnitude wholly necessitated by the extensive world order. Or at least it tugs on me just the way I like.

2
The Unironical in the Age of Irony

Seth Vannatta

Seinfeld reruns just aren't that funny any more. Between 1996 and 1998 my friends and I would gather on Thursday nights to watch *Seinfeld* before hitting the bar. The host was a high school classmate of mine and a liquor wholesaler, who would serve us his free "breakage." It didn't seem to get any better than that, and we thought each new episode of *Seinfeld* was a gem—sophisticated, clever, and racy.

This was before television programs on cable became brilliant, before the return of the primetime game shows and before Reality TV began to dominate the ratings. Watching *Seinfeld*, we felt like we were in on something with Jerry, George, Elaine, and Kramer. They were mostly annoyed by the everyday, and we could relate. We were all single, went on bad dates, and we liked good parking spots as much as they did, although they were more plentiful in Oklahoma City than Manhattan. That foursome glided over the surfaces of life, avoiding commitment, lacking sincere emotional attachment, and laughing their way through their Manhattan middle-aged existence. Jerry and Elaine encountered people who did give a damn about life, but those folks, with their ugly babies and "Desperado"-mesmerized, Carl Farbman obsessions were laughable. We laughed at them too, as if we were a part of the *Seinfeld* foursome.

But something has happened since then. Now, when I see Jerry overtly roll his eyes to indicate that he is being oh so obviously insincere (and I hear that damn laugh track roll with insider hilarity), I feel like I'm in a prisoner camp being forced to watch *Everybody Loves Raymond*. What the hell happened over the last decade? Why and how had the best show on TV lost its luster?

The Unironical

I think Chuck Klosterman gives us some insight into this phenomenon, which turns on the concept of irony. Well, for Chuck, it actually hinges on his use of the neologism, "unironical." Klosterman effortlessly writes and says "unironically" often. He writes *unironically* unironically. Chuck refers to himself watching the E! network *unironically* in *Sex, Drugs, and Cocoa Puffs*. I guess he was really serious about it. He said in an interview with David Grazian that the only people who visit Disneyland *unironically* are very small children. Their parents, or teens who visit the park, at least according to Klosterman, must be thinking, "This is all so fake and commercial and unmagical, but I am still here and the whole affair is fun in a detached, aloof sort of way." Klosterman describes going to a karaoke bar, which serves two general classes of folks: the locals, who genuinely, that is, earnestly and unironically, enjoy singing and watching others sing, and young kids from the nearby college town who make a farce of the evening, as if anyone could take karaoke seriously.

Why does Klosterman obviously need this word, unironical, or at least its adverbial cousin, unironically? Only when irony itself has become so pervasive and difficult to detect could we need to declare that something has *not* been done ironically. Klosterman refers to the work of David Foster Wallace to illustrate that we live in an age of pervasive irony. Wallace wrote in 1993 about the tyranny of an irony which is all-encompassing and elusive, pervasive, but difficult to pin down and define. In *Chuck Klosterman IV*, we're told that the Age of Irony is not dead, that it is alive and well in California—because Goth kids love Disneyland! In *Killing the Dinosaur* Chuck likens irony to Jason Vorhees. It cannot be killed, not even by the terrorist attacks of September 11th, 2001, not even by the election of Barack Obama, which were both supposed to usher in new eras of sincerity. After about five weeks of seriousness, the hockey-mask wearing killer was back, walking intensely, but very fast, and lurking around every dark corner. But the tyranny of irony cuts not with a madman's blade but with subtlety, constantly undermining the sincerity of human expression, spreading not fear but mistrust, cynicism, and posturing.

No one means what they say.

The cut of irony's blade creates a gash, but the wound never heals. It only grows wider, creating a distance between language and its meaning. Whenever this gap appears, the irony becomes metastatic, spreading like a cancer, building upon itself. The Danish philosopher, Søren Kierkegaard, describes this as a gap between the phenomenon and the essence. The phenomenon is the language, and the essence is the meaning, the thought. When thought is expressed in words, but the words do not express what is thought, but its opposite, irony materializes.

But wasn't *Seinfeld* funny and brilliant and cutting and edgy because of its irony? The characters were jaded, mistrustful, and utterly superficial. Jerry could not express the emotion of anger. When he tried, his voice pitched high, squeaky and effeminate. His friends—were they friends?—just laughed at him. Jerry's catch phrase in the face of human suffering and misfortune was a shrugging, "That's a shame." Jerry's best hope of understanding anything was by way of reference to comic books and Superman.

The Bizarro World

To see the irony of *Seinfeld* clearly, we have to enter the Bizarro World. And strangely, we have to meet the Bizarro Klosterman. Chuck tells us about archenemies and nemeses, the former helping us define ourselves as our complements, and the latter giving us something to root against in a primal, evil way. But he has not told us about a third archetype, the Bizarro—that person who occupies a parallel universe, whose every decision has been the opposite of our own. George Costanza embodied this universe for an entire episode of *Seinfeld*, and by making the opposite decision he would ordinarily make, he became instantly successful, snagging dates with attractive strangers and a choice job with the New York Yankees. Of course, Jerry remained Even Steven, because he had one friend ascend to success and another sink into failure: Elaine lost her job and her boyfriend, as she "became George," in the same episode.

Elaine, herself, entered the Bizarro world in another episode, meeting the anti-George, the anti-Jerry, and even the anti-Kramer. Her new Bizarro foursome read for fun, was kind to one another, and ate at the anti-coffee shop which served only Sanka and no big salad.

Klosterman doesn't know it, but he has a real life Bizarro world counterpart. His name is Jedediah Purdy. Klosterman, born in 1972, grew up in Wyndmere, North Dakota, was raised with deer-hunting brothers and feverishly Catholic parents. Purdy, born in 1974 in Chloe, West Virginia, was home-schooled on a farm by a mom who had a PhD in Philosophy. Chuck went to public school and listened to KISS and Van Halen in his spare time. Jedidiah entered the prestigious boarding school of Exeter at age thirteen. Klosterman matriculated to the flag-ship institution of the University of North Dakota. Purdy went to another famous university, Harvard. Chuck wrote a column aimed at Generation X, unironically called *Rage*. Purdy went to Yale Law School.

But both of these two dudes churned out publications. Chuck wrote *Fargo Rock City*, a humorous memoir about glam rock. Jedediah wrote *For Common Things: Irony, Trust, and Commitment in America Today*, in which he cites Michel de Montaigne with the ease that Klosterman equates his exes to members of KISS, in *Killing Yourself to Live*. Klosterman reads like late night bar conversation, Purdy like an over-studied GRE aspirant. Chuck cusses a lot; Jedediah eschews such sym-bols of disenchantment. While they are both popular culture

Chuck Klosterman   Jedediah Purdy

anthropologists, their conclusions are polar opposites. Chuck bathes in low culture, while Purdy wants only to sanitize us of its debilitating irony. They have both become quite successful: Chuck through his musings on Pamela Anderson giving head on screen and Jedediah through his tenured professorship at Duke Law School and his publications on liberty, violence, property, law, and civil disobedience. By the way, they look alike, at least if you ignore their costumes.

The Bubble Boy

I think Purdy's West Virginia farm-philosophical home schooling sheltered him a bit. Perhaps Purdy was like the Bubble Boy of *Seinfeld*, the germs of low culture could not enter his protected realm—only volumes of Edmund Burke's and Ralph Waldo Emerson's speeches were allowed to enter. And the other germ to which Purdy never developed any antibodies was irony. Klosterman was exposed to this early, and his system became immune. But when Purdy first encountered it, he broke out in reflective hives. Perhaps this is why Klosterman writes about the unironical, which to him is a strange and foreign creature, while Purdy sees irony as the standout. Purdy was probably the misfit from a West Virginia farm at Exeter, but he does have insight into irony.

Purdy describes irony as an attitude of detachment and disengagement from "the world." He tells us that Jerry Seinfeld is "irony incarnate." He writes, "Autonomous by virtue of his detachment, disloyal in a manner too vague to be mistaken for treachery, he is matchless in discerning the surfaces whose creature he is" (*For Common Things*, p. 9). The point of irony is a quiet disbelief in the depth of relationships and the sincerity of motivations. In *Seinfeld*, Jerry does not really believe in anything, except his own very simple set of self-interests. He constantly doubts the existence of social authenticity. But Jerry is not quite a cynic. Purdy tells us, "[Realizing the pretense of it all], the cynic stays home from the party. The ironist goes to the party and, while refusing to be quite of it, gets off the best line of the evening. An endless joke runs through the culture of irony, not exactly at anyone's expense, but rather at the expense of the idea that anyone could be taking the whole affair seriously" (p. 10).

Purdy says that irony, this attitude of detachment, of aloofness, of coolness, is most prominent among media-savvy young people. He says the more time spent in school, and the more expensive the education, the greater the propensity to irony. What he means is that if young people are well-read, have seen all the movies, and the ads, then they realize that there is a certain level of self-reference and repetitiveness to our emotions, to the very themes of humanity. So instead of having faith in the genuine expression of these truths such as love, fear, courage, and sacrifice, the ironist suspects that all emotion and opinion is imitation, an endless string of *Caddyshack* quotations, sports metaphors, and insider indie-rock references. Purdy says the ironist, "offers up the suspicion that we are all just quantum selves, all spin, all the way down" (p. 10).

No one means what they say.

Where Purdy is entranced by this phenomenon, Klosterman is so immune to it that he only refers to the unironical. Irony is so pervasive that he must strain to point out its absence. Klosterman's opinion is that since about 1991, irony has become an everyday element in the American sensibility, and irony has become the primary type of humor, so much so that people in their twenties today do not even remember or understand humor that is not ironical. Klosterman attributes this in part to *Seinfeld*, where irony becomes a normative way to experience comedy. Since the heyday of *Seinfeld*, the disease of irony has only spread. Surely the process of taking a video of a young person getting tased, turning it into a rap and posting it on YouTube, has made irony a more pervasive paradigm. But, for Klosterman, the triumph of irony in the world of comedy is a kind of loss and sort of a problem. Not a loss in the sense Purdy meant it. Purdy longs for sincerity and commitment. Klosterman only fancies something better than *Seinfeld*. Chuck thinks irony has become such a dominant paradigm of entertainment media discourse that consumers are confused by literal messages. We're all like the two slackers in the crowd at the Homerpalooza concert on the *Simpsons*. When one comments on the performance by the Smashing Pumpkins, "These guys are cool," the other asks "Are you being sarcastic?" According to Chuck, his response is like we all feel, "I don't even know any more."

But the sarcasm expressed by those slackers is often just an imitation of irony. Perhaps when Purdy thought he saw irony everywhere at Exeter and Harvard from his media-savvy schoolmates, he missed some of the nuances and contours to irony, confusing irony with mere sarcasm. Common in young students, this unsophisticated version does not understand itself. Investigating and questioning this ironic attitude in a young student often reveals that the student is not sure why she is being ironic, if she is being ironic, or even if she has a specific object of irony. Often they are merely imitating the sarcasm of their older siblings, parents, teachers and those embodying the dominant paradigm of thin *Seinfeld* sarcasm in entertainment. It imitates a disbelief in authenticity even if the student does not actually disbelieve. Another level of irony in young people is just teenage fear. Young kids avoid sincerity because being earnest is such a risk. It's so much easier to act aloof and play it safe. Reading Purdy's accounts of his experiences at Exeter, I imagine Purdy lacked some of the subtle social skills of keeping his cards close to his chest, a skill his supposedly ironic classmates at Exeter had honed.

Old School Irony

If we can dismiss some irony as just teenage imitation or social posturing, is it really as tyrannical as Jason Vorhees, slashing at us and widening the gap between our words and their meaning, our language and our thoughts? Has it hindered our access to know our own thoughts because, as we articulate them, we generate the gap between language and meaning? Perhaps we have forgotten the value of irony. Maybe in order to retrieve it we've gotta go old school and kick it with the original ironist, Socrates.

Kierkegaard actually wrote his dissertation on the concept of irony, and he sums up the way Socrates, not Seinfeld, is irony incarnate. Kierkegaard shows an ironic freedom in Socrates. He writes, "We have irony as the infinite absolute negativity. It is negativity because it only negates; it is infinite because it does not negate this or that phenomenon; it is absolute, because that by virtue of which it negates is a higher something that still is not" (*The Concept of Irony*, p. 261).

Socrates's life represents this negative freedom of irony; that is, the message of Socrates's life, the theme of his constantly negative freedom, is a macrocosm of irony. He parades around engaging in dialogues with various students, Thrasymachus here, Glaucon there. But he does not dedicate himself to one or the other. Like Seinfeld, Socrates never commits. Jerry brakes up with a new woman every week for reasons as shallow as the way she consumes her peas (one at a time). Similarly, Socrates does not love Alcibiades in particular; he loves the pursuit of the ineffable ideal of love, whose servant he is, and by whom he is called never to engage himself positively, because so doing, would undermine his service to the idea. The content of Socrates's life is ironic because each of his dialogues ends in emptiness. Socrates, oh so annoyingly, refuses to define the idea being discussed. He never tells us what courage, love, or piety are. In fact, Socrates claims he cannot define the idea he serves. If you read these Socratic dialogues, Socrates never gave us an answer, he only questioned others, slaying his interlocutors with the knife of irony, as if Jason Vorhees had traded in a hockey mask for a snubbed nose.

Chuck the Gadfly

Is this Klosterman's task? Doesn't he wander around asking celebrities their intentions, their thoughts, and the meaning of their art? Doesn't he expose the gap between self-image and self-portrayal? Socrates was called a gadfly, because he buzzed about nagging the sophists and political high-ups. He was so annoying, that the Athenians eventually swatted him dead, or at least forced Socrates to off himself with a poisoned cocktail.

Isn't Chuck a bit of a gadfly, buzzing about asking penetrating questions to our pop culture heroes? If one of the signs of irony, according to Purdy, is coolness, and one of Klosterman's most central objects of inquiry is the coolness of rock stars, perhaps Klosterman is telling us something about the gap between outer persona and inner self created by irony. In *Chuck Klosterman IV*, he refers to supposedly authentic Morrissey fans, who don neckties and posture as sufficiently dour to qualify as the fans Morrissey would have wanted. At one point, Klosterman refers to a fan momentarily dropping his veil of irony only to express "a grain of semi-sincere annoyance" (p. 56).

Consider Klosterman's theory of "Advancement," which he claims bears no resemblance to irony. Rock stars can advance themselves if they move beyond the rules created by their habitual iconography. Of course Chuck really only defines advancement denotatively, pointing to its exemplars, Lou Reed, Davie Bowie, David Byrne, and Joe Walsh. If their atypical artistic moments diverge too much from their routine templates—like a crappy episode of *Seinfeld* being played scene by scene in reverse, (and including in it a trip to India),—the move is overt. If the artistic gesture is done as a play or a farce on the artist's persona, then it is ironic. Klosterman's musings on the EKG charts of rock stars' artistic modalities exposes irony in a nuanced way, revealing its contours and defining them in contradistinction to Chuck's other made-up categories of rock careerism.

The Veil of Irony

Consider Klosterman's experience with Bono, in which Bono picked up several kids in his car and played his album to them, while playing air drums and harmonizing with himself. Klosterman asks:

> Did this really happen? Am I supposed to believe that he does this kind of thing all the time, even when he doesn't have a reporter in the front seat of his car? And does that even matter? Was that car-ride the greatest moment in those four kids' lives? Was this whole thing a specific performance, or is Bono's entire life a performance? And if your entire life is a performance, does that make everything you do inherently authentic? Is this guy for real, or is this guy completely full of shit? (*Chuck Klosterman IV*, p. 24)

Chuck's asking about the gap between Bono's thoughts, his inner sense of self and his persona—his mask and his performance as Bono-for-the-world. Bono responds to Klosterman's question in a way that is completely natural and completely rehearsed, and Chuck likens Bono's responses to Bill Clinton's inspirational speech at the Oklahoma City bombing. Bono wears a veil of irony, but it's as if the veil has become stitched to his face, and the distinction between inner and outer has been effaced.

Chuck gives us insight into the pervasiveness of irony by illustrating one of its peculiar qualities. These days, detecting irony is like looking at your own eyes without a mirror. One cannot identify irony as the foreground structure if irony is also the background. Instead, we can only discern moments of unirony, tinges of semi-sincerity, amid a picture framed by the ironical. The Gestalt has shifted. Chuck knows he is in the middle of the picture, framed by irony, so he can only bob and weave his way toward catching glimpses where earnestness discloses itself.

If Chuck's task is to highlight the unironical where it shows itself, Socrates's was to use the blade of irony to get at the truth, to give birth to the true idea, which he claimed to serve but did not know. Kierkegaard writes, "When Socrates declared that he was ignorant, he nevertheless did know something, for he knew about his ignorance; on the other hand, however, this knowledge was not a knowledge of something, that is, did not have any positive content, and to that extent his ignorance was ironic." Kierkegaard goes further to assert, "His ignorance was simultaneously earnest and yet again not earnest" (*The Concept of Irony*, p. 269). Was he writing about Socrates of ancient Athens or about of Klosterman of contemporary America?

Socrates knew that the objectivity of the culture of oracular proclamations had lost its validity, and he knew that the sophistic response to inconsistency of oracular law demanded his ironic scrutiny. Klosterman knows that the people he meets imitate reality TV characters, such as Puck and Pedro from the *Real World*, that they are performing the personas of reality TV archetypes. But what in Chuck's experience draws out his ironic scrutiny?

Both Purdy and Klosterman see irony as pervasive. Jedidiah wants to revive sincerity and commitment. Chuck merely notes when the unironical makes its rare appearance. Socrates wanted to show that a loss of actuality demanded more than phony argumentation by paid teachers of rhetoric. Chuck wants to know if we can ever have more than the veneer of our language, which is so thoroughly refracted through media and popular culture, that literal messages are now just confusing. Maybe all we can do is float through life on its surfaces, responding to every human drama with another *Star Wars* reference.

But if irony creates the gap between our fraudulent words and our inner thoughts, it also exposes the fissure, and at least allows for the possibility of an unironical experience. We may not retrieve the sincerity of Purdy's idyllic West Virginia home-schooled upbringing, but we may have a better understanding of what the wound of irony is, even if Klosterman's contribution to our understanding of irony is to show us why *Seinfeld*, once the summit of TV achievement, now falls flat.

Purdy and Kierkegaard give us different versions of irony. Kierkegaard writes of the ironist, Socrates, who knows that there is pretense in the world, seeks to disclose it, but still believes in something. Purdy's description portrays the ironist, Seinfeld, who because of his culturally mediated, sophisticated existence, is defeated by disbelief and has succumbed to irony. Where Kierkegaard portrays Socrates as master of irony, Purdy characterizes Seinfeld as mastered by it.

Master of His Domain?

Where does Klosterman belong? Is he master of his domain . . . of irony? Or has he been mastered by it? Is Chuck detached and disloyal, or does he serve an idea of which he is ignorant? If he has been defeated by irony, like Seinfeld and like the sophists Socrates battled with, Chuck will employ insincerity because he supposes that reality is not at all what it seems. The sophists profited from the distinction between appearance and reality; Seinfeld makes a joke of it, offering the disbelief that anyone could take our cultural institutions seriously. Purdy claims that the ironist, having been nurtured by media's overuse of irony and by art's imitation of life, sees all of actuality as ironic and therefore disbelieves. He succumbs and falls towards a self-interested nihilism.

But Kierkegaard thought that irony is a part of every genuinely human life. Each of us has the ability to detach ourselves from the particularities of actuality. Socrates remains ironically afloat because he repeatedly disengages from his dialogues in which he pursued truth. Constant attention to any particular student or argument would represent an investment in actuality that could not be universalized by his own ironic method. The Purdyan ironist, Seinfeld, remains afloat as well, free from engagement, cool and aloof. He has achieved a certain level of sophistication in his realization that insincerity exists; he sees the gap between phenomenon and essence. Yet he is hopeless to bridge it, so he treats it comically and never looks for more. The first of these, the genuine human life, searches for the truth. The second of these does not believe it exists. For the true (or "absolute") is the bridge between phenomenon and essence.

Kierkegaard maintains that irony is a means, not an end. To master irony means to use irony to detect deceit. It also means being able to employ irony's negativity in order to expose pretense or dishonesty, even if this use participates in the insincerity on one level by using language that does not accurately represent thought. The Purdyan ironist has realized that deceit exists but chooses to participate in it fully by only discerning its surfaces. Seinfeld treats irony as the end, the goal, not the path or the means to the truth. The master of irony understands that irony is the way, but not the truth.

Where authenticity demands self-knowledge and knowledge of one's environment, irony maintains the self amid the environment because it lifts the self above its surroundings by disengaging when the search for truth falls short, when irony detects deception. The master of irony is more than a product of his environment, more than a slave to the veiled self-interests of others. The ever-present gap between the phenomenon and the essence births irony, and irony allows humans to live authentically amid the constant void.

Which life does Chuck lead? Is he master of irony or has he been mastered by it? Does Chuck serve an idea, even if he cannot define it? Does Klosterman believe in an idea? Does he have a cause?

I think Chuck resides in the middle, between the extremes offered by Socrates, the master, and Seinfeld, the mastered. Like Socrates, Chuck does know something. He's sure of his own ignorance. Chuck knows that he does not know who he is, and he has helped us understand that we, too, do not know who we are. I think the idea he serves is self-understanding, but his pursuit of it does not begin from a privileged perspective. He cannot retreat to the Bizarro World and live inside Purdy's bubble, judging the world from inside that immunity to low culture and irony. He cannot live amid the clouds, as Aristophanes thought Socrates did. Chuck has to start in the middle of things. Chuck is a comedic ironist in the vein of Seinfeld in that he can understand the world only through constant play of its resemblances to the pop culture he grew up with and that composes the soundtrack of his life. Where Seinfeld refers to Superman, Klosterman refers to KISS. But Chuck also knows just how blurry his vision is, how media and art and culture have so clouded his vision, that he has no choice but to look for himself through the tint of their lenses. He investigates the relationship between phenomena—rock star personas, coolness, and over and underratedness—and essence—the inner being, thoughts, self-understandings of those rock stars. His inquiries do cut with the blade of irony. But he knows he cannot master irony, any more than he can bite his own teeth.

Seinfeld and Socrates Get the Death Penalty

The first shitty episode of *Seinfeld*, its last, inaugurated the age of every *Seinfeld* rerun sucking. My friends and I awaited the finale of *Seinfeld* in 1998 alongside the rest of America. And we were utterly disappointed. It wasn't funny. There was no soup for us in that debacle. Half montage, half reunion, the episode ditched its habitual formula and tried, failingly, to advance itself. Instead, it was overt. We stared at the episode completely confused, especially by its ending. But that was its brilliance. In that episode we were shown the anti-social, cold-hearted jerks we thought we loved. We were forced to see that perhaps a jail cell was their proper domicile.

Seinfeld's prison

Socrates's prison

Both Socrates and Seinfeld, the character, ended their lives in jail. The master of irony and the one mastered by it succumbed to a similar fate. Jerry avoided the death penalty, which was perhaps too harsh a penalty for Socrates, who accepted his death in service of the truth and obedience to state law. However, Jerry's character did die, (as the show ended), and he ended his existence commenting on the mundane and telling another joke. (The second button on George's shirt was too high).

Happily, Chuck is still with us, searching for himself and helping us do the same. We do not know how *unironically* he will serve his idea, but we do know that it will be funnier than a *Seinfeld* rerun.

Culture can
be wrong?

Culture can be wrong

GEORGE A. REISCH

"What depresses you more—being betrayed by an individual, or being 'betrayed' by your own culture?" It's a trick question because Klosterman believes you can't be betrayed by your own culture. Culture, he argues, can't be wrong. This is a towering truth that we all overlook. As he puts it,

> There's a peculiar disconnect between how people exist in the world and how they think the world is supposed to exist; it's almost as if most Americans can't accept an important truth about being alive. And this is the truth to which I refer: Culture can't be wrong. That doesn't mean it's always "right," nor does it mean you always have to agree with it. But culture is never wrong. People can be wrong. Movements can be wrong. But culture—as a whole—cannot be wrong. Culture is just there. ("Culture Got You Down?" *Esquire*, December 31st 2004)

His argument is this: people can be wrong because they exist in a larger context of laws or traditions that they can defy or offend, like a criminal breaking a law. A movement, just a collection of people, can be wrong in the same way. But culture, Klosterman seems to think, is the largest context out there. And that mean's it can't be wrong. There's no larger framework or setting outside of culture. His suppressed premise seems to be: for something to go wrong, it has to go wrong inside of, and with respect to, something larger than itself.

But that's not true. There are other ways that something can 'go wrong' that have nothing to do with offending some larger, superior framework or context. You can go wrong with respect to your own context or container—yourself. If my reason to live is to paint, or create music, or grow my business, then I could easily go wrong simply by turning my back on that goal or doing things to sabotage myself. I've gone wrong and betrayed myself only because I've veered away from values and goals that I personally hold dear, not because something larger is looking at me and shaking its head.

Culture can do that, too. Culture can chug along for years with its movies and books, laws and debates, trends and fads, songs, economic cycles, military conflicts, and what not, each of which is connected to the others in the big cultural stew that sociologists write books about. All these things hang together and form the culture we live in, talk about, and argue about. Then, the bottom can drop out. The whole thing can betray itself, the people in it, and everything that culture stood for in all its former integrity.

I refer of course to the release in 1981 of "In the Air Tonight" by Phil Collins. Phil and Atlantic Records opened the bomb bay doors and let this baby drop down on a world that would never be the same. It's been thirty years and *everyone* knows and, I trust, loathes this constipated dirge that slowly repeats the same three chords over and over. When the first verse is finally squeezed out, it has all the punch of an argument between second graders:

> Well if you told me you were drowning
> I would not lend a hand
>
> Good because you're so ugly
> I'd rather drown than have you touch me

From there we move on to cliché—it's been "a pack of lies" and "How could I ever forget?"—as the song's awfulness builds and snowballs. After the drums kick in, Collins sounds tortured— his "Oh Lord, Oh Lord"s snarling and squealing like Joe Pesci at the hands of Macauley Culkin in *Home Alone*.

Musicologists refer to the popular music vapidity index. It's the ratio of a song's drama, pathos, and emotion to the substance of what the song is about. You want these numbers to match, more or less, giving good songs a ratio of about one. For example, Springsteen bellows "Born in the USA" at about a 7 (out of ten) because, as the verses inform us, his character's got some serious stuff to bellow about—Vietnam, alienation, ruined lives at the hands of Nixonian politicians, joblessness. I'd eyeball these, taken together, at 7 or 8. So, on the awfulness index, as you'd expect, Bruce does well. Around 1, maybe 0.9.

Collins, on the other hand, squeals and shrieks at around 9, possibly even a historic 10 by the time Culkin has got pliers on Phil's fingers and has set his cap on fire. To have a hope of matching Springsteen, Collins's song needs to up the denominator a notch or two—to keep some sense of artistic proportion and credibility. But what number should we put in the denominator? What is it that has got Collins so torn and worked up, tearing his shirt off his chest and yelling "Oh Lord, Oh Lord" as it's "coming in the air tonight"?

[*sounds of crickets chirping*]

Nothing. It's just "it". A mere pronoun. "It" will be arriving later "tonight" but we know nothing about it. We know that Phil's upset, that he's more and more agitated as he feels it coming, that it's so important God needs to know about it. But we, the listeners, are left with "it." A placeholder. The something that is not really anything.

On the vapidity index, therefore, we've got a 9 divided by a nothing, a zero. That means "In the Air Tonight" becomes, by the time it is over, hyperbolically, *infinitely* vapid. There is no number you could put on the incongruity between the pathos and the emptiness of the lyrics. The performance is a directionless tantrum, like a balling child at the Walmart wailing through his tears, "But I waaaannnnnaaaa. I waaaannnaaaa"—making anyone with a human heart wonder, "what?" "What is it that this child wants? Can't mom or dad just *buy it* and make them shut up?"

Is it gum, candy, a squirt gun? Whatever it is, the child can at least point to it so we can have a number, a 1 most likely because squirt guns and the like are not really that important. So, a 9 divided by 1 gives us a vapidity index of 9 for this kind of tantrum. That's up there, but *it's a child* so there's nothing terribly wrong or out of whack here. But "In the Air Tonight" wails even harder, with a full complement of drums, synthesizers, gated reverbs, and state of the art studio effects to help a grown man push himself to the brink of existential anguish in the face of. . .

[*more chirping*].

Were this just a deep track from an obscure band, Chuck's theory might be right. In that case, it would just be a bad song, perhaps written by a mediocre singer-songwriter. But because the song is (as they say) "a classic," one that is so loved and adored that it nearly broke the *Billboard* 100 a *second time* in 1984 (Wikipedia says), one that has been sampled, quoted, referenced, covered so often, it's a part of our cultural wallpaper. As much as a song can be, it's the flag of our culture. One that's gone wrong.

> Why, I wondered, do people so often feel let down by popular culture? Why do serious film fans feel disgusted when another Tom Hanks movie earns $200 million? Why do record-store employees get angry when a band like Comets on Fire comes to town and only twenty-two people pay to see them? Why do highly literate people become depressed when they look at the *New York Times* best-seller list . . . ?

It's because they feel betrayed by their culture. You, Chuck, claim that there's no basis for this feeling, but I believe there is. I agree there's no reason to be upset if people like a movie that you don't like, or people don't like a band that you love. But "In the Air Tonight" and other let-downs are not ultimately about the people who feel let down. That is accidental and secondary to the culture's betrayal of itself and all the people in it. It has happened. It may happen again. I think I can feel it coming.

BOOK II

Know Thyself and Thy Cocoa Puffs

3
Glam Rock Identity

Bruno Ćurko and Ivana Greguric

Long, unkempt hair, tight pants, cowboy boots, lacquer nails, frilled shirts—when we read Klosterman's books, we thought Klosterman would look like an authentic glam rocker.

If you're like Klosterman and have a fascination, if not love affair with, glam rock, then you're in the right place. Prepare to face your own glam rock identity. Are you ready for the transformation from anonymity to fame and from poverty to wealth? If so, the tabloids will write about you and photograph you, and your fans will scream at your every guitar riff and hip thrust. But who will they be following? You? Or some phony persona? Will your identity be a mere mask?

What Is a Glam Identity?

Well, a real glam rocker has an extravagant style. "Glam" stands for glamour, as in something glamorous, sensational, and alluring. Glam rock, also known as glitter rock, is a genre of the rock music born in the UK in the 1970s. The glam-rock scene was concentrated in Los Angeles and centered on bands such as Guns N' Roses, Ratt, Motley Crüe, W.A.S.P., Quiet Riot, Dokken, and Cinderella. The list of glam-rock legends goes beyond LA, including Poison and Heavens Edge from Pennsylvania, KISS, Twisted Sister, White Lion from New York, Alice Cooper from Detroit, Bon Jovi and Skid Row from New Jersey.

Besides simple and effective guitar riffs and melodious solo-parts, those bands also share a peculiar fashion style. They rock with long and unkempt hair, with purple guitars, polyphonic singing. Their lyrics celebrate a hedonistic lifestyle. Glam rockers are famous for their enchanting fashion style—sparkly clothes, tight tiger-print glitter suits, platform shoes, sparkling jewels, and dramatic make-up. No wonder that a superficial rock critic, or an indifferent audience might say that this kind of music is just a provocation intended only to shock the public, making use of a superficial and external form, while the quality of music and poetics of these bands is rubbish. But fans of this kind of music, Klosterman and the rest of us, consider glam rock to be artistically valuable. Of course, there is a certain amount of trash in glam rock as well, but at its heart glam rock does have creative value. In his first book, *Fargo Rock City*, Klosterman skillfully turns a story of childhood in North Dakota—and the history of the glam rock bands he grew up with in 1998, such as Twisted Sister, Guns N' Roses, Motley Crüe, and Poison—into a serious philosophical contemplation of the joys and paradoxes of rock music.

The growth of glam rock was mostly unrecognized from the perspective of high-class rock criticism, but that lack of attention from the mainstream has just fueled its rebelliousness. But aren't all rock musicians rebels of a sort? We can say that today there are two kinds of rock fans, ones who are truly addicted to the hell rhythm of rock, and others who, from a more detached perspective, consider rock'n'roll to be a legitimate rebellion against the social conventions. We can see glam rock as a social movement powered by a lower-class ideology for young people. In their affinity for rock music, middle-class kids deliberately adopted lower-class values to oppose the values of their parents. Young people felt that rock musicians were "one of them," people who shared common interests and attitudes with their audience.

But is glam rock a truly unique phenomenon, or is it a movement with limited social significance? For example, long hair is one of the characteristics of the rocker. What's the role of the long hair in the everyday life of the rock fans and musicians? Can we say that wearing our hair long is a way to identify ourselves as a rocker, or it is just a part of the concert ritual through which we become a part of the noisy and colorful atmosphere of a rock spectacle?

We assume that readers of *Fargo Rock City* have done some rocking in their days. In *Fargo Rock City: A Heavy Metal*

Odyssey in Rural North Dakota, Klosterman tells us: "You know I've never had long hair" (p. 1). Never had long hair, but exhilarated with the long-haired musicians and their music? Hmm. Many readers might jump to conclusions and say: "Okay, he's well shorn, but he likes rock music. Long hair is not an important characteristic for rock music." Wait a minute. Is this true? How essential is a long hair to rock music? Maybe it is necessary only in order that the fans at concerts can shake their ratted out mops and create one of the symbols of glam metal followers? Is that head-banging some kind of a ritual, a festivity of the fact that we're part of the loud and noisy atmosphere of the rock concert? Still, Chuck did not identify with glam rock in that way, despite his merits in promoting glam rock. So why did he avoid the visual identification with the rockers?

We have noticed that ol' Chuck is well shorn, in that sort of thirty-something Justin Bieber-quaffed look. Is this an accident or a purposeful attempt to be the calm, unassuming rocker? Maybe in his early years, Chuck's mother was a great role-model. She must have taught him to cope stoically with all the troubles in life. That could be the main reason why Chuck took a reasonable and measured approach to rock music. The Stoics, from their founder in Athens by Zeno, to the more famous expounders such as the emperor, Marcus Aurelius of "Gladiator" fame, and the slave, Epictetus, have received little attention from glam rock fans. The Stoics considered destructive emotions to be the result of errors in judgment, and that a sage, or person of "moral and intellectual perfection," would not suffer such emotions. Stoics were concerned with the active relationship between cosmic determinism and human freedom. They believed that it is virtuous to maintain a will that's in accord with nature. Because of this, the Stoics presented their philosophy as a way of life, and they thought that the best indication of an individual's philosophy was not what a person said, but how he behaved. Perhaps Chuck values this stoic way of life, and views rock through the more measured and self-controlled lens of stoicism.

If so, he's got a bone to pick with the famous German philosopher Friedrich Wilhelm Nietzsche, who says that there are two main kinds of art—Dionysian and Apollonian. Apollonian art (think Joe Satriani—more on him later, Mr. Big) symbolizes Apollo, a Greek god of profound dreaming symbolizes self-control, healing, and general common sense. On the other hand, there is Dionysian art (think G N' R, Motley Crüe), which symbolizes Dionysus, is a god of wine, excess, wildness, anger, emotion and passion. Yes, glam rock and metal are Dionysian arts that celebrate wine, women and song (think Whitesnake song, Coverdale, Moody, Marsden, Murray, Lord, Paice). Chuck is an Apollonian with Stoic values, who writes about modern Dionysian art—glam rock. Quite the combo!

Whose Identity Would Chuck Steal?

If Chuck could change his identity and become somebody else, who would Chuck become? The one and only Joe Satriani! He would identify with the one of the best virtuosos of the Eighties and Nineties, just to play the guitar in Satriani's way for the first time in his life. Isn't that every guitarist's dream? Every musician has said at least once: "One day I would play like . . . (Van Halen, Kirk Hammet, Steve Vai . . .)."

So when stealing identities, you should go all the way, and take their entire spirit, not just their guitar playing talents. But since this is not possible, we can imagine that most musicians spent many hours in their rooms and garages to learn to play like their idols, and in this way they do take some of their identity. I also practice to play Satriani songs because I have also wanted to play like Satriani, despite the fact I am a girl (Ivana). Incidentally, my nickname, "Ibanez," is the name of the guitar that Satriani plays. In 1990, a company named "Ibanez" started a Joe Satriani series, selling guitars bearing Satriani's signature. Not only was Satriani a lead guitarist in Mick Jagger's first solo-tour in 1988, but his playing technique attracted Deep Purple, so he joined them in 1994. Satriani taught many great guitarists, and I wish I could have been one of them!

The fact is that all the great music heroes influenced one another, either directly (by being students in this case) or indirectly (through the media that surround us). What would the world look like without musical heroes that we admire? If we take a visual identity of our hero and imitate his style of play, soon we will become just a pale imitation. Instead of mere imitation, we should incorporate his style and idiosyncrasies. Then we should strive to surpass him, we should creatively add our own uniqueness to his, and create a new identity, developing our own style on the foundations of our rock hero. Chuck directs us to understanding the function of celebrities, who rule the media. From Chuck we can learn a lot about ourselves, how to achieve our own desires, but never forget to stay ourselves and be unique! Chuck manages to do this—thieve parts of identities while creating his own unique one. Perhaps we should learn from him.

So, if you want to be wise like Chuck, you need to forget about stealing Satriani's identity and go about the life you were given. By all means, take in what you want from your glam rock heroes, but do not strive for the unattainable. Control what you can, and know what is out of your hands, (your rep and your time of death among them). Don't serve the passions, learn how to handle your destiny, let your good sense prevail over your emotions, and be happy with what you have.

So Who Needs a Glam Rock Mask?

Some people think that glam rockers are exhibitionists with a bizarre fashion style, or just modern clowns with no musical value. Others think that the mask worn by the glam rocker has a hidden message, which conceals the shame of the musician and his fear of self-exposure.

René Descartes once said that an actor puts his mask on, so that no one can see shame on his face. Is the glam rocker ashamed of himself? Descartes's thesis indicates a relation between an actor's shame in playing himself, and the absence of shame in playing someone else. Descartes does not think that an actor puts on the mask in order to represent his character to an audience. On the contrary, he claims the mask represents something far bigger than that. Not only does the mask serve the actor, hiding the discomfort of his own skin, but it serves the audience, protecting them from the same discomfort of seeing oneself at the event. If the actor's face were disclosed, an actor would no longer be an actor, and for that reason the audience would transform from the viewers into the participants in disclosure of the others and themselves.

Klosterman's chapter "Appetite for Replication 0:56" in *Sex, Drugs, and Cocoa Puffs* adds another layer of intrigue to this question of glam-rock identity. Klosterman observes the phenomenon of "tribute bands," more specifically, a Guns N' Roses tribute band, Paradise City. When you watch Paradise City, you are watching a "real copy"—a paradox if there ever were one—of Guns N' Roses. Their songs, stage performance, image, and personas meticulously mimic the members of G N' R.

Klosterman goes on to argue that tribute bands are actors who get hold of a band's musical reality and then pretend to be something they're not. Chuck writes: "If a tribute band were to completely succeed, its members would no longer have personalities" (p. 58). But is the tribute band's embodiment of the character of the actual band really that complete? The pleasure the audience gets from such a performance is doubly dubious. Is the person screaming at a Paradise City concert screaming because of Paradise City or at the G N' R songs they are performing? Is the experience based on the performers, or has there been a mental flip, which reversed the faux-performance to the original artifact in the mind of the duped fan?

About five hundred people have paid $12 to watch Paradise City. At the same city, original band Dokken can't reach five hundred people. Klosterman wonders "how the real guys in Dokken feel about being as popular as five fake guys in Guns N' Roses" (p. 67). Therefore, it is not unusual for people to pay the same amount or even more to see a copy as they would to see a different original. But we do imagine that the popularity of the original band drives the ticket sales of the tribute band's shows, which plays set lists from the band's most popular phases.

But we also wonder how much self-identity does a band member acquire by playing in a band such as Paradise City, if he plays Izzy Stradlin, for instance? Does he lose a part of his own personality by taking on someone else's? Do they even ask themselves: "Who Am I? Or (Perhaps More Accurately) Who Else Could Be Me" (p. 13)?

Are Our Identities as Twisted as Twisted Sisters'?

Chuck warns: we are living in a world of media satiety. He also confesses: as he gets older, Chuck seems less certain about the world, writing "It's interesting to think about this and to understand this world. People are mad on culture and saying— I don't understand the world. But nobody totally does, of course it seems strange, especially when it is about things that become commercial" (thesocietypages.org/officehours/2010/02/07). Does anyone here understand the world?

The omnipresence of media changes our sense of reality and our understanding of self-identity. Media create a monoculture, so the structure of our existence becomes increasingly similar to everyone else's in the world, and cultural particularities get flattened. As a result we have a feeling of alienation and loneliness among the crowd. And Klosterman thinks that such alienation can grow into a big cultural problem. Media seduce us through radio, TV, newspapers; they manipulate our consciousness, shaping our identity according to current trends. In a way we become copies without the original, identical to everyone else, but not ourselves. When this happens, our identity is completely effaced, because we are no longer self-same. (After all, the word identity comes from the Latin word for oneness, which means that some being, phenomenon or attribute is equal to itself).

The appearance of information technologies, especially the Internet, enabled the creation of a new Internet culture, a new identity. We enter into a virtual reality where we can be whatever we want. He can make his dreams come true and have the identity he wants. But where is our identity when we are online, in the virtual communities such as Facebook or MySpace? One of the basic questions in the conception of the virtual worlds is: *Who are we when we are online, how far can we enter the virtual worlds and still remain ourselves*? Chuck answers: "I guess I've just really become comfortable with the idea that none of this is real, and that we're not quite in the Matrix, but it's close, and that all the things we're doing are constructions" (thesocietypages.org/officehours/2010/02/07). We can conclude that our brave new world calls into question the notion of self-same identity by the virtualization of our egos in online technologies. But glam rock bands, in their real and copied incarnations, also raise this same question. Who are the rockers, who are their imitators, and who are the fans of each? What is the relationship of our own identities to the masks of Facebook and glam rock?

Chuck—a Modern Socrates?

Chuck has noticed this conundrum in our search for self-identity amid the masks of musicians and MySpaces. Chuck concludes that our search for ourselves is a function of our alienation and isolation. Chuck is aware that we are all alone, isolated, and lonely. In response to this isolated loneliness we go on journeys, actual and virtual, as attempts to escape from ourselves, not to be here, not to be who we are. Perhaps we long to depart from ourselves in our online journeys and our forays into the world of glam rock. We're just trying to protect ourselves from loneliness and find peace in our souls. But the anxiety that drives our self-escapism is really a fear, a fear to ever face ourselves and live up to the famous ancient philosophy, "Know thyself."

According to the legend, "Know Thyself" was written on the Temple of Apollo at Delphi. Apollo is a Greek god of music, the arts, and the sun. He has urged humans to perceive their own bounds and mortality, because that awareness allows them to communicate with god. Apollo was worshiped for being a god of light and the sun, life sustaining gifts for us mortals, and he was worshiped for being a god of the arts and beauty, that which gives life value. Through the Delphic oracle, Apollo called Socrates the wisest man. But what is wisdom? Do we have to be philosophers to be wise? Who is a philosopher anyway? We're told a philosopher is a person who loves and desires wisdom, but who does not claim that he owns it. For a philosopher no answer is final; the philosopher keeps asking questions. Socrates was always searching for meaning through the dialogues he had with his friends and foes. He used to say that he does not want to teach anyone about life, because he is also still learning how to live. His followers wrote his thoughts down, but he was against that, telling them that they should not memorize his thoughts because that only proves they don't have their own thoughts. It's necessary to think, to make one's own conclusions, to believe in one's own mind, one's own common sense. Without conscious cognition about yourself, not even gods can help you.

Socrates remained loyal to his thoughts and to himself until his whole life. In 399 B.C., when democracy was blossoming in Athens, Socrates was accused of disrespect for the gods and corrupting youth. His death penalty, meant to suppress his influence, actually became the triumph of his calm, consistent thoughtfulness. Even though his friends made his escape possible, Socrates stayed in prison and drank the poison, respecting the laws of his state. Can we say that Socrates succeeded in knowing himself? We can't say that for sure, but he raised awareness of the need to know ourselves, and we all must realize that this is our ongoing philosophical pursuit, to know ourselves.

Looking at the sentence "Know thyself," some other questions appear. How do I know myself? Who am I? Is it possible to know oneself when we are not even able to understand the world around us, nor our role and purpose in it? How do we know ourselves in a world that constantly changes, and causes changes in our identity? Chuck answers this question for us: all the things we learned and understood seven hours ago are now out-of-date, so we have to start all over again.

When talking about love and rock music, Chuck makes another point about shifting identities. He considers that most popular rock music produces false images of ideal love, like Coldplay. He blames crappy bands like Coldplay for ruining his love life, as he can never live up to their phony fantasy love images. But if we know that Klosterman is well aware of the influence of society in forming and changing our understanding of identity, how can he and we not escape the tail-chasing twist of searching to know ourselves amid both a shifting identity and an anxious fear impelling us to quit the search altogether?

Lucius Seneca, a Roman Stoic philosopher, once said that the life lived best is not the longest life, but the life that lasts long enough to be fulfilled. Is your life fulfilled? Socrates's certainly was, and Chuck is trying to follow him. It's only necessary to dare, to be brave enough to make your wishes come true, and to realize the life you have always dreamed of. Consider Chuck as our exemplar, our modern Socrates, a person who dares to write about popular culture. Chuck reflects on the relations between rock music and social frameworks, and dared to publish a book about metal rock at the nexus of rural culture and the search for self-identity. Chuck actually created what he was looking for. He says of *Fargo Rock City*: "It was the kind of book that I always wanted to read, and could never find" (thesocietypages.org/officehours/ 2010/02/07). So he wrote it!

Seneca said that it is not true that we don't dare because things are difficult, but things are difficult because we don't dare. Chuck's creative exploration of today's pop-culture helps us to understand American culture; his provocative attitudes, written in plain language, seduce his readers while making make them think. These are the things that made him an icon of post-modern culture, a modern day Socrates, and an exemplar of stoic virtues!

Socrates was the wisest of men, not because of his knowledge, but because he understood his ignorance. Understanding that we do not know who we are, and appreciating that the quest for self-knowledge is a mysterious and puzzled one is the condition which makes the daring search possible. Chuck inspires us to reflect on the relationship between our love of glam rock music and the difficulty of knowing ourselves. Our reflections do not give us the definitive answer to the question, *Who am I?* But this isn't a reason to quit asking the question. Instead, Chuck inspires us to ask the question whose answer is elusive and ever shifting. Perhaps our glam rock identity is not a superficial search for money or fame, but the more important task of finding ourselves amid the masks we wear and the masks worn by our glam rock heroes.

4

Reading, Writing, and Thinking with Chuck

SETH VANNATTA

Chuck cops to his own BS in *Sex, Drugs, and Cocoa Puffs*. He admits to contriving his personality through a limited number of consciously selected conversational devices. He writes:

> My witty banter and cerebral discourse is always completely contrived. Right now, I have three and a half dates' worth of material, all of which I pretend to deliver spontaneously. This is my strategy: If I can just coerce women into the last half of that fourth date, it's anyone's ball game. I've beaten the system: I've broken the code; I've slain the Minotaur. If we part ways on that fourth evening without some kind of conversational disaster, she probably digs me. Or at least she *thinks* she digs me, because who she digs is not really me. (p. 7).

Is Chuck just a phony, trying to get into his dates' pants, or should we cut the guy some slack and figure out if he's telling us something deeper about the human condition?

Chuck's Full of It (But at Least He Knows It)

I think that Chuck's just admitting to the inevitability of being slightly inauthentic in our relationships. I mean, who could really "be themselves" on a first few dates? After all it's really hard to be ourselves when we don't really know who we are. I once told a group of middle schoolers at Casady School in Oklahoma City, where I used to teach, that they should break certain rules. The most important of these rules was "Be Yourself." Telling a twelve-year-old to be herself, when she is in the hormone-drenched flux of change and socialization, is as futile as attempting to avoid contriving one's discourse on a first date.

Baring your soul on a first date isn't really realistic, and it's not necessarily more authentic than just admitting that your conversation on that date is somewhat staged. We're in a constant struggle to know who we are, and so part of that struggle is going through the contrived banter of first and second dates. So what's the best path to this elusive self-knowledge?

When I taught junior high in Oklahoma City, one year our theme was "self-discovery." We had the slogan posted on the wall in colorful construction paper as the background to famous quotations by great thinkers of the past from Socrates to Einstein. Perhaps we were suggesting that the purpose of education is to discover ourselves, and so maybe we thought that we could find out who we are by doing our homework.

Reading Is a Bore

Chuck secretly suspects that he hates reading. Like many of my seventh graders and like some of us, Chuck feels as though reading is something that he forces himself to do. And he suspects that many people might consider him irrelevant because of this. I'm not sure this is the case. I *do* find Chuck relevant, and his remarks about reading don't piss me off or disappoint me as if I were Chuck's junior-high English teacher. Chuck tells us that since he writes at roughly the same speed as he reads, he feels as if he should be writing, which is what he is paid to do. This makes sense.

I suspect that many of us actually feel the same way Chuck does. I admit that just because reading is boring doesn't mean that reading is not the route to self-knowledge. But must we bolt ourselves to desks in libraries to figure out who we are? Surely not. Since Chuck suggests that writing, not reading, seems a more valuable way to spend his time, and since so much of his writing is in the service of self-understanding, perhaps we can write our way to self-knowledge.

Often I feel just as Chuck does, that reading is almost passive, a "neutral, reactive way to spend an evening" (*KYL*, p.

166). (By the way when people hear what I do for a living, they often ask me if I "love to read." This question always strikes me as strange, and I almost never know how to answer. I do not "love to read" any more than Chuck does, but I certainly like reading more than *not* reading. But in this way, I do not "love breathing" either. And I have never and will never use the phrase, "curl up with a novel," which makes my skin crawl).

Is Writing Difficult?

Instead of reading and getting diminishing returns on my reading, I feel I need to write. People often ask me if writing is difficult, which is a tough question. My inclination when asked about the difficulty of writing is to search for some underlying assumption in the question about writing. I suppose those who ask about the difficulty of writing mean to ask me whether or not it is hard to hold all of your ideas inside your head in an organized way and then exert them onto a computer screen. If such a rephrasing of their question is acceptable, then a false premise in their question emerges. Writing is *not*, as they assume, a process of transmitting the inside of oneself onto the outside world. Rather, writing is a function of attending to one's thoughts.

What Is Thinking?

If writing means attending to the thoughts in our heads, then what does it mean to think? What is thinking? Is the process of thinking an application of an organized concept in our heads onto the messy particularities of our experience? Do I organize my world in thought, and do I exert some thinking power over my external environment? Such a conception of thinking subtly suggests that there is a little me inside myself doing the thinking, a ghost in my bodily machine.

Many philosophers have worked with such a conception. Plato offered us the idea that our soul is like a chariot, whose driver was our capacity for rationality. The rational part of our soul, which does math and makes sensible arguments about how to rate rock bands, drives the horses to pull the chariot, and these horses represent our appetitive and spirited natures, these last two horses doing all of the Cocoa Puff eating, SoCo and Lime drinking, and nemesis fighting.

René Descartes told us that there is a thinking substance, the mind, which is separate from the body and unlike the body, is not extended in space. Descartes thought that there were really only two things in the world, minds, which do all the thinking, imagining, and doubting, and bodies, which include all the tangible stuff of the world. Immanuel Kant figured that the only way we could make any sense of the world was if all of our judgments about it were accompanied by an "I" that does all the thinking. (He called this the unity of apperception, an ego which necessarily accompanied all of our thoughts).

The philosophical question accompanying the supposition of a thinking self or a rational subject is *how do we have access to ourselves as thinkers*? Chuck seems to wonder this all the time in his writing. He is mesmerized by Britney Spears's seeming lack of insight into who she is and what she represents. Britney seems oblivious to the fact that she represents an icon of unavailable sexuality, that society fantasizes about her veiled and protected sexuality (at least at the time of his interview).

In *The Visible Man* Klosterman's character, Y———, the arrogant "scientist," who has the ability to cloak himself and "objectively" observe people without being seen, seems to think that he can discover who people *really* are by watching them when they're alone. Y——— is convinced that his subjects play a variety of roles in their lives of work, of friendships, and of relationships. Y——— thinks that beneath this all, he'll find these subjects' "essence," their true selves. Y———'s therapist and we readers are left speculating on how Y———'s quest for a true understanding of someone else is a mirror, reflecting the opacity of ourselves to ourselves. Do we really know who we, ourselves—independent of our work selves, social selves, and romantic selves, our personas—are?

Chuck is befuddled by Val Kilmer's inflated sense of self-knowledge. Kilmer claims to know what it is like to shoot a man *better* than Doc Holliday, who really gunned people down, and Kilmer claims to know what it is like to fly a fighter jet *better* than those who have actually been ejected from an F15. The paradox of how an actor could think he knows himself better than someone who actually does the things that the actor portrays in a film brings us again to the difficult question of how we know ourselves at all.

Philosophers have offered all sorts of answers at this question of how we know ourselves. Descartes answered this question by saying that we do have a clear access to our thinking selves. All we need to do to be sure of the mind that does the thinking is try to doubt it. Descartes doubted everything that could be doubted, the world around us, the concepts of science and math, and more. But he could not seem to doubt the fact that he himself was doing the doubting, the thinking. Hence, he famously said, "I think, therefore I am." The thinking self, the mind inside the bodily machine was just that self-evident to him.

Kant argued that our understanding of the world is the result of our application of some concepts in our minds to the world that we experience through our sights, sounds, smells, and feels. According to Kant, when we blow off our reading and sit to watch *Saved by the Bell* or listen to Wilco on our iPods, those objects of our sense perception, our eyes and ears, conform to the concepts in our minds. The problem is that we don't have access to these concepts while they're working. What we see, the trite lessons learned by Running Zack or the underrated semi-geniusness of Jeff Tweedy, occurs right at the intersection of our reception of the these things through our senses and our application of concepts to them. Without the concepts these things would be meaningless, but since they always mean something, our concepts are always working. Kant seemed to be saying that we cannot figure anything out about our own thinking while we're doing the thinking. We are blind to the working of our minds as our minds do the work.

So what are our alternative approaches to self-knowledge? Do we even know who is doing the thinking? How do we go about grasping the *I* that thinks? Do, we, as Chuck does, drive around and wonder about the meaning of our relationships with former lovers? Do we just reflect on the stuff we like, such as crappy *Saved by the Bell* reruns and transcendent Wilco tracks? That seems to be part of the story, but philosophers have been trying to figure this out for quite some time.

Who Am I?

Philosophers in the twentieth century tried to answer this question in many ways. Sigmund Freud suggested that consciousness, the mind, was in reality an *effect* of a structured unconscious, to which we have a sort of indirect access through interpretations of our dream-life, interpretations of our relationship with our mothers, (what did it really mean when she called us "nice bugger?"), and interpretation of our unconscious habits, (such as our self-reflexive laughing when thing are not actually funny, as when we find ourselves without exact change in Germany).

Michel Foucault showed that the rational subject, the *I* that does all the thinking, (which Descartes and Kant had been presupposing as a continuous foundation for thought), was in fact a constructed product of language and discourse. The thinking self was not continuous through each cultural epoch, but instead a construction relative to the discourse of each social sphere. Foucault doubted that some neutral rock critic, Klosterman or otherwise, could float through time making judgments about which band rocked the hardest, (Led Zeppelin, not AC/DC, Chuck). Instead the language we use to describe the world somehow shapes our conception of who is doing the describing. Chuck does not criticize Coldplay as some sort of king standing above his realm of rock. Rather, Chuck is just a construction of the language he uses to characterize them, that is, "the shittiest fucking band I've ever heard in my entire fucking life" (*Sex, Drugs, and Cocoa Puffs*, p. 3). (I'm not sure what this says about Chuck, but I do not mean to suggest that the critic inside his head is made only of foulness and filth).

Another philosopher, Martin Heidegger, offered the idea we should abandon the attempt to retreat inward to discover ourselves. Instead, we're always thrown into the world, a world of things, relationships, people, trends, and culture. For Heidegger, we are a unique sort of being, (the human kind), for whom *Being* is a question, and this *Being* includes our *own* being. For Heidegger, we can only recover ourselves through our engagement with the world of things. One way he puts this is that instead of doubting or casting aside all the inauthentic, everyday ways of engaging in the world, including obsessing over *The Real World* or watching ourselves die while playing

The Sims, we must restore ourselves in and through all that inauthentic junk. Heidegger suggested that following the crowd was one of our inevitable activities, but an activity shot through with the possibility of finding our own authentic possibilities. We inevitably fall into a mode of anonymity, watching the shows that everyone watches and following fashion trends or counter-fashion trends along with the crowd.

Thinking about Thinking

What we see through this brief history of thinking about thinking is that the process of thinking is tied up with the question of self-identity and self-knowledge. If we give up the notion of a stable, certain, self-transparent *I* who exerts my understanding on the world, then we are left with a sort of unstable, transient activity of attending to things in the world. Through these things, we learn about ourselves. Such a notion brings us back to Chuck, who once said, (and I paraphrase), *My writing is different because it's things I'm interested in, and I'm really just writing about myself and using those subjects as a prism.* Chuck is writing about himself, but he is using things to refract his thoughts through. For Heidegger, this is not a fault; this is an inevitability. What things does Chuck like? Chuck likes what everybody likes. Chuck likes pop culture. And nothing is more inauthentic and crowd-following than pop culture.

But what is thinking? I suggested above that thinking is the process of attending to our thoughts, which might seem utterly circular. But if we give up the notion of a thinking self doing and exerting the thoughts, then what are we attending to when we think, and how does such a process work?

Thinking Is Daydreaming on a Long Drive through Montana

Consider why reading is so often an activity that we feel we're forcing ourselves to do. Many of us encountered problems reading as young, or old, students. Why was reading so difficult? For me, and for almost all of my students, reading was and is hard because our minds wander away from the narrative on the assigned pages and toward something else. As a young student

I thought I was alone, the only kid in class who had this problem. I was not alone, and it has taken me over thirty years to realize that the tendency to drift in thought did not have to be a shortcoming as a student. Drifting in thought could be a potential virtue. The proper skill I needed to cultivate was in fact thinking, but thinking meant putting the book down and attending to these thoughts with a level of active engagement. The stuff of thought, the content of our daydreams, is a potential goldmine. Attending to these thoughts, this stream of consciousness, as William James called it, is the first step in writing. The next step is walking to the computer and documenting the stuff of that realm.

What Goes On Inside Chuck's Head

If to say that when we're thinking we are *in thought* is more than mere metaphor, then we need to attend to the logic of being-in-thought. How do thoughts connect with one another in the stream of consciousness? Such a question brings us back to those modern philosophers (such as Descartes and Kant). The logic at work in much of the philosophy of these moderns, those who presupposed the continuous foundation of the thinking subject, was a logic of classification. Aristotle gave us this propositional logic, in which we find subjects connected to predicates by linking verbs. The subject is the particular of our experience and we put it under a category, a predicate. *U2 is overrated*, in this way of thinking, just means that the particular band, *U2*, belongs to the category of all things overrated. U2 is the same as those other bands in that category and different from others not in it.

Classificatory logic, however, is not the only logic available to our thinking, and I am offering the hypothesis that when we attend to our thoughts the way Klosterman does when driving across the country visiting the places where famous rock stars died, our thoughts are connected not by the logic of classification, but by the logic of similarity. Foucault, one of those philosophers who questioned the continuity and self-sameness of the thinking subject, refers to the logic of Petrus Ramus. Ramian logic was the Protestant Reformation's alternative to the Aristotelian logic inherited by the Catholic theologians and modern philosophers.

Foucault was attracted to this logic in part because he thought that the logic of classification was a mode of discourse which made possible all sorts of dividing practices, a logic which erected walls and cells into which we could categorize types of behavior and people. The modern world, moving with the momentum of classificatory logic, divided up things into all sorts of binary oppositions, sane and insane, healthy and unhealthy, male and female, normal and deviant, civilized and barbarous, even overrated and underrated. Foucault viewed the modern subject as a sort of striving *not* to be the marginalized other of all of these binary oppositions. The thinking self was a product, a construct of the culture whose mode of discourse was this type of dividing language and logic. According to Foucault then, the mind inside Chuck's head is just the attempt not to be as shitty and fake as Coldplay.

The alternative logic, the logic of similarity, views the world as an ongoing play of resemblances and similarities. The structure of the world, on this account, is analogy, and the philosopher who writes analogically that *life is robbery*, for instance, discloses something structural about nature. Foucault uses the character of Don Quixote as an example of someone wandering in the modern world of classificatory logic, and by his constant search for similarities, appearing to be crazy. Quixote is convinced that windmills are giants to be attacked. Classificatory logic had banished all resemblances into the impoverished realm of mere imagination. In such a culture, Quixote is insane, living only in his head.

Perhaps it's too easy to dismiss this logic of similarity and say with the crowd that Quixote was in fact crazy. But does such a dismissal discount our actual experience of attending to our thoughts? When we think about our daydreaming, how does one thought lead to another? Our thoughts seem connected by an endless string of resemblances, which re-present that which they signify. When Chuck signs Luke Dick's copy of his book, (See "How Chuck Got Chicks") the signature is meant to re-present the actual author, Chuck.

This re-presentation of the objects of our thought is like Klosterman's experience of walking down the stairs of dead Replacements guitarist Bob Stinson's apartment after failing to learn much about Stinson's death in *Killing Yourself to Live*. Klosterman recalls listening to "Bastards of the Young" on his car radio, weeks after the funeral of his friend who had died of cancer. He burst out crying because "Bastards of the Young" was his friend's favorite Replacements song, and the song lyrics discuss burying people and struggling with the memory of the death of loved ones. The remarkable trend on which Klosterman reflects is that eventually, any Replacements song would trigger his memory of "Bastards of the Young," which would trigger the memory of his friend. The way his thought connected was by resemblance, and the similarity in Chuck's thoughts and memories bore the presence of his friend, and the entirety of his painful loss, even if the signifiers had been removed chain link by chain link from the actual cause of his sadness.

When Klosterman listens to the four KISS solo albums in *Killing Yourself to Live*, he reflects on his potential over-reliance on pop culture as a prism through which to understand the world. Chuck writes:

> Has it really come to this? Have I become so reliant on popular culture that it's the only way that I can understand anything? (p. 214)

Klosterman hopes that he would have the better sense not to relate the potential death of his mother or a Rwandan genocide to rock music resemblances. And I feel sympathy for his hesitation. But he proceeds to reflect on his many romantic relationships through the prism of former members of KISS. The structure of his thinking is that of analogy. Chuck writes: "Yet here I am in Montana, and this is what is on my mind" (p. 214). He could have written, "This is the realm of my thinking. I am *in* thought, and as I attend to the play of resemblances therein, this is what presents itself to me." He proceeds:

> Diane is sort of my own personal Gene Simmons . . . Lenore is more like Paul Stanley . . . Quincy is, of course, Ace . . . Dee Dee would be Peter . . . And this process does not end with these four, either; I once had an extended fling with an actress named Siouxie, . . . I mentally compare her to Eric Carr, a man who actually played drums for KISS longer than Peter Criss . . . I dated a photographer in Ohio . . . she was like guitarist Bruce Kulick . . . There was a woman in Fargo whom I met at the mall . . . Tina was my Vinnie Vincent. (pp. 214–16)

Now, this goes on for three pages, and I have cited Chuck enough to let you see the string of resemblances which present themselves to him and that he lets his readers in on. Now, you're saying to yourself, this is just a writer's device, a conceptual scheme through which he can refract his self-involved obsession with his sexual history. Yes and no. The logic of similarity expresses the nature of things by revealing their structure as analogy. The logic gains its momentum by our attention to it. But this does not detract from the fact that our thoughts are connected by it. That it enables us, after we had attended to our thoughts, to make use of it as a consciously applied schema speaks to its richness and power, not to its poverty or weakness.

Two things are going on here. One is the question of thinking, the logic of our thoughts. The other is about the thinker, the one who first attends to her thoughts and then appropriates their logic of similarity and resemblance as a powerful plan to understand the world.

Recall that Chuck said that he was really writing about himself and using popular culture as a prism. Why could he not just write about himself directly and spare us the details of the history of the members of a band, whose bassist front man was most known for his uber-long tongue wagging?

Know Thyself through Your Favorite Band

Could it be, thinking against Descartes, that we do not have such an easy access to ourselves? Klosterman takes up this question explicitly in his first chapter of *Eating the Dinosaur*. During an interview with the American documentary filmmaker, Errol Morris, Klosterman wants to know why people answer questions in interviews when asked. Klosterman has spent most of his career in journalism *asking* the questions in interviews, but in his more recent fame, he has been on the other end of the dialogue, *answering* questions of interviewers. He wonders why he answers the questions. In one of Morris's responses, we get a gem of philosophical speculation quite relevant to my musings in this chapter.

> I'm not sure we truly have privileged access to our own minds. I don't think we have any idea who we are. I think we're engaged in a constant battle to figure out who we are. (p. 5)

If Morris is correct, and I think he is, then Heidegger was correct as well. We are inevitably thrown into a world and can only recover ourselves through our engagement in the mode of anonymity, the mode of following the crowd. Klosterman has built his young career following the crowd. He likes what the crowd likes, and this is, of course, popular culture.

However, Chuck does not pretend that by his conscious selection of which pop culture trapping to appropriate that he can stylize himself as authentic. He admitted to being fully contrived on his first few dates. He only has three and a half dates worth of material, which he pretends to deliver off the cuff. But since Chuck doesn't know who he is, how can he be himself on the date? We are in a constant struggle to know who we are, just as Morris said, and so part of that struggle is going through that contrived banter of first and second dates, although I think we should avoid "coercing" women into anything, including just staying into the last half of the fourth date.

Is Chuck a phony through and through, or does Chuck also strive after the authentic life? I think that Chuck's admission of his BS on his first dates is a wiser confession than some might think. Chuck *knows* he's ignorant of who he is. And he knows he's trying to figure out who he is. Self-knowledge is the condition for authenticity, surely. But Chuck also knows that an authentic existence cannot be had by any direct approach, as that would only register as fake. Nor can authenticity be achieved only by a rejection of tradition, authority, and all that a counter-culture has deemed co-opted by the mainstream establishment.

This is especially true since the idea of authenticity by way of rejection of the mainstream has itself been co-opted and sold back to youngsters at the mall repeatedly. Even attempts to be genuine by coloring one's hair purple can seem as inauthentic as drinking Mountain Dew because we self-identify with NASCAR driver, Dale Earnhardt, Jr. Since we're all thrown into this world, (we did not choose to be here), and we are all fallen in the Biblical sense, (we are imperfect), we must inevitably take up a relation to the world of fleeting things, tenuous relationships, and shifting projects.

The world of fleeting things includes the junk of pop culture, such as *Saved by the Bell* reruns. (By the way, much like Chuck, the summer of 1993 included for me the routine of, after bussing tables from 6:30 A.M. to 2:30 P.M., watching four *Saved by the Bell* reruns in the afternoon . . . instead of reading. My four went for ninety minutes, the middle portion of which contained two episodes, to which I would flip back and forth until I could give full attention to the last episode. Tracking the plot development of two episodes of *Saved by the Bell* simultaneously was, well, not difficult).

The world of tenuous relationships includes our own personal narratives reconstructed through the filter of rock music icons. I, too, went through my Led Zeppelin phase, and I declared as Chuck says every adolescent male does, "Wow. I just realized something: This shit is perfect. In fact, this record is vastly superior to all other forms of music on the entire planet, so this is all I will ever listen to, all the time" (*Killing Yourself to Live*, p. 200). While we're on the topic of Zeppelin, recall the logic of what makes them so popular. Their "rib-crushing" qualities are their resemblances:

> They sound like an English blues band. They sound like a warm blooded brachiosaur. They sound like Hannibal's assault across the Alps. They sound sexy and sexist and sexless. They sound dark but stoned; they sound smart but dumb; they seem older than you, but just barely. Led Zeppelin sounds like the way a cool guy acts. Or— more specifically—Led Zeppelin sounds like a certain kind of cool guy: they sound like the kind of cool guy every man vaguely thinks he has the potential to be, if just a few things about the world were somehow different. (p. 199)

Now granted, in *some* of Klosterman's logic of similarity, he swings and misses, but I think he did tap into some structure of nature revealed by way of analogy.

Our own shifting projects include those phases of our rock band tastes which seem to embody the structure of our experience by analogy. But we do still have an existential task. We must recuperate ourselves and achieve authenticity in and through these transient styles. This is our ongoing project, and through an exemplification of the attention to one's thoughts, Chuck illustrates the insights of attending to our thoughts and the logic of similarity which give them order. Furthermore, Klosterman shows the wealth of value they provide as prisms to know ourselves.

Finally, what Heidegger gives us as a description of authenticity concerns the realization of our mortality. We must question the direction of the crowd when we are called as if by another voice, our conscience, to do so. If we attend to this call, we become individuals and we realize our ownmost possibilities, as we anticipate the possibility of our own death. We project authentic existence in anxious resoluteness toward our deaths. Klosterman's anxiety and obsessive writing over death suggest that he is on a long path and constant struggle for the authenticity which he knows cannot be had by any easy formula.

I think his writing helps us travel the same path. He realizes, alongside Heidegger, the intimate relationship between living and dying. We live towards our own deaths. The more this possibility is a reality to us, the better chance we have of living up to our ownmost possibilities. Chuck writes, "We are always dying, all the time. That's what living is; living is dying, little by little. It's a sequenced collection of individualized deaths" (*Killing Yourself to Live*, pp. 112–13). Now, we do not need to break up our experience into little atomic parts as Klosterman does to understand that living is a living toward our own death. But perhaps the extent to which people strive *not* to know the reality of their living as dying is coextensive with their living in an inauthentic rut. Their fear of death causes them to blind themselves to themselves. Their thinking self is, as Foucault suggested and as Freud intimated, a retreat from the marginalized Other, represented by decay and death. Owning up to the inevitability of our own deaths helps us recover ourselves from the crap which we are always caught up in.

Writing, Thinking, and not Reading

Is writing difficult? If Descartes was correct, and, in order to write, our thinking mind must hold its knowledge inside in an organized way and then transmit it onto a computer screen in an exertion of magical proportions, the writing is more than difficult—it is impossible. Writing, as a product of attending to your thoughts, is not hard. You just need to put down your reading and attend to your thoughts and the logic that structures them, much like Chuck does for us.[1]

---

[1] I'm indebted to Kenneth Stikkers for his work on the logic of similitude which I incorporated in this chapter.

5
Fake Love Lives

CRAIG ROOD

"No woman will ever satisfy me," he says. And with a title like "This Is Emo," it's easy to suspect Chuck Klosterman wallows in self-pity. But he doesn't just spew out his faults and frustrations. He says that when it comes to love, many of us fall short of our ideal and are left frustrated and confused. Klosterman claims it's not his personal problem, but a cultural one.

On the surface, Klosterman's argument makes a lot of sense. While most sixteen-year-olds writing English reports can articulate that the mass media creates expectations that are difficult—and often impossible—to fulfill, Klosterman goes beyond the traditional analysis of the media's influence on body image and violence to claim that the media manipulates the way we view relationships and love. He blames Coldplay for songs that "deliver an amorphous, irrefutable interpretation of how being in love is supposed to feel" and for persuading people to want that feeling for real (*Sex, Drugs, and Cocoa Puffs*, p. 4). He blames actors like John Cusack for creating a cult following among women for his role as Lloyd Dobler in *Say Anything*. He blames all of us for letting art and life become interchangeable.

Klosterman's claim is intriguing, but what does it mean beneath the surface? Philosophically, what does Klosterman mean when he says no woman will ever satisfy him?

She Loves Him, She Loves Him Not; She Loves Him, He Is Not

Klosterman claims that others can't satisfy us because we judge them against the impossible standards set by movies, love-songs, and sitcoms. We screwed up by letting art become the ideal that we hopelessly stumble toward. And we're going to be frustrated and a bit anxious as we constantly fall short.

In Klosterman's Lloyd Dobler/John Cusack example, he claims that viewers mistook the role of a character for the actual person who did the acting, and viewers fell in love with the person in the role. In "This Is Emo," Klosterman writes, "It appears that countless women born between the years of 1965 and 1978 are in love with John Cusack. . . . But here's what none of these upwardly mobile women seem to realize: They don't love John Cusack. They love Lloyd Dobler. When they seek Mr. Cusack, they are still seeing the optimistic, charming, loquacious teenager he played in *Say Anything*" (pp. 2–3). The women, including Melissa Vosen (See "Killing Myself to Live in Carnival Square"), love a role played by a man, not the man himself. Klosterman continues:

> And these upwardly mobile women are not alone. We all convince ourselves of things like this—not necessarily about *Say Anything*, but about any fictionalized portrayals of romance that happen to hit us in the right place, at the right time. This is why I will never be completely satisfied by a woman and this is why the kind of woman I tend to find attractive will never be satisfied by me. We will both measure our relationship against the prospect of fake love. (*Sex, Drugs, and Cocoa Puffs*, p. 3)

In philosophical terms, Klosterman's point illustrates the distinction in metaphysics between appearance and reality, between what seems to be and what is. In everyday terms, it means the love-deprived twenty-something is living in a fantasy world and doesn't realize it. Lloyd Dobler doesn't exist, and the women seeking him are bound to be disappointed. Furthermore, men will become disillusioned because they will be judged against a standard that is based in fiction (and men do the same to women). Klosterman explains:

> If Cusack and I were competing for the same woman, I could easily accept losing. However, I don't really feel like John and I were 'competing' for the girl I'm referring to, inasmuch as her relationship to Cusack was confined to watching him as a two-dimensional projection, pretending to be characters who don't actually exist. Now, there was a time when I would have thought that detachment would have given me a huge advantage over Johnny C., inasmuch as *my* relationship with this woman included things like 'talking on the phone' and 'nuzzling under umbrellas' and 'eating pancakes.' However, I have come to realize that I perceived this competition completely backward; it was definitely an unfair battle, but not in my favor. It was unfair in Cusack's favor. I never had a chance. (p. 2)

Klosterman could never be Cusack. But what's worse: women would always want him to be like Cusack and—without realizing this—he would try to be like Cusack (or maybe Zack Efron, Vin Diesel, or Morgan Freeman).

Klosterman, played by Chuck Klosterman

Klosterman's point about the influence fictional characters have on our own sense of self and character raises questions about individual identity and how someone becomes who they are. To a large extent, identity seems learned. Who we are and who we want to be are constantly influenced by our surroundings, including those around us. To some extent, we're all actors, trying to play parts. A passage from existentialist Jean-Paul Sartre's *Being and Nothingness* helps to illustrate this point:

> Let us consider this waiter in the café. His movement is quick and forward, a little too precise, a little too rapid. He comes toward the customers with a step a little too quick. He bends forward a little too eagerly; his voice, his eyes express an interest a little too solicitous for the order of the client. . . . All his behavior seems to us a game. . . . He is playing, he is amusing himself. But what is he playing? We need not watch long before we can explain it: he is playing *at being* a waiter in a café. . . . This obligation is not different from that which is imposed on all tradesmen. Their condition is wholly one of ceremony. (p. 82)

The waiter in the café plays a part, a role he's learned from experience—from movies, from watching other waiters, from being a waiter and adjusting to customers' expectations of waiters. Beyond his first day of work, I doubt he ever thought, "I need to figure out how to be like a waiter." Still, he tries. And the fact that he tries makes his actions seem unnatural and inauthentic.

Several contemporary philosophers would argue that we all role play. We're always acting or performing (hence this theory of identity is called performativity). Performing in this context does not necessarily mean deceit, though some roles are more sincere than others. Judith Butler, a feminist philosopher, claims that this is what happens with gender. Echoing Simone de Beauvoir's claim that "one is not born a woman, but becomes one," Butler asks:

> Does being female constitute a 'natural fact' or a cultural performance, or is 'naturalness' constituted through discursively constrained performative acts that produce the body through and within the categories of sex? (*Gender Trouble*, pp. xxviii–xxix)

Butler's question gets at the fact that women are not born with an innate desire to wear makeup or paint their fingernails. Women learn their gender (or choose to rebel against gender norms as did glam rockers in the 1980s). Through repeated performances—by themselves, with others, and in fictionalized portrayals—and feedback from others, women learn what it means to be a woman; for the most part, women try to fill this role and other men and women expect it.

Just as gender is performed, so are other aspects of our identity (like our jobs, as the passage from Sartre suggests). As I compose this essay, I think and act like a writer (and so does Klosterman). I've developed my own approach, but this approach exists within the context of what I was taught in school, what I've seen in movies, accounts of famous authors (many of which are tragic, including Sartre's addiction to Corydrane), and narratives I've learned from friends. I cannot sit down at a computer without this background, without this knowledge of the writer's role.

Likewise, you, as a reader, come to this essay with expectations of what it means to be a reader. In part, your knowledge has been influenced by the culture you are part of: you have learned about the best environments for reading, how to hold the book, what kinds of things (if any) to write in the margins and when, and so on. (And you'll probably be self-conscious of this for at least the next paragraph—or stop reading out of spite.)

This point about our identity being performed shows up throughout Klosterman's work. In his analysis of MTV's show *The Real World*, Klosterman writes that by the third season both the characters on screen and his real life acquaintances "started becoming personality templates, devoid of complication and obsessed with melodrama" (*Sex, Drugs, and Cocoa Puffs*, p. 39). In the preface to his interview of Britney Spears, Klosterman explains that he doesn't feel like he knows the real Britney, and, what's worse, neither does she: she seemed "unable to differentiate between (a) the person who was famous and (b) the person she actually was" (*Chuck Klosterman IV*, p. 11). And in *Eating the Dinosaur*, Klosterman complains about fake laughter. He encourages readers to "Watch *The Daily Show* in an apartment full of young progressives and you'll hear them consciously (and unconvincingly) over-laugh at every joke that's delivered, mostly to assure everyone else that they're appropriately informed and predictably leftist" (p. 173).

Our identity and views of the world are largely learned and performed. We create who we are, and the project of identity creation is ongoing. Specifically, Klosterman suggests in "This Is Emo" that our understanding of love is learned. And he is right that the mass media often isn't the best teacher. From our favorite movies and television shows, we can learn what a romantic evening and first kiss should be like, and how people communicate and look at each other. One of the problems, Klosterman notes, is that "The mass media causes sexual misdirection: It prompts us to *need* something deeper than what we *want*" (*Sex. Drugs, and Cocoa Puffs*, p. 6). If identity is a performance, the roles we cast for each other are often unrealistic (insane, perhaps); it's like expecting a third grader to play Hamlet—or expecting that woman in the coffee shop to be as emotionally clichéd and flirty as women in all *Lifetime* movies and romantic comedies since at least 1989.

The problem of fake love affects all of us. Klosterman laments that whenever meeting others, "I notice that they all seem to share a single unifying characteristic: the inability to experience the kind of mind-blowing, transcendent romantic relationship they perceive to be a normal part of living" (*Sex Drugs, and Cocoa Puffs*, p. 2). Later on, he tries to analyze the cause of this phenomenon:

> The main problem with mass media is that it makes it impossible to fall in love with any acumen of normalcy. There is no 'normal,' because everybody is being twisted by the same sources simultaneously. You can't compare your relationship with the playful couple who lives next door, because they're probably modeling themselves after Chandler Bing and Monica Geller. Real people are actively trying to live like fake people, so real people are no less fake. Every comparison becomes impractical. This is why the impractical has become totally acceptable; impracticality almost seems cool. (pp. 4–5)

We're in love with fiction, according to Klosterman. We expect ourselves and those living and breathing before us to act and feel like the projections we see on the screen. They do, to an extent, but they also fall short. And we're disappointed.

Can we ever experience others for who they truly are? Can *they* ever be truly authentic? Can *we*?

An Authentic Performer?

"Real people are actively trying to live like fake people, so real people are no less fake" Klosterman writes (pp. 4–5). But what does *real* mean in this context? Is there a natural self, a self immune from the media? A self immune from others? (The obvious answer is no. But keep reading; the detailed answer is worth your time. For real.)

Klosterman claims that "art and life have become completely interchangeable" (p. 8)—that is, fiction and reality have bled and neither is completely separable. Our lives are like Plato's allegory of the cave: we're all trapped in a cave, watching shadows on the wall, thinking these shadows are really real, not understanding that they are imperfect reflections of what is real. To modify Plato slightly: the cave is now a movie theater with reclining seats—but we are no less deceived. Surfer kids in California and Emo kids in New Jersey (and even farm kids in North Dakota) see fake love and think it's real love.

Klosterman says we all confuse real and fake love. But "love" in the movies is a kind of love that doesn't work outside of the movie theater (Plato scorned art as being an imitation of an imitation). We aren't John Cusack and the girl walking on the street isn't Anne Hathaway (at least not on my streets; and yes, the streets in North Dakota are paved; and no, there are only about eleven people in the state who actually sound like the characters in *Fargo*). Yet we pretend and maintain the delusion that our everyday life should be like the lives we see in sitcoms and movies, according to Klosterman. We continue to choose the fake world over the real world, and we continue to be disappointed.

Klosterman explains, "But this is how media devolution works: It creates an archetype that eventually dwarfs its origin. By now, the 'Woody Allen Personality Type' has far greater cultural importance than the man himself" (*Sex, Drugs, and Cocoa Puffs*, p. 5). We both act and expect others to act like Woody Allen (or anyone else famous), though, for most of us, we aren't completely aware. From our experiences, we learn what it means to be funny, what it means to be an interesting person, and what it means to have an exciting relationship. But when such meanings are modeled after fiction, we're likely to be disappointed. We fail to meet our expectations because our expectations come from movie scripts. Trying to adapt these scripts to our three-dimensional world is often impractical. (Klosterman's argument rests on the premise that fictional relationships are unattainable because the expectations are too high, when, in fact, they may be too low).

In light of Klosterman's 2009 marriage, we might say Klosterman was mistaken: he thought he would never be satisfied, but now he seems to have found someone. We might be tempted, but the version of his self that wrote *Sex, Drugs, and Cocoa Puffs* anticipates such an objection. After explaining that no woman will ever satisfy him, he continues:

> Should I be writing such thoughts? Perhaps not. Perhaps it's a bad idea. I can definitely foresee a scenario where that first paragraph could come back to haunt me, especially if I somehow became marginally famous. If I become marginally famous, I will undoubtedly be interviewed by someone in the media, and the interviewer will inevitably ask, "Fifteen years ago, you wrote that no woman could

ever satisfy you. Now that you've been married for almost five years, are those words still true?" And I will have to say, "Oh, God no. Those were the words of an entirely different person—a person whom I can't even relate to anymore. Honestly, I can't image an existence without _____. She satisfies me in ways that I never even considered. She saved me, really."

    Now, I will be lying. I won't really feel that way. But I'll certainly *say* those words, and I'll deliver them with the utmost sincerity, even though those sentiments will not be there. . . . But here's the thing: I *do* believe that. It's the truth now, and it will be in the future. (p. 1)

Saying this (rationalizing this?) makes his argument apply across time. He claims that no woman will ever satisfy him—not in two months, two years, or two decades. Never. His claim isn't about love and identity for a particular person at a particular time and place, but for everyone, always. This makes his argument philosophical—and makes Klosterman's angry critics call him arrogant (or an "ass-head," but seriously, who calls someone an "ass-head?"—answer: Mark Ames).

Authenticity Is Dead—The Media Killed It

The issues of individual identity and love relate to the nature of reality (philosophers call this metaphysics) and knowledge and our way(s) of knowing (philosophers call this epistemology). Klosterman's analysis raises two basic philosophical questions. A. What's real? B. How do we know?

    There are about as many different answers to philosophical questions such as these as there are philosophers. Thales, the father of Western philosophy, claimed that reality was ultimately made of water (ironically, he fell into a well while staring at the sky; I suppose this gets back to my earlier point about identity being learned: philosophers have been accused of having their heads in the clouds ever since). Heraclitus claimed that reality is constant flux. Parmenides said that reality is one, complete, and unchanging. Plato is a hybrid of Heraclitus and Parmenides: for Plato, this world is constantly changing, but that is because we are deceived by our senses; we can acquire knowledge, but only through our reason in contact with another complete and unchanging world—the world of forms. Modern scientists will likely claim an atomic theory, echoing Greek philosophers like Democritus and Empedocles, in which there is only one, material reality.

Klosterman's most obvious intellectual kin is none of these thinkers, but rather, a contemporary cultural critic, Jean Baudrillard. Baudrillard has a more abstract (and obscure) take on Klosterman's point, though their views of reality are basically the same. Rather than say what reality is made up of, Baudrillard claims that we cannot know reality because our experiences are always filtered by language and culture. One of his best known works is *Simulacra and Simulation*. While conventional uses of "simulation" imply intentional deception or artifice, Baudrillard's use suggests that the deception is a necessary part of all our experience. Baudrillard writes:

> Today abstraction is no longer that of the map, the double, the mirror, or the concept. Simulation is no longer that of a territory, a referential being, or a substance. It is the generation by models of a real without origin or reality: a hyperreal. The territory no longer precedes the map, nor does it survive it. (*Simulacra and Simulation*, p. 1)

In Klosterman's analysis, Woody Allen represents what Baudrillard calls "the generation by models of a real without origin or reality." Allen is everywhere—with traces found in subsequent movies, your behavior, your neighbors, your friends. According to Klosterman, Allen "made it acceptable for beautiful women to sleep with nerdy, bespectacled goofballs; all we need to do is fabricate the illusion of intellectual humor, and we somehow have a chance" (*Sex, Drugs, and Cocoa Puffs*, p. 5). But, as Klosterman points out, few realize that Woody Allen (or anyone else famous) is what they are attempting to imitate; in other words, though the original role or archetype is continuously imitated, we are not always aware of or able to identify this origin. To take this a step further, the actors we see in movies today are trying to be in some sense like real people— but they are also trying to act like an actor (a role shaped by other actors from other movies). At the same time, we try to be like them. Given all of this, it's not exactly clear what it means to be authentic.

Baudrillard's phrase, "the generation by models or a real without origin or reality," gets to the heart of post-structuralism, a contemporary take on language and reality. In post-structuralism, the old view of a clear relationship between a word or sound-image (signifier) and a concept (signified) becomes fragmented; more precisely, the relationship between signifier and signified is mutually reinforcing, yet constantly changing. It's like saying that reality influences our language and reality is influenced by language—except the relationship is much messier than that. In Klosterman's terms, "Real people are actively trying to live like fake people, so real people are no less fake" (pp. 4–5). Baudrillard explains that there is "No more mirror of being and appearances, of the real and its concept" (p. 2). Or, to use the linguists' terms, simulacra do not represent a connection between a concept (a signified) and ultimate meaning (a transcendental signifier); simulacra can only point to an endless web of signifiers because there is nothing real and stable to refer to. According to Baudrillard, we are stuck in a world of the hyper-real, deluded by mass culture and unable to access anything directly.

Baudrillard's argument is a new take on Kant (bear with me; it will all make sense in just a bit). Immanuel Kant, an eighteenth-century German philosopher, is best known for what he called his second Copernican Revolution. Just as Copernicus showed that the Sun, not the Earth, was the center of our solar system, so Kant wanted to make a similar inversion for philosophy. (And tragically, Kant succeeded). Many philosophers before Kant's revolution thought reality was the center; a human mind needed to conform to or perceive reality to acquire knowledge. (Our concepts conformed to the objects of our perception according to this paradigm). However, Kant argued the human mind was at the center; knowledge was not acquired, but rather, constructed by the human mind. The mind actively constructs or shapes reality by means of the mind's lenses (what Kant calls forms of intuition and categories of the understanding), like space, time, and causality. We cannot know things-in-themselves (the *noumenal* world) because our mind is always imposing structure on the world; all we can ever know is things as they appear to us (the *phenomenal* world), and thus, our knowledge is incomplete. (The objects of our perception conform to our concepts according to Kant's paradigm).

Baudrillard's metaphysics and epistemology are similar to Kant's. However, rather than claim the existence of *innate* categories of the mind like Kant, Baudrillard claims that the categories or lenses are *social constructions*. All of our past experience imposes on our present experience. If there is an ultimate reality, or things-in-themselves, we can't know it. According to this view, we can only access hyperreality, a world constructed by us through our language and culture.

Baudrillard's views of culture, language, and reality are notoriously controversial. His book *The Gulf War Did Not Take Place* (1995) is introduced by a scene in which CNN reporters on the front lines of the Gulf War are watching CNN to figure out what is going on in the war. Baudrillard goes on to argue that the media has simulated our experience of battle and destruction to such an extent that it is impossible for there to be any sense of an underlying reality of the war. Now, I don't think Klosterman is this outrageous, but I do think his analysis of love in the media assumes views similar to Baudrillard's about the nature of reality and the power of the mass media. For instance, in *Eating the Dinosaur*, Klosterman writes, "I get the sense that most of the core questions dwell on the way media perception constructs a fake reality that ends up becoming more meaningful than whatever actually happened" (*Eating the Dinosaur*, back cover). For both Klosterman and Baudrillard, reality is socially constructed through experience, including images and language. But whereas Baudrillard seems content with this, Klosterman seems to retain hope for authenticity—a reality, he implies, that is immune from media.

Media(tion) and Authenticity

Movies, music, and television are all forms of media; they mediate, or are the means by which we connect to plots, lyrics, and characters, all of which can teach us about things like self-identity and relationships. For Klosterman, the mass media makes everyone a bit artificial: we always perceive others and adapt to be like or unlike them. Klosterman's argument seems powerful until we ask a really basic question: Can we ever be absent from the media? In asking this, I am obviously referring to the mass media, as he does, but I am also pushing his argument a bit further to ask whether the media—both overtly fictional and not—really refers to all of our interactions. In other words, is all of our experience mediated or situated? By making this shift, the question really becomes: Can we ever exist apart from a context, apart from things in the world?

Aristotle and the empiricists claim that to be alive is to be able to perceive—to see, hear, touch, taste, and smell—and to think. Our mind at birth is *tabula rasa*—a blank slate, upon which experience writes and from which we form our understanding. Our knowledge is learned, and so it has to come from somewhere. We cannot know concepts like "intelligence" or "love" without coming in contact with conceptions of these in the world, conceptions likely to have been influenced by movies, music, novels, sitcoms, our neighbors, and so on. We might create a new concept of love, but the roots of such a concept are ultimately traceable back to experience. *To be* is to be in the world.

Most of us recognize the increasing influence of the mass media, and Klosterman is right to be concerned about its pervasiveness. He jokes that "in the nineteenth century, teenagers merely aspired to have a marriage that would be better than that of their parents'" (*Sex, Drugs, and Cocoa Puffs*, p. 4). The Internet, movies, and sitcoms didn't become part of everyday life until the twentieth century, but haven't there always been media, even if not on as massive and pervasive of a scale? Hasn't all of our knowledge been mediated by the sum of our experiences, including books, plays, newspapers, our neighbors, our past, and our present situation? Doubtless, neither Plato nor Aristotle knew of Kelly Kapowski or Monica Gellar, but don't you suppose their judgment of women was at least influenced by Helen of Troy or Antigone?

Klosterman wants real love, and thus, real people. On one level, this makes sense: fictions perpetuated by the media can be destructive if we try to enact them in our everyday lives. What's problematic, philosophically, is that he counts on readers having a clear division between "that which comes from the mass media" and "that which doesn't," and his tone suggests that the latter is better. But his main point is that the distinction is false; as he says, "art and life have become interchangeable" (*Sex, Drugs, and Cocoa Puffs*, p. 8). Yet, by implication, Klosterman longs for a reality that is non-mediated, one that is cut off from context. "A relationship," Klosterman claims, "based on witty conversation and intellectual discourse" is just another gimmick, and it's no different than wanting to be with someone because they're thin or rich or the former lead singer of Whiskeytown. And it actually might be worse, because an intellectual relationship isn't real *at all*. My witty banter and cerebral discourse is always completely contrived. (pp. 6–7)

Shortly after, he continues, "she *thinks* she digs me, because who she digs is not really me" (p. 7). What, then, is a *real* basis for a relationship? What, then, is the *real* self?

In fairness to Klosterman, I don't think he would state this outright, but the argument he puts forth in "This Is Emo" implies a Platonic ideal of a pure, unchanging self. Klosterman—like Plato, Kant, and Baudrillard—presumes a lost paradise of pure being (whether the world of forms, the *noumenal* world, or a world apart from culture). The problem is that no such world exists. We can't escape from the media—and more broadly, we can't exist apart from mediation or context. Nor should we try. There is no "real" self completely cut off from the self that sees, breathes, listens, and speaks.

We should not disparage our process of being and knowing as inauthentic or fake, nor flounder in emotional angst. Culture and context do not create a fake world, nor do they disqualify our knowledge or way(s) of knowing. We must exist and know by some means. Our real, "authentic" self—our only self or selves—is one that has to be in this world, the world of people, pop-culture, and everyday performances. The point is not to escape from the mass media or mediation, but to be in control of it. Self-control, Aristotle suggests, means we must not be guided primarily by emo(tion), but by reason and the perceptual evidence of this world—a world which we can understand and change.

What's frightening about Klosterman's diagnosis is that we seem trapped. Everyone's conceptions of love are mediated and, according to him, delusional. Klosterman explains that "Fake love is a very powerful thing" (*Sex, Drugs, and Cocoa Puffs*, p. 3), though he fails to question whether fake love is the only thing with power. But let's ask the question now: Is culture destiny—or do we have the power to act?

When taking in conceptions of love (or gender, work, and so on), or when mimicking the interactions between Diane Chambers and Sam Malone (or Monica Gellar and Chandler

Bing, Diane Court and Lloyd Dobler), do we have the freedom to stop and say "No, this isn't right—this is nonsense"? Do we have a center of control apart from the scripts for the roles we attempt to perform? If we can enact such a power—and if others do the same—we might be able to establish standards for relationships that others and ourselves can satisfy—or surpass.

Klosterman proclaims, "No woman will ever satisfy me," and he then explains, but "I know it's not my fault. It's no one's fault, really. Or maybe it's everyone's fault."

The response should be, "How fatalistic!"

Turn off the CFL?

Turn off the CFL

MATT SIENKIEWICZ

Someone builds an optical portal that allows you to see a vision of your own life in the future (it's essentially a crystal ball that shows a randomly selected image of what your life will be like in twenty years). You can only see into this portal for thirty seconds. When you finally peer into the crystal, you see yourself in a living room, two decades older than you are today. You are watching a Canadian football game, and you are extremely happy. You are wearing a CFL jersey. Your chair is surrounded by books and magazines that promote the Canadian Football League, and there are CFL pennants covering your walls. You are alone in the room, but you are gleefully muttering about historical moments in Canadian football history. It becomes clear that for some unknown reason you have become obsessed with Canadian football. And this future is static and absolute; no matter what you do, this future will happen. The optical portal is never wrong. This destiny cannot be changed. The next day, you are flipping through television channels and randomly come across a pre-season CFL game between the Toronto Argonauts and the Saskatchewan Roughriders. Knowing your inevitable future, do you now watch it?

—*Sex, Drugs, and Cocoa Puffs*, pp. 131–32

Chuck's question here hits upon a profound concern deeply engrained in both the history of religious thought and moral philosophy. What he's described, in fact, outlines almost perfectly the manner in which traditional Jewish and Christian thinkers have conceived of God's all-knowing, timeless perspective on the world. It's a moment that will smack anyone who believes in an all-powerful Creator harder than a couple of too-strong Witty Chuck cocktails at one point or another. If God knows everything, then He is not only aware of the contents of my web history, but also knows what unsavory things I'm going to do in the future. This is not simply embarrassing—imagine your mom could walk in and catch you doing unspeakable things you haven't even done yet—but it's also a direct and rather horrifying assault on your freedom. If God knows you're going to do something, do you really have any freedom when you do it? Is it fair to say you have any freedom at all? Does this get you off the hook for throwing up those Witty Chucks at your hipster buddy's ironic Val Kilmer film festival party?

Here Chuck seems to be providing what might be described as the "movie" solution to this theological problem. As you watch yourself watching the CFL's fourth-downless football (seriously, someone thought it was a good idea to have only three downs, great if you love punting) you're sort of seeing a movie of your future self. But that doesn't mean it was scripted.

Think of the chest-wax scene from *40-Year-Old Virgin*. Just like God watching you surf the web or Chuck's hypothetical future, you're watching guys who couldn't make the Oakland Raiders bumble across the field. When you watch Steve Carrell get the hair ripped out of his chest, you've been temporally displaced from the event you're watching—just like God always is. Remember, an all-powerful God is thought to have invented time, thus everything that's ever happened or ever will happen is essentially part of God's DVD collection, to be watched whenever He's bored with running the universe. Similarly, you can watch the waxing scene now or watch it later, it's never going to change. But none of that changes the fact that Carrell's yelps and expletives emerged from his own free will. They may or may not have been written in the script but the fact that you're seeing it in a form that ensures it will never change does nothing to change that fact. As long as your vantage point has a different relationship to time than whatever it is you're watching, it's at least logically possible that free will remains in play.

So, Chuck's magic portal doesn't have to strip your life of all meaning or make you one of those guys who talks about *The Matrix* as if it's important. Which is really good, 'cause you'd probably have to re-watch those terrible sequels if it were. But this doesn't quite answer the question. So what should you do?

Well, we live life with a degree of certainty about our future anyway, no? I hate to break it to you, but one way or another, we all end up in a similar place, physically at least. So, you've lived your whole life knowing you're going to die and nonetheless decided to devote your limited time and resources to learning what some guy with too much time on his hands thinks about Chuck Klosterman's weird filler material about Canadian Football. If that major revelation hasn't thrown you off of your game, knowing you're someday going to take seriously a bunch of guys who collectively go by the name "the Alouettes" probably shouldn't be more than a hiccup.

Or, to put it more straightforwardly, no, you shouldn't watch Canadian Football. That'd by like saying "Hey, I'm gonna die one day, might as well just jump in the box now." Seriously, they play with only three downs.

BOOK III

Eighty-Five Percent of a True Philosophy

6
Death Takes a Road Trip

CHAD FLANDERS

Somewhere, at some point, somehow, somebody decided that death equals credibility.

—CHUCK KLOSTERMAN (*Killing Yourself to Live*, p. 13)

The old philosophical saw goes: if a tree falls in the woods, and no one's around to hear it, does it make a noise? That's the basic version. There are variations, of course—including the recurrent lament of the Introduction to Philosophy student: If a tree falls in the woods, and no one is around to hear it, *does anyone care*?

Here's the variation that Chuck Klosterman hits us with in his book *Killing Yourself to Live*: if a rock star dies, and no one really cared about his music before, is dying something that can totally transform his career, making a nothing into a something? If a rock star dies in a plane crash, is his music even more worth listening to?

Case in point #1: Jeff Buckley. Before his death, his album and his career were okay, decent, respectable, even somewhat notable. But his catalog was hardly extensive. At most, he was someone to watch. This was all before he drowned in the Mississippi River, which apparently changed everything.

After his death, Jeff Buckley becomes classic, deep, and "real," a messiah (p. 123). People—you know them, whether they admit it to you or not—listen to his cover of "Hallelujah" over and over and over again after they've broken up with their girlfriend or after some similarly major life event. The song now "speaks to them." The same song, written by Leonard Cohen, but now sung not by a living but by a *dead* Jeff Buckley is haunting instead of languid and meandering, full of a new and significant meaning, *even though the lyrics are the same as when Cohen sung them.* Every pause, every breath, is like Buckley's last. He hangs on. Or at least he did hang on, until he didn't. We can hang on. Maybe.

And in a way, strange as it sounds, it's *actually* true that the song becomes different, even *sounds* different, after Buckley's death. Of course, this has a lot to do with *us* changing, but the music seems to have changed, too.

But even weirder, Buckley's death didn't just change his music, make it more freighted with meaning, it changed *Buckley's whole life.* Buckley's whole life becomes *different* now that he died young. His life becomes tragic and profound, rather than routine and mundane. It becomes something it wasn't when Buckley was alive. For Buckley, dying was a pretty brilliant career move: he only started living when he died. There are other examples, and *Killing Yourself to Live* is full of them: Elvis, Buddy Holly, Duane Allman and ultimately, Kurt Cobain.

This gives us two questions.

1. **How is it possible that dying could be really good for someone? I mean, isn't death pretty bad?**

and

2. **Should we care that death can be good for someone? Or is it really a question not worth asking? Does it matter for us, who go on living?**

And this leads inexorably to a question about the two questions, viz., why should we read a book and then set about to answer a question the author is unsure is really worth asking?

Can Our Lives Go Better (or Worse) after We've Died?

Killing Yourself to Live is pretty much about these two questions. Klosterman takes a road trip to figure out why rock stars, or a lot of them, seem to do so much better after death. But he's also on a road trip to see whether this is a question worth thinking about. He's always oscillating wildly between whether he's asking himself a really deep question, and whether it's really pointless to keep on asking it. Is it, Klosterman asks himself at several points, a question that serious people are interested in? Or is it a question only for flippant folks?

We might think of the question Klosterman is asking as a sort of secularized version of the question of what happens when we die. It's secularized because Klosterman isn't asking the religious question of what happens when we die—whether we'll be joining a chorus of angels singing the original chorus to Hallelujah by Handel, or whether we'll be with Judas Priest and Van Halen in hell.

No, Klosterman's asking whether *down here, on Earth*, it can be a good thing for people, particularly rock stars, to die. And not just a good thing for the people who keep on living, but *good for the people who actually die*. The question, we ought to admit right up front, is pretty strange. How could it be a good thing for a rock star's career, for his music, for his *life*, to *die*? Can good things keep on happening to us, when there's no "us" around anymore?

What, in short, could it possibly mean to say that people are benefited or hurt by something that happens after their death? If we stipulate that this life is the only life we have, and that when we die we're *dead*, then it would seem to follow that *nothing* can be good or bad for us after we die. All that's happened to us has happened already: there's nothing *new* that can be added to our stock of experiences, for good or for ill.

As Klosterman knows, however, this isn't true with rock musicians—sometimes, their story only really begins when they die. Their death somehow gives their life meaning that it might not have had already. This is, to say the least, weird. How can you get something from *dying* that you couldn't get by *living*? And how can this make your life actually go *better*? It worked for Jeff Buckley, anyway.

Aristotle, referred to by many in the middle ages as simply "The Philosopher," wrestled with a version of Klosterman's question in his classic, *Nicomachean Ethics*. He suggests the following example. Suppose a businessperson spends his entire life building up his empire—he's made the connections, built up the relationships, staffed his company with the best people. He runs it well, and then he dies. But then his sons take over his business, and through a combination of bad luck and careless decision-making, they squander his fortune and his empire. Aristotle's question was, can we say that the failure of his business was a bad thing for the father, even though he was dead? Aristotle wanted to allow at least some force to the thought that people really can fare better or fare worse, even after they have lived out their lives. "It would be odd," Aristotle says, "if the fortunes of the descendants did not for some time have some effect on the happiness of their ancestors" (*Nicomachean Ethics*, p. 16). Especially, we might add, if the ancestors put a lot of weight on the fortunes of their descendants.

This phenomenon seems to make sense. We might put Aristotle's point this way. At various times, we are all the authors and the subjects of several stories. Some of them indeed come to an end when we die and when we cease to be able to influence our story in any active way. But some of those stories have a life that outlives the death of their authors. We can still be the subject of our stories, even though—because we're dead—we cease to be in any meaningful way the ongoing authors of those stories. If this is so, then even when those *lives* end, our "stories" are in some sense still ongoing. So what happens after we die may have some bearing, big or small, on how well our life story goes. The businessman whose business collapses after he dies has been, even in a small way, hurt by that loss. His happiness has waned. And that's because one of the stories of his life—starting a successful business empire—didn't end when his life did. It went on, for better or for worse.

This is how rock stars might go on to be helped or hurt after they've died. Buckley's music gets discovered, or noticed, and all-of-the-sudden (or so it seems) his life is a success, his songs are meaningful, deep, and worthwhile. All of the suffering has paid off. His life, we might say, was not lived in vain (as he might have lived, had he not drowned, and remained relatively obscure). Buckley becomes immortal, not by not dying (which is the way Woody Allen wants to be immortal), but by having the most important part of him live on: his music. "Lesson: To live in the hearts of those we leave behind is not to die" (*Killing Yourself to Live*, p. 108).

Now, we have to be careful here because we might not want to say that *all* of what happens to a person after their death will change the meaning of the person's life. In fact, Aristotle seemed reluctant to give much weight to things like fame and celebrity status. Those things, Aristotle says, we can't really control even when we're alive, and if we can't control them then, it's an open question whether they should really be credited to us. Aristotle was big on virtue, and we *could* control whether we were virtuous enough. No one could give us virtue (Aristotle sometimes called this "greatness of soul"), and no one can take it away from us, even after we die. On the other hand, if we haven't lived virtuous lives, then no amount of success can make up for that. Think of Michael Jackson, whose death has resulted in even greater fame, but still wasn't able to remove the sense that the guy was, although a great artist, pretty messed up. So there is still something about *our lives* that can't go better for us after we're dead. If we've lived terrible, vicious lives, no number of posthumous fans can make *that* go away. We're stuck to a large extent with the lives we've actually lived.

However, Aristotle did contemplate the possibility that our lives might go better or worse after we die, even if only in a limited way. Rock stars can live on in the hearts of their fans. And this is the important point: their lives can go better or worse, not in just some objective sense, but in a way which is really better *for them*, even when they've died. Jeff Buckley's life has actually gone better since his death, strange as it may sound. Death might not be the end of a musician's career, but only the beginning.

There Are No Stupid Questions, Except the Stupid Ones

So it seems possible that our lives could actually, in some meaningful way, *go better* even after we die, and not in some spooky sense. Rather, our lives can go better insofar as our projects live on even after we die, in the hearts and minds of those who come after us.

But there's the rub. Whether our lives go better or not will depend on whether there are people who carry on after us, and in a way that actually *fits* with the way we lived our lives—or wanted to live them. In other words, our success in our life-after-we're-dead depends on our fans, those who remember us after we're dead. And this can be a problem.

Killing Yourself to Live is book-ended by fans' reactions to two events. One, which nearly consumes the book and hovers over all of it, is the death of the fans at the Great White concert in West Warwick, Rhode Island. What's interesting and important about the people who died at that concert was that they were not famous—indeed, they were made fun of by those who weren't at the concert, practically moments after they passed away. But the people who went to the concert weren't there to be seen or to *say* that they had gone or that it was amazing, or that it sucked. Nor did they go in some self-consciously ironic mode, which treats it as a laughable event but fun in its disingenuousness, as when some folks go to karaoke bars and treat the evening as some sort of laughable event, even alongside those who are there in an earnest way to sing and hear their peers sing. (For more on that see Chapter 2 in this volume, "The Unironical in the Age of Irony"). Rather, these folks at the Great White show were there in earnest because they were just *fans*. They had that particular sort of integrity that a person has when he's *really into* a band, and doesn't care what anyone else thinks.

More importantly—at least for the lesson Klosterman is eventually going to draw—are the people who mourn for those who died in the Great White tragedy. They have had family members die, but they seem happy, as happy as any people Klosterman has ever met (*Killing Yourself to Live*, p. 35). Klosterman becomes fast friends with them; he does cocaine in one of their pick-up trucks. Their memorials to those who died that night, simple crosses, as well as the attitudes of those who mourn the dead must seem to Klosterman as exemplary ways to deal with death. There is no pretentiousness to them, as one of the mourners says of those who would go to concerts by Great White or Warrant. There is a sense that these mourners will go on with their own lives, as indeed even the members of Great White have decided to go on with theirs (p. 136). They seem to be genuine both in their remorse and in their happiness, and above all, in their dedication to those who have passed away.

By contrast, Klosterman is scathing about the reaction of "fans" to Kurt Cobain's death. The people who mourn Cobain did not know him—except perhaps in some fantasy (p. 233). They have theories about why he died, but they don't really know why Cobain died, and it doesn't really matter to them. That's because ultimately, Cobain's death isn't about Cobain. It's about *them*, about what Cobain means to *them*.

In general, Cobain's death is "poorly remembered" (p. 244). In fact, it's so poorly remembered that people tend to *falsify* the past, and not remember it. The way many of Cobain's fans "remember" Cobain is to invent a past about what they think might have happened—what Cobain might (but probably didn't) mean to them. We tend to forget, Klosterman reminds us, that at the time of Cobain's death, Pearl Jam was the more popular band. There is a lot of "reverse engineering" going on, both culturally—what did Nirvana mean for *us*?—and individually—what did Cobain mean for *me* (p. 123)? We recreate the past—Cobain's and our own—in our own image.

With the death of the fans at the Great White concert, the memorial to them was really about *them*, the dead. But the death of Cobain isn't really about Cobain—it's more about the people who think that his death gave them something they were missing in their own lives. By having Cobain's death *mean something* to them, somehow, retrospectively, those who mourn Cobain gain depth: they gain an identity. By attaching yourself to Cobain, it "was now possible to achieve credibility simply by mourning retrospectively," Klosterman says (p. 226). You could become *cool* just by identifying yourself as a fan of Kurt Cobain, even if this only became true after Cobain died.

And here Klosterman flashes back to a conversation he had earlier in the book, at the Chelsea Hotel, where he first hears the lesson it takes him the whole book to really *learn*. There, he is trying to find the room where Sid Vicious's girlfriend had died. He is not the first one to look for this room. Some coming to visit even want to *stay* in the room where she died. The manager of the Chelsea Hotel, interjects, and says that those looking for the place where Sid Vicious's girlfriend died are people who have nothing to do: "If you want to understand what someone fascinated by Sid Vicious is looking for, go find *those* people. You will see that they are not serious-minded people. You will see that they are not trying to understand anything about death. They are looking for nothing" (p. 9).

What Klosterman learns at the beginning of the book, but only really understands at the end, is that the people who are fans of rock stars after their deaths are not serious people, that they are looking for nothing. They are trying to find something that just isn't there. These misguided fans are trying to find meaning in someone else's death, and somehow have that meaning make *their lives* better. Klosterman, too, has been looking for nothing the entire road trip, by trying to find the meaning of the death of rock stars. There is no meaning to it. The dead, he says at the end, are simply dead, and everything else we can say about them is just a "human construction" (p. 230). The scales fall from Klosterman's eyes.

When we look at those who follow the famous rock dead, what they're doing has "nothing to do with the individual who died and everything to do with the people who are left behind" (p. 230). They are not serious people. Neither was Klosterman, prior to his revelation. He spends the entire book going to the places where rock stars had died. What was he looking for? He was looking for nothing, after all. He was ignoring the truth that dead people are simply dead, and the rest is human construction.

This does not mean, necessarily, that the question Aristotle was concerned with—can we be benefited after we die?—has no answer. But it does suggest we are better off not asking the question. We have to ask, instead, why we are worried about whether people can benefit after they die. Sometimes, we really are worried about *them*: this is the lesson we learn from the Great White fans. Those who mourn *them* are authentic in their mourning, they aren't trying to create anything that wasn't there. Rather, they were trying to remember what *really was* there.

But the lesson we learn from the fans of Kurt Cobain is that we should be pretty suspicious of why we mourn people we don't know, or had nothing to do with our lives. We should worry that we are looking for something that was never there in the first place: we are fooling ourselves, and in a way, doing a disservice to those we are supposedly mourning.

And this brings us back to Jeff Buckley. It may seem that in his death, he is having a better life. But what gives him this better life? Fans. Those who are inventing a mythical present for him, creating something that wasn't necessarily there, imbuing his songs with meaning they don't necessarily have. The fans are taking as much from Buckley as they are giving him.

So Klosterman leaves us with a profoundly ambivalent message about rock stars like Buckley and Cobain. By worshipping them, and mourning them, we are extending their lives—we're making their lives longer, and in some sense, better, than they would otherwise have been. But at the same time, such "life" is manufactured, invented, *not really authentic*.

The fans of those who died at the Great White concert give us a better lesson. Remember what was actually there. Don't make things more than they were. Don't give things more meaning than what they have. There was—and is—enough meaning in what was actually there. Buckley wrote some good songs. So did Cobain. But Buckley was no messiah, and Cobain didn't die for our sins. Nirvana was just a rock band, you know?

The Death of This Chapter and the Meaning of Its Existence

Killing Yourself to Live is in the end a subversive book. It's a book by a rock critic—and in many ways the archetypal rock *fan*—going on a road trip to see the landmarks of the famous rock dead. But the book ultimately concludes that it's not worthwhile to go on road trips to see the famous rock dead: only unserious people do that, the ones who find meaning in the lives of others and not their own lives. Klosterman is critiquing a certain way of *being a fan*.

This is a subversive thing to say about rock fans, the people Klosterman needs to survive as a rock critic. But it's a message made palatable by the fact that Klosterman needs to hear that message too. *He* needs to be reminded of the limits of worshipping the mighty dead, of imagining that they are more than they really are, and most of all, imagining that *they* can make us something we're not. He, after all, is the one going on the road trip.

In the end, Klosterman needs to kill himself as an unserious rock fan, to live as a more serious person. And by doing it to himself, Klosterman hopes that he can maybe save us having to make the trip ourselves.

7

Celebrity as the Sickness unto Death

JOHN THOMAS BRITTINGHAM

Am I for *real*, or am I full of shit? And what does it mean to be *real* anyway?

Am I only *real* when I cast aside my fancy gadgets, my social responsibilities, the vices I've come to cherish, and the so-called virtues I pretend to cultivate?

Am I a phony if I consider my electronic doohickeys, Don Draper-esque stunning good looks and soul-crushing self-confidence, my important (or at the very least self-important) and well-known friends, and my work successes as the most important parts of who I am? Is my self something that is constructed from all of the above-mentioned elements—a kind of fake ID for life—or is there something more to my self? Oftentimes, I don't ask myself these questions because I'm too busy concerning myself with the lives of others, be they musicians, actors, or tabloid queens. But even celebrities can't escape questions of a real or fake self—even if I always assume that they are as authentic as a Hostess Cupcake.

So, what are celebrities *really* like? As a journalist for several prominent music and culture magazines, Chuck Klosterman has had the opportunity to interview quite a number of celebrities. Inevitably, this question of what they're *really* like comes up whenever Chuck, himself, is being interviewed. Reflecting back upon these interviews, Klosterman notes how the identity of the artist *as* a celebrity is often as much a constructed artifice as their albums, films, and books. Some of these celebrities are aware of themselves as constructing an identity (Jeff Tweedy), while others appear to be completely oblivious (Britney Spears). Some are obsessed with their celebrity identity (Billy Joel), while others seem like they couldn't care less (Robert Plant).

Still, before we can look at the relation between the celebrity image and the person who bears that image, we have to ask ourselves a deceptively simple question that we have yet to ask: what is a self? One way of thinking about what makes something "a self" is by understanding the self as a synthesis. Or, as the nineteenth-century Danish philosopher Søren Kierkegaard put it, the self is a relation which relates itself to itself.

But what the hell does that mean? Is such a relation composed of just two parts or of more than two parts? And these parts are made of what exactly? Which parts are the *real* parts, and which parts are not parts at all? Kierkegaard is talking about a synthesis or relation between the temporal and eternal, finite and infinite, actual and possible parts of ourselves. It's not just a synthesis of who we've been, or who we are right at this moment, but of who we're capable of being.

Yet, bringing these two parts of the self together and recognizing them as actually the same self that we, ourselves, are requires some distancing. It requires being both an observer of the self and being the observed. Who better than our friend Chuck Klosterman to tell us about the experience of observing those who are observing themselves? And who better than some of the celebrities that Chuck has interviewed to tell us a little bit about ourselves by telling us a little bit about their selves? There is something interesting to note about our relation as readers to Chuck Klosterman as the author and as the interviewer. In a sense, we (the readers) are observing Chuck's observances of celebrities—observances that incorporate both the self-reflection of their famous subjects and the comments and interpretations of Chuck himself. Not only do we have the possibility of learning about ourselves from inquiring into these famous subjects, but we stand a chance at learning a little about Chuck too. We'll follow Kierkegaard's itinerary as we explore how celebrities manifest these sicknesses of the self, all the while trying to find out whether or not we are for real or if we are full of shit.

Behind the Britney Curtain

How is it possible that someone could be ignorant of having a self? It seems like the most obvious bit of knowledge in the universe. To be a human being that is still living is to have a self. End of story. Actually, it's not the end of the story—in fact, it's more like the beginning of the story. If the self is a synthesis or a relation as Kierkegaard thinks it is, then there are going to be multiple parts of the self that are in relation. For someone to be ignorant of having a self would be for such a person to be ignorant of one or more of these parts brought into relation with the parts that they do recognize. They would, for example, emphasize their obsessive consumption of profane amounts of television as an indication that they have become a keen observer of the human condition all the while remaining completely in the dark concerning the condition of their own personality. This person would then be someone who is completely unaware of their self as a whole, only recognizing those parts that are most immediate to them (and yet, at the same time, being ignorant of that which is so immediate it is overlooked—the self).

The perfect example of this first type of sickness of the self is Britney Spears. During his interview with Ms. Spears, Chuck recognizes this very paradox of identity almost immediately. In his descriptive setup to the interview, Chuck tells us that there is a risqué photoshoot with Britney where she's hidden behind a curtain. He knows that she is more or less naked behind the curtain but he, like the rest of us, is forbidden to go past this barrier.

Chuck says, "Apparently, the reason I am here is to be reminded that the essence of Britney Spears's rawest sexuality is something *I will never see*, even though I know it's there. This is why I am a metaphor for the American Dream. Culturally, there is nothing more trenchant than the fact that Britney Spears will never give it up, even though she already has" (*Chuck Klosterman IV*, p. 13). Keep in mind Chuck wrote this before the proliferation of photos of Brit's not-so-shrouded undercarriage on the Internet.

Britney's "rawest sexuality" is itself a metaphor for that part of the self that remains in question. Chuck points out that we're clearly not allowed to peek behind the curtain and see that part of Britney which is excessively and intensely hers. However, Chuck also notices that this metaphor operates at another level. It's as though Britney herself is unaware of what is going on behind the curtain. She's the one being exposed, but she doesn't understand it that way. In fact, she doesn't even think about it.

"I ask her questions about her iconography", Chuck says, "and she acts as though she has no idea what the word *iconography* even means. It's not that Britney Spears denies that she is a sexual icon, or that she disagrees with the assertion that she embodies the "Madonna/whore" dichotomy more than any human in history, or that she feels her success says more than any human in history, or that she feels her success says nothing about what our society fantasizes about. She doesn't disagree with any of that stuff, because she swears *she has never even thought about it*. Not even once" (p. 13).

No matter what Ms. Spears might think about herself, anyone with a television in the first decade of the twenty-first century would say that it's undeniable that Britney Spears is a sexual icon. She is more than just her concrete, immediate self. We might even say that she symbolizes an idea that goes beyond herself. Klosterman says as much when he ruminates that "She is not so much a person as she is an *idea*, and the idea is this: you can want everything, so long as you get nothing. The western world has always been fixated with the eroticism of purity: that was how Brooke Shields sold Calvin Kleins, and that was how Annette Funicello sold the beach. But no one has ever packaged the schism like Britney Spears" (p. 14). Yet, as we've been saying, the schism doesn't immediately affect Britney because she doesn't even recognize it in the first place. The symbolic part of her self, the part that exists as an idea of the "wet-hot virgin," doesn't even enter her thoughts. She remains steadfast in her naiveté, not unlike a prudish girlfriend who's never even heard of blue-balls, be they philosophical or otherwise.

It would be understandable if Britney were the first instance of someone monumentally famous being completely ignorant of her public perception of what she has come to symbolize. However, Chuck identifies Britney as both another member of the blonde icon archetype that proliferates in American popular culture and as something new. "This is what makes Britney so different," Chuck tells us, ". . . she refuses to deconstruct herself. That falls in stark contrast with the previous generation of blonde icons, most notably Madonna (who makes it clear that she controls every extension of her existence) and Pam Anderson (who refuses to take her own Barbie Doll bombast seriously)" (p. 15). Britney, therefore, is a self that fails to recognize any part of herself that might extend beyond just her immediate goals and surroundings. She appears to live a fundamentally simple existence. She is an entertainer, and she amuses people by shaking her booty and singing songs that they like. There is nothing more to it than that.

Still, what might it mean for Britney to "deconstruct herself" as Chuck says? Would she have to recognize that her handlers are making her into a sexual icon in the manner of her predecessors despite the fact that she perceives herself as a pure entertainer? Would she have to accept that she is popular only partially because of her talent and partially because she fits into a role that American popular culture has perennially carved out for a select few of its more attractive young ladies? Or maybe she'd have to admit that she's really good at working out and confusing bathing suits with formalwear. Perhaps, but Britney refuses to recognize these parts of herself. In fact, they entirely fail to describe Britney Spears—according to Britney Spears. There is no need to look behind the curtain because, according to Britney, there is nothing behind the curtain to see.

Regardless of how Britney views herself, we can recognize that Britney, as a brand or as a cultural symbol, is more than just the southern-born mouseketeer turned pop artist. And we can wonder, along with Chuck, if she is truly ignorant of herself as something more than just the immediate, unabstracted Britney that she's always been to herself or if she has pushed the denial of this symbolic part of herself to such an extreme that we are all fooled into believing that she is ignorant of it. However, if we're keeping with Kierkegaard's diagnosis of despair, it's almost undeniable that the Britney who Chuck interviewed was suffering a sickness of the self. Kierkegaard puts it this way:

> This is the state in despair. No matter how much the despairing person avoids it, no matter how successfully he has completely lost himself (especially the case in the form of despair that is ignorance of

being in despair) and lost himself in such a manner that the loss is not at all detectable—eternity nevertheless will make it manifest that his condition was despair and will nail him to himself so that his torment will still be that he cannot rid himself of his self, and it will become obvious that he was just imagining that he had succeeded in doing so. (*Sickness unto Death*, p. 21)

What Kierkegaard is emphasizing here is that a person such as Britney, no matter how hard she tries to remain ignorant, cannot remain in ignorance about her self forever. In fact, it's not the case that there is nothing behind the curtain, that there is no deeper, more symbolic part of Britney. Rather, it's that she has lost that part of herself which is like an archetype, which is symbolic, which is an idea, which does go beyond the immediate image she has of herself. And that eternal part of her, that part of her that is beyond just her body or her person but is nevertheless still very much her—that part of her lays claim to the part that she does recognize.

So, is Britney for real, or is she full of shit? In a sense, she is very much for real, at least, to herself. But we can see that she might be full of shit. We're the ones that recognize that there's this whole big Britney brand which is connected to the sexy blonde or "wet-hot virgin" archetype that is perennial in American popular culture. So is Britney still full of shit if she doesn't think she is? And what about ourselves? If we deny the eternal and symbolic parts of ourselves—those parts of ourselves that push us beyond just our immediate, concrete situations—do we suffer a sickness of the self? Do we even have a part of ourselves that pushes us beyond ourselves? If we deny this driving part, this symbolic, eternal, or infinite part of ourselves, are we still for real? Or are we full of shit?

Imagine being in Chuck's shoes during this interview in 2003. Imagine listening to somebody completely deny anything other than what is most immediate to her regarding a career that is full of sexual symbolism and teenage fantasies. The very part of Britney that drives her to sing "Baby One More Time," wearing pigtails, a bare midriff, and a Catholic school girl uniform, emanating infantilized sexuality throughout, is the same part of herself that she seems to be denying. She *is* the sexual icon, the quintessential American product—sexy, sleek, and addictive. Imagine thinking, 'What's going to happen when you realize that you're all these things people say you are? Are you going to freak out? Are you going to shave your head and attack cameramen with an umbrella? Are you going to run from bad choice to bad choice trying to anesthetize yourself to who you have come to recognize as being, in fact, you?' What went through Chuck's mind is unknown to us, as is what went through Britney's mind. It remains in question whether or not she was actively deceiving herself. However, as Klosterman recognizes, she still might be a genius for having maintained the deception for as long and in as steadfast a manner as she did.

Meditations of a Former Rock'n'Roll Messiah

While Britney Spears represents someone whose defining feature, at least in Klosterman's interview, seemed to be an unrelenting naïveté about herself as anything more than just an entertainer, this is certainly not the case with U2. More specifically, when Chuck interviews U2's lead singer, Bono, in Dublin on the eve of *How to Dismantle an Atomic Bomb*'s release, he formulates the question of identity as follows: "there is only one question about U2 that actually matters, and I'm still trying to figure it out . . . is Bono for real, or is Bono full of shit?" (*Chuck Klosterman IV*, p. 23).

With Bono, we have a celebrity that is both an extreme construction and someone who is desperately trying to be authentic. There is the Bono of rockstar posturing, of 3D concerts and messianic imagery, and then there is the Bono of the One campaign, of Jubilee 2000, and of countless other humanitarian causes he championed. But the question that we have to ask ourselves right now is this: "Is Bono someone who suffers from a sickness of the self where both the humanitarian advocate and the messianic rock'n'roller are artifices? And if they are performances, then what part of Bono is for real and what part is full of shit?"

What's most interesting about Klosterman's assessment of Bono and Bono's assessment of himself is how they both recognize that the most symbolic and self-consciously caring part of U2's career is precisely that part which is most inauthentic. How could this be? How could the heart on sleeve, advocate of the underdog, politically active U2 actually be less authentic

than the ironic, always sunglasses and skullcap wearing, iPod
endorsing U2 of the 1990s and beyond? Klosterman identifies
this desperation for authenticity as what made U2 so important in the 1980s. He says, "The reason U2 were (arguably) the
most important band of the 1980s was because audiences felt
they *always* took a side. What makes "Sunday Bloody Sunday"
a powerful song is that something seemed to be at stake, even
if you had no idea what happened in Northern Ireland during
the winter of 1972. If anything, U2 seemed to care about things
too much; there was no middle of the road on the drive toward
Joshua Tree" (p. 30).

That U2 cared was undeniable. That they wanted us to *know*
they cared is what remains questionable. What separates the
early U2 from someone like Britney Spears regarding selfhood
is that they acknowledged the symbolic, infinite, side of their
band. U2 knew they were becoming symbols for something more
than four lads from Ireland who played music together, and
they wanted that almost as much as they wanted us to know
that they wanted it. Bono assesses the situation like this:

> I don't think anyone who's famous didn't *want* to be famous. The peo-
> ple who hide in the shadows and cover their heads with their coats
> when they're being photographed by the paparazzi probably think
> being famous is more important than it actually is, and—in a way—
> probably need fame more than anyone else. I've gotten to the stage
> where I almost forget I'm in a rock band, which was never the case in
> the 1980s. And that was annoying, because that wasn't sexy. Self-
> consciousness is never sexy. I mean, I've watched myself being inter-
> viewed on TV, and I just think to myself, *What an asshole.* (*Chuck
> Klosterman IV*, p. 30)

While Bono was never one to hide his light under a bushel, he
does admit to taking fame far too seriously. In this statement
Bono reveals to Chuck and to the rest of us that he is able to
see the symbolic, iconic part of himself, and he casts it aside. In
a way, Bono is saying that who he was in the 1980s, with all
that grandstanding and posturing, was inauthentic. He admits
to the symbols but he appears to lack the will to embrace them
anymore.

Bono becomes a representative of Kierkegaard's second
level of the sickness of the self: despair in not willing to be one-

self. Kierkegaard explains it as follows: "This form of despair is: in despair not to will to be oneself. Or even lower: in despair not to will to be a self. Or lowest of all: in despair to will to be someone else, to wish for a new self" (*Sickness*, p. 52). Kierkegaard sees a tension between those parts of ourselves that we want to acknowledge and those parts that we'd rather not admit are a part of who we are (for example, acting like a messianic figure who fronts an extremely popular rock band). So when Bono is disparaging his 1980s self for his seemingly self-righteous posturing, he is also suffering from despair. He sounds as though he wishes to be a different self than that iconic, flag-waving front man from Live Aid, as though he despairs in having been so self-conscious.

Acknowledging that such posturing is involved in the creation of an identity is something that another less famous musician, Jeff Tweedy of Wilco, spoke about with Klosterman in another interview. We might say that part of the reason why such posturing goes on in the first place is that, by creating a persona or an identity with passionate symbolic aspects is, in a way, quite cool. This is what KISS did with aplomb, but the same could be said for others such as Prince or Morrissey or Jack White for that matter. Tweedy, however, sees things quite differently. "It's just that I'm uncool," Tweedy says when asked about the overt normalcy of his middle-class life.

> I have a great life but it's an uncool life. It was a wonderful revelation to move to Chicago and make music and just be normal. So many artists reach a certain level of success, and then they cross over; they surrender everything to the service of their persona. Take somebody like Madonna, for example; you could never get to be that huge unless you surrendered every other impulse in your body to the service of your persona. Even with Bob Dylan, there was clearly a point early in his career where he was completely able to immerse himself inside that persona. And I think it's disastrous that so many people destroy themselves because they can't do it. They don't have the intestinal fortitude. I mean, how many fucking people has Keith Richards killed? How many countless people has Sid Vicious killed? How many young girls has Madonna made insane? (p. 146)

To surrender one's self to the symbolic or iconic part of the self is so common in rock'n'roll that it seems like a cliché. Yet, what

Tweedy is getting at is that one has to give up on that part of the self in order to retain any level of normalcy. The pursuit of a personality like that of Sid Vicious or Madonna is, in many ways, the pursuit of a self that is externally cool. And this pursuit of external coolness exacerbates the distance between the immediate self and the symbolic self. Both Tweedy and Bono go beyond ignorance of any self that is other than what is most immediate, but they both have reservations about the consequences of cultivating those parts of the self.

In like manner, Kierkegaard paints a picture of *the man of immediacy*, that is, the person who retreats from their symbolic, infinite self and hides in his or her own normalcy. "Imagine a self", Kierkegaard says, "and then imagine that it suddenly occurs to a self that it might become someone other— than itself" (*Sickness*, p. 53). For example, imagine four young lads growing up in Dublin playing punkish music together. Now imagine that they, themselves, imagine that they could be something other than just four guys with three chords and the truth. That they imagine themselves as musical missionaries, bringing the listening masses anthems of social protest. They imagine themselves as a band that is not only famous, but one that matters. Or, in Kierkegaard's words:

> . . . yet one in despair this way, whose sole desire is this most lunatic of lunatic metamorphoses, is infatuated with the illusion that this change can be accomplished as easily as one changes clothes. The man of immediacy does not know himself, he quite literally identifies himself only by the clothes he wears, he identifies having a self by externalities (here again the infinitely comical). There is hardly a more ludicrous mistake, for a self is indeed infinitely distinct from an externality. So when the externals have completely changed for the person of immediacy and he has despaired, he goes one step further; he thinks something like this, it becomes his wish: What if I became someone else, got myself a new self? Well, what if he did become someone else? I wonder whether he would recognize himself. (*Sickness unto Death*, p. 53).

These celebrities, such as Bono, who recognize themselves by externalities—even if these externalities are things like heart-on-sleeve desperation or flag waving self-importance—these celebrities choose to become something else because they see that their symbolic/infinite self has become something they despair over. They seek a respite from their infinite self because their immediate self is embarrassed.

And this is precisely the part about Bono that is so interesting; he is embarrassed about his behavior in the 1980s when everything appeared to matter and he seemed to care *too much* because it appears now to have been just posturing. But no one would say that the Bono of the 1990s or even the sunglasses-wearing elder statesman of this past decade was any less a posture. Klosterman, himself, seems to believe that

> Bono thinks rock'n'roll is so shallow, in a way. He has always enjoyed the trappings of fame, but he feels the urge to balance it with something more substantial. He really is a walking contradiction. It's always all or nothing with him. There is almost nothing in the middle. (*Chuck Klosterman IV*, p. 31)

Still, the "substantial" part of Bono, the one that cares about AIDS victims in Africa but doesn't confuse that with rock stardom isn't so different from the Bono of the 1980s who did confuse, or at the very least conflate, the two. Bono wants to escape from the self-consciousness of his 1980s self but, in expressing this desire for escape, only reveals further self-consciousness. He is self-conscious about being self-conscious.

The despair which takes the form of willing not to be oneself recognizes that the symbolic or infinite part of the self— that part of us which is not immediate—does exist. One in this stage of despair just wants nothing to do with that part of the self. However, desiring to escape the trappings of fame or the symbolic parts of the self does not, in itself, make one authentically a self. Regardless of whether we are as famous as Bono or nearly unnoticeable, trying to escape that public or iconic part of the self is still a denial of who we really are. Besides, Bono in the 1980s seemed to really believe that U2's music was a force for social change. He seemed to believe in the ideals proclaimed so strongly by their ambient anthems that he could gesticulate on stage like a rock'n'roll messiah without the slightest hint of irony. So was Bono of the 1980s for real or was he full of shit? Is the Bono of our era, who looks back with embarrassment at his former behavior and seeks to escape it for real or is he full of shit? Was it that, in the end, those ideals

Bono proclaimed were wrong, or that they were just uncool and Bono would rather be cool than right?

In contrast with Bono, Klosterman regards Tweedy as the least pretentious rock star he's ever met. Tweedy's life is certainly uncool with its suburban home, kids in softball, soccer-dad milieu with complementary minivan and "proud parent of an honor student" stickers, but one cannot say that it is an inauthentic life. Tweedy understands the allure of that self-conscious desire for fame and all of its trappings, and he wants nothing to do with it. With Tweedy, there isn't any lingering embarrassment about his past or the unsexiness of his suburban lifestyle so much as there is recognition and acceptance of those parts of his self that are symbolic (and in a sense silly) and those parts that are concrete and downright "dad-like."

And what about us, for that matter? If we deny the parts of ourselves that are constructions, ideals, and symbolic—that is, those parts of ourselves that go beyond what is most immediate—are weeding out inauthenticities or are we simply in denial about who we really are? If we deny the iconic parts of ourselves, are we still for real? Or are we phony?

The Master of Puppets Is the Master of None

If the last form of despair was a weakness of the self through the denial of the symbolic or iconic (what Kierkegaard would call infinite) part of the self, the third form of despair embraces that side. In fact, this third form of despair embraces the eternal part of the self to the point that it becomes the only part of the self that matters. This is why Kierkegaard calls this form of despair "defiance;" it is a form of despair that defies its own finitude and limitations. In defiance, the self refuses to allow its limitations to lay claim to itself and refuses any limiting of its possibilities. There's perhaps no better example of this third form of despair than the lifestyle that rock'n'roll celebrities apparently enjoy. And there's no better example of why this lifestyle leads to despair than Metallica.

In his write-up about the Metallica documentary *Some Kind of Monster*, Klosterman attempts to drive home the point that "rock'n'roll manufactures a reality that's almost guaranteed to make people incomplete" (p. 108). Granted, his choice of subject matter makes emphasizing this manufactured reality quite an easy task, but it is still one that we, as consumers of popular music, television, and film, tend to overlook. Perhaps it is not that we overlook that rock'n'roll in particular manufactures a reality all its own; rather, we overlook that such a reality leaves its participants fundamentally incomplete.

"I think most people in rock bands have arrested development" Metallica lead guitarist Kirk Hammett says. He continues:

> "Society doesn't demand people in rock bands do certain things. You're able to start drinking whenever you want, and you can play shows drunk, and you can get offstage and continue to be drunk, and people love it. They toast their glasses to an artist who's drunk and breaking things and screaming and wrestling in the middle of a restaurant. Things like that happened to us, and people cheered."
> (*Chuck Klosterman IV*, p. 109)

"How many people has Sid Vicious killed?" wondered Jeff Tweedy, and rightfully so. The consequences of the creation of an identity which is iconic are often far greater than one anticipated upon entering into the world of rock'n'roll. It also appears that we consumers of their artistic projects encourage such drastic behavior and then also turn up our noses to them when they reveal the hollowness of their lives.

Metallica is going through a drastic transition during the filming of their documentary, *Some Kind of Monster*; a transformation, which includes a stint in rehab for lead singer James Hetfield and sessions with a therapist, named Phil Towle. In the midst of this transition, the band's identity as a hard rock juggernaut begins to fray, resulting in disillusionment, anger, and despair. That people under a considerable amount of stress would begin to notice their relationships beginning to break down is nothing new. When that same thing happens to hard rock bands, it can be perceived as extremely odd. These bands are supposed to be brutal forces of nature more akin to a hurricane than a hurt puppy. This is why what happened to Metallica is so interesting: they broke down and did it all on camera. Metallica showed us what it means for forty-somethings to finally begin the process of maturing after having lived inside the symbolic or iconic self that they cultivated over decades.

"If you strip down all human beings to their core, you'll find the same stuff," Towle says,

> you will find fear of rejection, fear of abandonment, fear of being con-
> trolled, fear of being unloved, and the desire to love and be loved.
> That becomes more complicated with hard-rock bands, because—
> when you exist in a mode of instant gratification—you're never hungry
> for depth of intimacy. Sex, drugs, and booze are glorified in rock'n'roll,
> but those are really just symptoms of the desire for relief." (*Chuck
> Klosterman IV*, p. 104)

Part of the process of cultivating a hard rock identity manufactured to be cooler or more brutal than the lives of most hard
rock fans is that such an identity feeds off of debauchery. This
debauched lifestyle becomes an identity all its own where "rock
gods" can defiantly live like children and get paid millions of
dollars to do so. It is almost as though, because they possess
talent in other areas, we are all the more willing to concede
that rock stars are above the consequences of the manufactured reality they enjoy.

"Metallica's evolution as real people was aborted by their
surreal existence," says Towle. "Kirk Hammett once told me
that coming off tour was like experiencing post traumatic
stress syndrome; he said it was like leaving a war and re-enter-
ing real life. When I asked him why he felt that way, he said,
'Because now I have to empty the trash.' The profundity in that
statement is its simplicity: rock stars are infantilized by people
who do everything for them. We insulate them from a reality
that would actually be good for them" (*Chuck Klosterman IV*, p.
109).

Having to take out the trash is not merely an element of
maturing into what is commonly referred to as adulthood but
represents the immediate and concrete forms of existence that
rock stars appear to be continuously escaping. "Almost everyone that is really famous has cultivated personality. I can
safely say that no one who has ever won an Oscar didn't want
to win an Oscar" says the actor Val Kilmer in another
Klosterman interview (p. 45). Celebrities, it appears, always
wanted to be that famous personality, as though they were a
character in a performance piece about their own lives.
However, such cultivation of a personality is not without its pit-

falls. Even when one lives behind the veil of one's own making, be it as a celebrated hard rock band member, an Oscar-winning actress, or a novelist, the concrete everyday part of the self lays claim to this ego-centric dream world of a self.

Kierkegaard pointedly remarks that, "The self is its own master, absolutely its own master, so-called; and precisely this is the despair, but also what it regards as its pleasure and delight. On closer examination, however, it is easy to see that this absolute ruler is a king without a country, actually ruling over nothing" (*Sickness unto Death*, p. 69). A "rock god" who can amaze with his bravado, excess, and talent at playing more notes than seems humanly possible but laments at having to take out the trash is, in Kierkegaard's eyes, a king without a country who rules over nothing. This is why Metallica tearing away the veil and revealing their bifurcated selves, alienated from their everyday concrete lives and yet no longer able to find fulfillment in their manufactured identity, is such a bold move and also such a terrifying prospect. James, Kirk, and Lars reveal that they are not only figures of strength, brutality, and coolness but also fragile human beings. And it is precisely the act of revealing this that is so terrifying.

Consider Kierkegaard's reflection on this phenomenon:

> Consequently, the self in despair is always building only castles in the air, only shadowboxing. All these imaginatively constructed virtues make it look splendid. . . . In despair the self wants to enjoy the total satisfaction of making itself into itself, of developing itself, of being itself; it wants to have the honor of this poetic, masterly construction, the way it has understood itself. And yet, in the final analysis, what it understands by itself is a riddle; in the very moment when it seems that the self is closest to having the building completed, it can arbitrarily dissolve the whole thing into nothing. (p. 69)

When we think about rock stars coming to terms with having to take out the trash or live "normal" lives, we tend to think that it is simultaneously good for them and extremely uncool. Coolness tends to be equated with a kind of unrealistic detachment; a kind of life lived amongst castles in the air, as it were. Yet, when we think about the revelation of our own frailty, the revelation that we, too, are shadowboxing and waiting for our symbolic or iconic self to arbitrarily dissolve into nothing, we are probably genuinely terrified.

So, is Metallica for real or are they full of shit? Are they for real because they recognized the fundamental poverty of living only in their manufactured and debauched reality? Are they full of shit for having hidden in said identity until the filming of *Some Kind of Monster* and now, having given up the conceit, have no idea who they are as people or as a band? In a way, they are the most "for real" of all the artists that we've focused on, save maybe Jeff Tweedy. Metallica finally acknowledges their frailty. They recognize that they are not just infinite, symbolic, iconic selves but they are selves that have a concrete, temporal, everyday part. Though the process is monstrous, they (well, at least James Hetfield) strive to reconcile these two parts of their selves.

However, this process of reconciling the self to itself is not, according to Kierkegaard, accomplished by any willing or action of the self. Such an act of the self would be done from the position of mastery, which is precisely the position Kierkegaard wishes to diagnose as a sickness of the self when he refers to it as despair in willing to be oneself. The self which believes itself to be the master of all it surveys, especially its own self, is deluded and cannot reconcile its self to itself. The only remedy for a self which either ignorant of its self, in denial about its self, or defiantly claiming mastery over itself has no recourse but to "rest transparently in the power that established it" (p. 14).

What might it mean to rest transparently in the spirit which gave rise to us? Might it be an admission of a fundamental human fragility, a recognition that we are not the masters of ourselves? Might it also mean recognizing that even the most embarrassing and mundane parts of our selves are still part of us, are still, at bottom, us? Might it also mean that we do attempt to deny who we really are and accept ourselves as a synthesis of mundane and iconic, temporal and eternal, actual and possible?

If I accept that I am a synthesis of my mundane, everyday, taking-out-the-trash existence and my symbolic, iconic, infinite, cultivated persona; if I accept that I am, as a synthesis, not the one who mastered myself nor a slave to the most immediate parts of myself; if I accept that I am still subject to the seemingly arbitrary forces of nature and culture which act upon me and challenge both the perception and the lived experience of myself, then am I, as Chuck Klosterman wondered about Bono, for real or am I full of shit?

8

Killing Myself to Live in Carnival Square

MELISSA VOSEN

Once your reality closes down to zero, you're no longer part of it.

—CHUCK KLOSTERMAN

I am twenty-eight years old, and I'm in love with John Cusack. And even though I've never met pop-culture critic Chuck Klosterman, he knows my secret crush. It's a secret I share with millions of other women my age across the United States.

If I were being completely honest and self-reflective, I would have to admit that I do not really love John Cusack; that, of course, would be silly. I love John Cusack's 1980s portrayal of Lloyd Dobler, a character in Cameron Crowe's cult classic *Say Anything*. In 2000, Mel Gibson starred in *What Women Want*, a mediocre movie in which his male-chauvinistic character Nick Marshall heard the inner thoughts of women. Throughout the movie, Nick used this ability to try to figure out exactly what women are looking for in a partner, among other things. (Ironically, with the 2010 release of audiotapes belittling and threatening his model girlfriend, it appears Mel Gibson has learned next to nothing from playing character Nick Marshall. He still clearly has no clue what women want).

The answer, however, is so simple. All Nick Marshall had to do was ask Chuck Klosterman. Women want Lloyd Dobler.

Most women, however, realize this desire is problematic; Lloyd Dobler is a fictional character, and even if one views Cusack as Dobler, the likelihood of dating, even meeting, the real Cusack is relatively slim. And because Dobler and Cusack are not one in the same, there would inevitably be some disappointment. Would Cusack really run ahead and remove glass from my path as we strolled passed a 7-Eleven in the early hours of the morning after an all-night kegger? Probably not.

But, if not Lloyd Dobler or John Cusack, Klosterman argues women want the next logical thing; they want their relationship to mirror the relationship of Lloyd Dobler and Diane Court. According to Klosterman, we *all* desire fake love, the love manufactured by Hollywood. While many women desire Dobler, I believe a good percentage of men, depending on sexual orientation, desire Diane Court, a character described in the movie as a brain "trapped in the body of a game-show hostess." Perhaps this is what explains Cusack's own notorious bachelor status. Does Cusack secretly desire Diane Court—and, unfortunately, even Ione Skye, the actress who played Diane, and does she even actually live up to his standards? Or, more likely, does Cusack not live up to the standards of millions of women across the United States? Does everyone that Cusack meets expect to meet Lloyd Dobler?

I don't think Klosterman would claim to have a greater understanding of women or the human condition than the average Joe; he is just a normal guy. In fact, I'm sure Klosterman would argue that all Nick Marshall (and Mel Gibson) had to do was turn on the television or watch *The Notebook*. We want the fairy tale; we want Hollywood's version of love. We want a little less of reality, a little less of ourselves. What we want is a little *more* fantasy, a little more of the one-dimensional television and movie characters, the systematic output of Hollywood, in our own life.

And, as Klosterman implies, none of us is immune to that desire. Our desire for fake love transcends gender, sexual orientation, race, and class. We are all susceptible, and we are all suspect. Klosterman notes that every time he meets an American who isn't profoundly boring or mentally handicapped, he notices one "unifying characteristic." Americans (sans the boring and sans the handicapped) have "the inability to experience the kind of mind-blowing, transcendent romantic relationship they perceive to be a normal part of living" (*Sex, Drugs, and Cocoa Puffs*, p. 2).

Sex, Drugs, and Cocoa Puffs focuses on more than just fake love, but its subject matter revolves around one thing: reality and our desire for anything and everything cliché. While many readers would never admit publicly their desire for fake love as Klosterman has, Klosterman presents a convincing argument by providing personal examples and drawing on popular culture; his argument certainly resonates with me. I own four movies—one of which is *Say Anything*. And if I were to venture a guess on how many times I have seen the movie, I would say into the hundreds, which, as my fiancé pointed out, is roughly eight days of my life. Ouch.

Why the incessant viewings? It's not because I don't subscribe to cable; it's because I love the idea of Lloyd Dobler and Diane Court—that and the WE channel has the movie on a fairly regular rotation.

Klosterman challenges how his readers view love and identity by providing humorous examples from his own life and popular culture. *Sex, Drugs, and Cocoa Puffs*, by all accounts, is a celebration of America's low culture and art. In one chapter, Klosterman argues that the teen comedy *Saved by the Bell* has meant more to its audience than many highly rated, award-winning television shows because of the audience's ability to relate to it (however unrealistic the show might be: see the Tori paradox or Zack's relationship with Mr. Belding). Klosterman writes, "I didn't care about *Saved by The Bell* any more than I cared about *The X-Files*, but the difference is that I could watch *Saved by the Bell* without caring and still have it become a minor part of my life, which is the most transcendent thing any kind of art can accomplish (regardless of its technical merits)" (p. 138). Klosterman's *Sex, Drugs, and Cocoa Puffs,* his "low culture manifesto," is an example of what Mikhail Bakhtin calls carnivalesque literature, literature that challenges traditional cultural views and hierarchies and champions low culture: Klosterman champions the low culture of women's undying love for John Cusack and Coldplay and an entire generation's fondness for Zack Morris.

Step Right Up 0:10

Bakhtin's carnival can best be described as a celebration of the subversive and the mixing of classes. Bakhtin argues that the carnival satirizes and undermines traditional views of culture by suspending the ordinary and the distance and hierarchies between carnival participants; Bakhtin believes that carnival-ization can have a liberating effect in literature (Bakhtin, "Carnival and the Carnivalesque" in *Cultural Theory and Popular Culture: A Reader*, p. 251). The carnival is also present in modern day television, movies, and other forms of media. Umberto Eco argues that the carnival still exists in different forms and beyond the town square; he writes, "Modern mass-carnival is limited in space: it is reserved for certain places, certain streets, or framed by the television screen" (Umberto Eco, "The Frames of Comic "Freedom" in *Carnival!* p. 6).

Television, an all too common subject for Klosterman, is often a place where traditional values are discussed and some-times challenged; in television, hierarchies between partici-pants (viewers) often vanish. How many different people, on any given Tuesday, watched *American Idol* in March of 2005? The answer is millions—from A-list Hollywood celebrities to minimum wage earning fast food workers (unless, of course, they worked the night shift). Around thirty million people from all walks of life tuned in each week to watch now pop-country princess Carrie Underwood take the Idol crown.

While popular cultural media such as television, the great equalizer, serve as a place or grounds for the carnival, Klosterman's book and analysis serve as a celebration of it. If you listen closely, you can almost hear Klosterman bellowing, "Step right up!"

Klosterman uses mostly sarcasm and humor to challenge and question traditional cultural views and disassemble hier-archies. When Klosterman is discussing Pamela Anderson's sex symbol status, he states, "We don't need Pam to know where she is; she helps us understand where *we* are" (*Sex, Drugs, and Cocoa Puffs*, p. 84). While many may find it uncomfortable—even ludicrous—to suggest that former *Baywatch* star Pam Anderson is the compass for our society (or at least when Klosterman wrote *Sex, Drugs, and Cocoa Puffs*)—Klosterman believes otherwise. In fact, he chastises critics who are unnec-essarily negative or snarky toward the 1990s blonde bombshell because we, as a society, have made her who she is today.

Klosterman believes that the reason many hate Anderson is because she represents an unrealistic image of the human race, an image that we as a society created and an image that many of us still desire to obtain. (I realize this still gives us no logical explanation for David Hasselhoff). We hate, however, to see this image in real life—which is very similar to how Klosterman feels about Cusack. For Klosterman, Cusack represents an unrealistic image of love—and even though he isn't actually Lloyd Dobler, many of Klosterman's potential love interests see him as such.

Bakhtin also argues that one of the primary characteristics of a carnival is the crowning and de-crowning of a king; in *Cocoa Puffs*, Klosterman, low culture carnival critic, is both carnie and king. Klosterman shows us over and over our desire for both the ridiculously unattainable and the absurdly simplistic—which explains, in a nutshell, both our lust and hatred for Anderson and our preoccupation with *Saved by the Bell*. People want their life to have one meaning, and as Klosterman argues, people usually imagine something "completely imaginary" or "staunchly practical" (p.184). Ultimately, Klosterman's self-awareness is what crowns him king of the unordinary ordinary, king of the carnival.

Meet the Huxtables 0:57

Klosterman claims that instead of worrying about violent video games and movies, a common concern post-Columbine, parents (and the public in general) should be worried about how love and relationships are portrayed in the media. Klosterman believes that adults mesmerized by Hollywood's portrayal of love are much more dangerous than preteens mesmerized by an action movie peppered with fight scenes, explosions, and car chases. It's true that parent groups often protest excessive violence on television and in movies; love, however, is rarely their focus—unless, of course, nudity or teenage pregnancy is part of the plot. Ironically, what these groups fail to see is how the media influences them as adults. Klosterman believes that love scripted by the media has impaired our ability, even as adults, to access what is normal in a relationship. He writes, "There is no 'normal,' because everybody is being twisted by the same sources simultaneously" (p. 4). Instead of desiring our real, complex partners, we desire Lloyd Dobler.

For most of us, Klosterman believes we model our relationships, probably depending on our generation, after Cliff and Clair Huxtable or Chandler Bing and Monica Geller, and even if we happen to model our relationship after our neighbors, a non-celebrity couple, it is likely that they are avid viewers of *The Cosby Show* or *Friends*. For Klosterman, everyone is vulnerable to the media; gender, sexual orientation, race, and class are irrelevant. Klosterman, despite his savvy critique, isn't even immune; he writes, "I wish I was Lloyd Dobler. I don't want anybody to step on a piece of glass. I want fake love. But that's all I want, and that's why I can't have it" (p. 10). Klosterman's über-self-awareness is what ultimately makes him carnival king. Rather than ignore the media's unfortunate influence, as many of us do, Klosterman recognizes the situation for what it is.

Many of us agree with Klosterman's accusation of John Cusack as responsible for the 1980s version of fake love. Who over thirty and under fifty doesn't love the iconic image of Dobler holding a giant 1980s-sized boom box to win back Diane? Admit it. You're humming Peter Gabriel's ballad, "In Your Eyes" right now. Most of us, however, might be a little less likely to admit we model our arguments after the arguments of Sam Malone and Diane Chambers. While we all occupy this carnival square, we all have different roles and degrees of awareness.

This Is the "True" Story 1:42

It isn't just relationships we attempt to emulate. Klosterman argues that MTV's *The Real World* is a successful franchise because it offers the public one-dimensional characters who are easy to imitate. He writes, "The show succeeds because it edits malleable personalities into flat, twenty-something archetypes. What interests me is the way those archetypes so quickly became the normal way for people of my generation to behave" (p. 31). It's easier, Klosterman argues, to adopt one of these one-dimensional personalities because it makes it easier for other one-dimensional personalities to understand you. It makes communicating with one another a lot less complicated. It is almost, in a way, essential for our survival. We must kill ourselves, sacrifice our personalities (and the personalities of our loved ones), in order to live.

Ultimately, Klosterman believes this flattening of characters into one-dimensional personalities is what makes *The*

Real World (as well as shows like *Saved by the Bell*) so successful. While smart teen dramedy *My So-Called Life* received rave reviews, it quickly was canceled because, as Klosterman argues, the main character Angela, played by a young Claire Danes, was too unique. Her feelings were too complex. This same phenomenon can be seen today. I mean, does everybody really love *Raymond*? Why were *Freaks and Geeks* and *Arrested Development* canceled while *Two and a Half Men* continues, to my thinking, its abysmal run?

The answer is archetypes. Angela didn't reflect any archetypes—nor did Jason Bateman's character on *Arrested Development*. Angela inhabited a world that was simply too real. Her love interest, Jordan Catalano, was illiterate, mostly due to undiagnosed dyslexia, but he also was a fairly talented musician who wrote, at times, profound song lyrics. He was messy. He was complicated.

We desire to model ourselves after the one-dimensional, and very unrealistic, characters we see on television, just as we desire fake love and have a propensity to model our relationships after the relationships of fictional characters. As Klosterman points out, Julie from the first season of *The Real World* was not an unintelligent, naive hick. And, even though I have never met Julie, I believe him. MTV, however, edited hours of footage, ultimately airing only a few brief clips, clips void of any context, until they molded her into just that.

The one-dimensional archetypes of *The Real World* simplify social hierarchies in general (*all* viewers aspire to be one of the seven cast members) while simultaneously making existing hierarchies more defined. But, as Klosterman points out, it makes communication between people easier. In 1994, youth across America began defining their sense of normal and their sense of self by sculpting their personalities after Puck, Pedro, Judd, Mohammed, Rachel, Cory, and Pam. What does it mean to be Puck and play the Puck role? For an entire generation who came of age in the mid 1990s, to play the Puck role meant being the guy who would eat his roommates' peanut butter with his bare hands while simultaneously picking his nose.

Despite the recent naming and branding of the "me generation" and the endless campaigns urging youth to embrace who they are, these archetypes have come to define a generation. We all know a Puck. We all know a Judd. We all know a Rachel.

A viewer watching *The Real World* or *Saved by the Bell* is like being a participant in a carnival. It is a celebration of the subversive because, as Klosterman writes, "*Saved by the Bell* wasn't real, but neither is most of reality" (p. 147). It challenges what we know and what we define as real and as normal—just like our notion of love. Many of us are partake in everyday what Klosterman calls "low culture." We do not have an elite social status, and we do not peruse high art. Yet, many of us are probably unwilling to admit—perhaps unwilling participants in carnival square—that we emulate twenty-somethings sexing it up (at least in more recent *Real World* seasons) on MTV. It's an awfully hard pill to swallow, but as Klosterman writes, "Important things are inevitably cliché, but nobody wants to admit that. And that's why nobody is deconstructing *Saved by the Bell*" (p. 136).

We want relationships that are unattainable; we want to date Lloyd Dobler or Diane Court. We want to be Flora from *The Real World*—even if she is the nosy roommate who crashes through a bathroom window because she is spying on her roommate getting it on in the shower. It's easier to be flat one-dimensional drone.

Klosterman as King 2:52

As I mentioned before, Mikhail Bakhtin argues that one of the primary functions of a carnival is to throne and dethrone an unlikely king. Bakhtin writes, "And he who is crowned is the antipode of a real king, a slave or a jester; this act, as it were, opens and sanctifies the inside-out world of the carnival" (p. 252). I would argue that Klosterman, with his witty critique and as a champion of low culture, is *this* carnival's king because throughout his text, he celebrates the inside-out world, challenging traditional views of love and identity—just to name a few.

Some of you may be wondering, how is Klosterman challenging traditional views of love when, according to Klosterman himself, we are all susceptible to the power of fake love and all model our personalities after a character in MTV's dismal, no-music programming? My answer is this: while we all may be susceptible to fake love, not all of us are willing to see it for what it is. Klosterman, in this sense, is quite unique.

It was only after I read *Sex, Drugs, and Cocoa Puffs* that I realized why I can watch *Say Anything* over and over again, year after year.

Knowing, however, is a burden all on its own, and knowing is why Klosterman has already been dethroned. He has already admitted, very publicly, that fake love will be a part of his life forever; he questions if he will ever truly satisfy a woman—and vice versa because of movies like *Say Anything* and women like me. He admits, even though he knows better, he wishes he were Lloyd Dobler. And regardless of where he goes, he knows that the cast of *The Real World* (doesn't matter what season) surrounds him; ultimately, he knows everything important in life, as he so delicately puts it, is cliché. This über-awareness is what makes him king of this carnival, slave to the media, and jester to the masses.

Throughout his book, Klosterman asks again and again, "What is reality?" Ultimately, he argues it is the only question worth asking. While some may disagree, I think Klosterman is right. It is *a* question worth asking, again and again. In a world filled with a fake love and archetypes, however, we may never really be able to find an answer. As Klosterman points out time and time again, just because we're aware— doesn't mean we're immune.

In the end, my desire for Lloyd Dobler and my fascination with Kelly Kapowski is why I'm a carnival participant and why I'm killing myself to live.

Watch
me
dream?

HYPERthetical Response #3

Watch me dream

SYBIL PRIEBE

At long last, someone invents "the dream VCR." This machine allows you to tape an entire evening's worth of your own dreams, which you can then watch at your leisure. However, the inventor of the dream VCR will only allow you to use this device if you agree to a strange caveat: When you watch your dreams, you must do so with your family and your closest friends in the same room. They get to watch your dreams along with you. And if you don't agree to this, you can't use the dream VCR. Would you still do this?

—*Sex, Drugs, and Cocoa Puffs*, p. 128

Well, I have to answer YES to this because, um, NO wouldn't be as much fun. Duh. However, before you label me as an exhibitionist or total weirdo, hear me out.

Okay, so just what the hell is a "dream"? Simple. It's a bizarre mini-movie with our unconscious as the director; he cooks up the plot with a recipe of the day's leftover tidbits, a dash of screwy things from our past, and, of course, tons of symbolism (snakes, teeth falling out, flying, etc. = things that make dream books sell like bestsellers!). Sigmund Freud and Carl Jung would probably agree with my definition. Okay, well, maybe they wouldn't, but they're . . . not here to defend themselves. And, honestly, Sigmund figured that dreams were straightforward events mixed with repressed thoughts; Carl knew we could attempt to understand them with the use of symbols and interpretation. I'm not that far off base, then.

130 Sybil Priebe

According to the anti-Sigmund+Carl, Sri Swami Sivananda, the "Dream world is totally different from the waking world. . . . Sometimes we have a dream within a dream. During sleep, sometimes we are conscious of the fact that we are asleep and we are dreaming. In dreams more often than not we assume a body that is the master of the dream world" (Sri Swami Sivananda, *Philosophy of Dreams*, http://www.dlshq.org).

Long story short, this director—my own unconscious—could easily keep me from showing a VCR full of "naked me at the office" scenarios. How? Easy. There's a strong possibility that I could control these dreams—mid-dream sequence, you know. I've done it, and you've probably done it. What if half way through the dream, I realize this will be seen by others? Bam! Change it up and suddenly clothing comes out of nowhere or the guy I was kissing turns into my current boyfriend.

What I'm trying to get at is that the philosophy behind dreams and dream-making is that they can be anything they want to be. And since I could control these dreams, I have an additional reason as to why I'd do this.

Money! This Dream VCR could lead to a taping of something better than existing movies and TV shows.

Think of the good dreams you've had—the insanely surreal ones with multiple meanings that you dissect with friends or haven't told a single soul about (not the dull ones where you jump from hollering at Aunt Sue about her potato salad to the kindergarten classroom when Billy pointed out your imitation footwear). Who wouldn't want to watch those wild rides? And think of the ways one could control this insanity to make the dream more insane!

Also, think of the horror flicks that wake you up with wet armpits. My sister can't understand why I detest watching horror films; well, now she can view the ones that make me shiver when I'm "counting zs." My sister could buy a copy of this VHS to view with her other horror-loving friends.

Now, think of the "bad" dreams you had to witness to alone. You will share it with a paying audience and that will make it easier to deal with, won't it? If you were going to have the bad dream anyhow, why not make some cash?

Plus, think of your post-drinking dreams. Those are like current movies on acid, right? What I mean is if you were to have me watch re-runs of *Real Housewives of New Jersey* and do five shots of Patron before zonking out, the dreams would be better than any reality show on right now! Bam! It would be pure insanity without a plot. Oh wait, that *is* most reality shows. Anyhow, they make a lot of Benjamins, so I definitely think I'm onto something. Or Chuck was. Whatever. You get our/my/his point. And, as I said before, what a bonus—I get a crazy night out with friends before pocketing the greens over the chaos I create when I'm unconscious.

Now, not only do I think I can control these dreams, but if my friends and family do watch—these dreams will explain my eccentricities. A side note to my original idea of the philosophy of dreams, is the idea that, well, we could really "see" what our family members are thinking and feeling. After my friends and family watch my weird-ass dreams, my attitude and oddness will only become more understandable and forgivable and obvious.

> THEM: Sybil, why do people's faces get fuzzy and change into other faces?
>
> ME: Um, you tell me.
>
> THEM: It's statistically impossible to walk into a store where everything is your size, you know?
>
> ME: Yeah, genius, I know. Tell my subconscious that.
>
> THEM: So, do you think that when you scream in your dreams and nothing comes out . . . that that means you feel like no one listens to you?
>
> ME: Good call, chief. Did you forget that I teach English to college students?
>
> THEM: Is it annoying to have dreams where your teeth fall out for no reason?
>
> ME: Yes. Totally. I want it to stop.
>
> THEM: Wow. You must like architecture with all those dreams about building and tearing down walls.
>
> ME: Yep. True story.

There is a slight glitch to this answer of mine. *Eighty-five percent percent of the time, I don't dream.* Nada. Zilch. Donut hole.

Talk about dream control! It would be a VCR recording filled with a 3:00 A.M. pee-break interruption and the occasional stop at 6:00 A.M. to check that I didn't miss my alarm. People would watch and fall asleep. I could potentially cure insomnia with my "somnia." Jeezus Pete—how great is that!

Lastly, this situation would eliminate me ever having to say again, "Oh my god, you'll never guess what I dreamt about last night." Because the reply would be: "Oh, yes. Yes, we *know*."

BOOK IV

The IVth
Critique

9
Only Chuck Can Save Us

MATT SIENKIEWICZ

On July 8th 2010, Lebron James provided Americans and the media pundits they love to hate with a unique opportunity.

For a long while it has seemed that the days of the public media event with moral consequence has been relegated to a semi-mythical past full of fireside chats, Lincoln-Douglas debates, and other things from tenth-grade social studies class. Today presidential debates are just mile markers in the horse race and the closest thing we've seen to a real discussion over an important, nationally-experienced media moment was the argument over whether Janet Jackson's mostly exposed nipple was the cause or merely the result of America's demise into a realm of Godless depravity somewhere between Sodom and Sweden. Sure, we've got *Meet the Press* and a million blogs that break down every moment of everything. But blogs are a type of fragmented, specialty media. It's hard enough to talk with your friends about what you watch or read, let alone have a national discussion.

Yet, Lebron, by renting an hour on ESPN and making the biggest *Decision* in basketball history since they got rid of those short-shorts worn by Chuck Klosterman's beloved 1980s Celtics, gave millions of Americans something to discuss. In front of tens of millions of people, Lebron shattered the collective heart of Cleveland, choosing to leave his hometown Cavaliers and join the Miami Heat.

It was a surprising, meaningful moment that said a lot about America's attitudes about individuality versus community, labor versus capital and race's relation to cultural power.

Lebron's moment captured the attention of people inside and out of the sports world, mixing business, entertainment, culture, and the ethics of personal behavior into a strangely fun cocktail reminiscent of the "wop" the North Dakotans chug in *Downtown Owl*. And yet, for the most part, no one on ESPN's vast family of media properties got into these deeper, more fundamental questions when talking about Lebron. No one except Chuck Klosterman.

For most commentators, Lebron's program, *The Decision*, was merely an opportunity to complain about the spoiled nature of the contemporary athlete or perhaps to preach a vaguely free-market perspective espousing personal freedom through sophomoric and often personal job-hunting metaphors. Skip Bayless, a particularly unctuous ESPN talking head, spent segment after segment talking about Lebron's "lack of remorse" about leaving Cleveland, never taking the time to explain what exactly the man should be sorry for. After a few days I had had enough of ESPN's missed opportunity to talk about something significant that garnered considerable attention by people who weren't hardcore sports fans.

Only God Can Judge Me

But then I stumbled upon Klosterman's appearance on the ESPN podcast, *The B.S. Report*. The exchange between Chuck and the program's host, Bill Simmons, featured virtually none of the annoyances of standard media fare. It was an in-depth discussion about Lebron's choice, unencumbered by either commercial interruption or a sense of score keeping. Whereas ESPN's long-running program *Around the Horn* literally gives points when one of its guests says something of perceived value, Simmons and Klosterman weaved in and out of a complex discussion without the need to one up one another or sneak one last word in before the ShamWow guy or a lime-flavored light beer bottle commandeered the screen.

And more importantly, Klosterman made serious points— things worth actually thinking about beyond the realm of mass culture in which he reigns so supremely. Whereas other commentators played "Who's to blame?", Chuck asked us to interpret Lebron's bold choice to dump a fledgling rust belt city with a vicious history of sports tragedy as the whole world watched in terms of our contemporary conception of confidence.

Most people saw James's attention-grab as a marker of profound insecurity, yet Klosterman, quoting Tupac, suggested that James's apparent heartlessness was instead telling the world "Only God can judge me." In other words, James's insistence on buying an hour block on ESPN to do what is traditionally achieved via a quick phone call and a signature wasn't a plea for attention; it was a statement of profound self-control. James was proclaiming his refusal to enable us in our addiction to vicarious living through stars like himself. He wasn't going to let the American public force him to become the kind of one-dimensional character that *Sex, Drugs, and Cocoa Puffs* argues is the real legacy of *The Real World* and reality TV.

Sure, Lebron was supposed to be a Good Guy. But he did this Bad Thing, Chuck argued, for our good as well as, his own. He did something "bad" because he wanted to, and he did it publicly because we should all know that the molds our hyper-mediated world wedge us into are neither healthy in the long run nor satisfying in the short term. It may sound simplistic, but for someone in Lebron's position of wealth and influence, the idea of truly "being yourself" is actually kind of profound.

Now, in the interest of full disclosure I need to point out that I don't think Chuck's right. Personally I believe, and believe that Chuck probably believes, that Lebron's just a youngish guy who came into the possession of a bad idea and some even worse advice on how to execute it. Nonetheless, I really, truly appreciate the fact that Klosterman was able to take this meaningful cultural moment and, through the new medium of podcasting, debate its more subtle elements less than a month after it happened on a program with millions of listeners. Klosterman's contribution strengthened our collective discourse not only about Lebron, but also about celebrity culture and the ways in which all of us are asked to play our roles as opposed to look more deeply and critically. Using the vocabulary of political philosophy and communication theory, Klosterman was contributing to what is known as the "public sphere," a concept that underpins much Western thought on the nature of democracy and productive public citizenship. And the Lebron podcast is just one example of Klosterman's uncanny ability to debate popular culture in public forums in ways that make us think about the nature of our society. So, yes, I'm making the claim that Chuck's ideas about the appeal of Abba in America or Val Kilmer being "advanced" make our democracy stronger.

Chuck in the Public Sphere

The idea of the "public sphere" comes from the seemingly immortal ninety-year old Jürgen Habermas, a German philosopher who not only is still alive fifty years after writing a book that changed political thought forever, but who also still produces new articles now and then.

As you might suspect, Jürgen Habermas and Chuck Klosterman are not writers who share space in many sentences. The former is compared to philosophers like Hegel and uses chapter titles like "The Paradigm Shift in Mead and Durkheim: From Purposive Activity to Communicative Action." His jargon-laden, *extremely* historically informed prose is the kind of thing I'd tried to make inside jokes about as a graduate student and is probably twenty-five percent responsible for me remaining single for the majority of the period. Klosterman, on the other hand, uses chapter titles like "Every Dog Must Have His Every Day, Every Drunk Must Have His Drink" and proceeds to give us fifteen pages on the genius of Billy Joel. He has perfected a style that projects intelligence without the baggage of pretension or seriousness that so often comes with it; he's obviously a smart guy, but he doesn't let that get in the way of a good time. If you ever bump into a group of people with .edu email addresses throwing back drinks and laughing too loudly, it's probably true that they a. think they are being as witty and down to earth as Chuck and b. are doing nothing of the sort. It's hard to be reasonably smart, reasonably funny, reasonably accessible, and still make your, hopefully reasonable, point. Trust me, I'm trying right now and the success-to-effort ratio isn't what it could be.

Klosterman's arguments are well considered and often surprisingly rigorous, yet they are also, in every sense, popular. Not only does his work sell many times more copies than Habermas's *The Transformation of the Public Sphere*, which went decades before even being published in English, but

Klosterman also focuses on things that people know and love. Whereas Habermas's arguments hinge on conceptions of eighteenth-century French bourgeois society, Klosterman uses Zack Morris and Larry Bird to prove his cultural points. Habermas, as we'll detail shortly, uses historical fictions for the sake of philosophical truth while Klosterman employs contemporary fiction to teach his readers about their own cultures. However, Klosterman's public persona, especially when combined with new communications methods such as podcasting, makes him just the sort of guy that Habermas, the champion of the public sphere, should be glad we have around.

Yes, Habermas wants people to discuss big issues like the future of democracy and the best way to achieve the public good. And, no, Klosterman doesn't much care if the discourse goes much beyond the realm of popular culture. However Habermas's theory of the public sphere suggests that perhaps even Klosterman's apparently trivial arguments have the potential to do just that. When Chuck and Bill Simmons argue about Lebron or do battle for two hours over the virtues of the *Lost* finale, they may well be encouraging just the sort of engagement that Habermas thinks produces better citizens and societies.

Grad students rapping about the canon of western philosophy over PBR represents just the sort of scene that Habermas evokes in his groundbreaking description of eighteenth-century Europe, a time during which, his most famous argument goes, the world's only truly functional "Public Sphere" existed. According to Habermas, this was a time in which open, public debate flourished because there was a space in which the people had the ability to identify the true nature of their collective interests in the best possible fashion—through logical reason. In other words, for one reason or another, people during this period were able to put aside their own agendas in order to pursue an absolute, objective truth. It's a questionable claim and one we'll take a closer look at later, but it's a key to Habermas's idea about the public sphere. If it seems like too much of a stretch to you that people could be so objective, think of one of the interludes in *Sex, Drugs, and Cocoa Puffs*. Klosterman asks you to envision a time portal through which you discover one day you'll fall in love with Canadian Football. Habermas's argument wants to look through one in which people were once supremely rational. Yeah, it's unlikely, but it's no sillier than a football league with a team called the "Allouettes." (For more on this read "Turn off the CFL").

The Crucible of Debate

Habermas's claim is that as the European Feudal system collapsed at the end of the Middle Ages and royalty lost its ownership of everything, spaces like pubs and parks emerged where people could meet a public and stop thinking of themselves as subjects of the king. The result was, according to Habermas, spaces of vibrant debate and intellectual engagement that served as the underpinning of a truly successful democratic system. In particular, he points to the salons and teahouses that emerged during this period and attracted a diverse group of individuals, considering the time period. Just as the citizens of Owl, North Dakota, in *Downtown Owl* only seem to talk meaningfully about anything at the bar or the diner, the European citizens of the time found these new public space as bastions of unfettered expression beyond the reach of the King. It's somewhat like the freedom of subject matter and mode of address that you'll find in Klosterman's various projects. While Chuck might toe the company line while writing in *Spin* and pull some punches, when he's talking only for himself on a podcast you'll often find he's freer in tossing out ideas. Yes, he's still in public, but the metaphorical king is off his back. In the Europe of Habermas's philosophy, the salon or pub gave the people a similar freedom, resulting in an informed and influential public able to smartly and effectively articulate its needs, desires, and opinions.

Essential to Habermas's conception of the Public Sphere's golden age was this lack of external interference. Without external meddling, people had the ability to focus on the one thing that really matters: a clear, unbiased argument. Think of the difference between two talking heads on cable TV versus the way that Klosterman debates with Simmons on *The B.S. Report*. The talkers want to score points and will appeal to the emotions of the audience and one another to score their point. When Skip Bayless argued about Lebron on ESPN, he built his case on James not looking "happy to join" Miami or "sad to leave Cleveland." These things might be true, but how can you have a meaningful discussion that starts that way? What can you say to such a thing, other than that it's irrelevant?

Klosterman, however, offered a definition of confidence via Tupac's "Only God can judge me" life-philosophy and went on to show how Lebron's actions suggest he fits that notion of confidence. You can disagree with Chuck, but to do so you have to argue logically about what it means to be confident or what Lebron actually did. This is the sort of rational debate Habermas locates as the heart of the public sphere of eighteenth-century social clubs and print journals. People knew that they had better check their personal preferences and prejudices at the door, and they forwent the sorts of petty, selfish motivations that impede people from really getting to the truths of matters. Their goal wasn't to be right on a personal level, but instead to discover, communally, what makes the best sense.

Now you're probably thinking Habermas is just a bit full of it. It's not hard to parody his picture of Europe's past as a Disney World for tweed-wearing professors and Mr. Bottomtooth from *Family Guy*. Not only is it hard to believe that such a time and place ever existed, but there aren't too many people for whom it even sounds like a great place to visit. Can we really take seriously the idea that people at some point in the past were truthfully able to put aside their social positions and personal preferences in order to focus entirely on the merits of one another's arguments? For example, if I were to bump into Klosterman at a Manhattan bar one night, and we were to get into a verbal battle over, say, the cultural significance of KISS guitarist Ace Frehley's obsession with UFOs, I'm fairly certain that Chuck's pop guru status would irreparably bias everyone involved in the discussion. The hipsters would appeal to the fact that he's said about a million smart things about KISS in his life, and I've never said any. They would then notice me drinking a beer that was either too ironic or not ironic enough and dismiss me altogether. Furthermore, as Chuck and I did battle over whether or not Frehley represents "alien" elements of American culture, I'd be desperately trying to score points at all costs. It's far cooler to tell your friends you beat such a pop culture guru in an argument. It certainly trumps the importance of accessing a philosopher's ideal of "objective truth." So is Habermas to seriously have us think that in similar, if perhaps more somber, arguments a few hundred years ago in Bavaria, things would have been so fundamentally different?

The Ideal Ideas Exchange

Probably not. Or at least no more than Klosterman is trying to convince us that one day we might wake up with our musical tastes "reversed," as per the chapter in *Sex, Drugs, and Cocoa Puffs*. Habermas knows full well that the picture he paints is an idealized one that, at best, glosses over some serious rough patches, not the least of which is the fact that minorities, the disabled, the young, the elderly, and females almost certainly couldn't have even gotten through the door of your average French salon. Instead, what Habermas is doing is establishing, through what is essentially a piece of historical fiction, the ideal form of discourse that he believes ought to take place in the public sphere of a well functioning civil society. It's a thought experiment, something that Klosterman fans are well-versed in. The past he paints is what we should aspire to if we really want a society that is based on providing the best lives for its citizenry as opposed to catering to the whims of the powerful. His point is not so much to say how great things were in the past, but instead to show us how many light years away our current environment is from how things need to be if we want a society that truly looks out for its own best interests. No, it's not as fun as the what-ifs in the Klosterman *Hyperthetical* party game, but what do you expect from a German guy named Jürgen?

But even if we acknowledge that the Habermas is idealizing the style of debate that took place during the period of his glorious public sphere, we're left with another nagging problem. Yes, there are people who like to go to bars and argue about politics, but there are lots of other things to discuss, many of which are a lot more fun. In the example above, I referenced an argument over Ace Frehley and Alien lifeforms as opposed to one over the virtues of stem-cell research mostly because in social settings the more engaging topic is one the most likely to evoke extended discussion.

Most of us don't get paid to compare Ralph Nader to Rivers Cuomo and daydream about chewing on a triceratops, so when we get home from work, we want our "intellectual" engagement to be fun. If you have trouble believing that Europeans a few hundred years ago had as much fun debating the merits of restructuring the local sewage system or the definition of justice than you do arguing about your favorite basketball team, you're not alone. Habermas, serious though he may be, not only acknowledges this phenomenon, but he even embraces the idea that there is value in talking about fun stuff. He may have had *Don Giovanni* in mind more than Nikki Sixx or Axl Rose, but the idea is there. Before the salons and cafes turned into bastions of debates over the public interest, there was, in the Habermasian narrative, a "public sphere of letters" that developed. French, German, and British citizens would gather together not only to talk about, say the best use of public land, but also the merits of new plays, the latest trends in musical composition and the superiority of certain authors. It appears that if a debate over the originality of Mozart sonatas could be a productive part of the public sphere, Klosterman's contention that Paradise City, a Guns N' Roses cover band, is the most "sonically pure" band in the world could be as well. After all, popular culture has always been popular for a reason—it's not clear that Axl Rose is one iota more obsessed with sex than *Don Giovanni*, lover of all things erotic.

And Habermas may well concede this point. In his account, debates over art and culture not only serve as a sort of training ground on which to try out the sorts of rhetorical strategies necessary for proper political debate, but they also play the very crucial role of teaching people that arguments don't always have to involve advocacy. For example, when you read Klosterman's article "Appetite for Replication" about Paradise City, the stakes are, presumably, very low. Unless you have a personal preference for dressing like Izzy Stradlin and doing shots of Jack Daniels until you can't see straight, the virtuosity or authenticity of people who do have such predilections probably isn't a matter of significant personal gain. However, in Habermas's way of thinking, this can be a good thing.

By personally evaluating Paradise City you're engaging in an activity much like the idealized citizens of the "public sphere of letters" were doing in Habermas's eighteenth-century Europe. The key is to contemplate something you have found enough interest in to take seriously and learn the facts about,

but which you have no apparent rooting interest. This may
sound simple enough, but it's not an easy thing to do. You could
pick up a scholarly tract on the essence of beauty that you have
no stake in, but it's unlikely that you'll really debate the merits of the argument if you're not at least an amateur expert in
the field. It's also easy enough to pick up the op-ed page of your
local newspaper and evaluate both sides of an argument over
school vouchers. But unless you have some personal stake in
the matter, it will likely be hard to delve into it fully. At the
very least, most people wouldn't have a very good time doing
so. But "Appetite for Replication," in arguing that a tribute
band can express an unparalleled purity of devotion to a set of
songs, gives the reader the opportunity and motivation to consider something with a relatively high level of intellectual rigor
without having any personal stake in it. In Habermas's portrayal of the ideal public sphere, people learn to think objectively and abstractly in large part because topics like art and
music provide motivations beyond personal gain to do so. The
fun one has in arguing about the band, in this case, matters, so
long as it brings along with it the virtue of rationality. Your
time dabbling in the "public sphere of letters" is training you to
put aside your personal stake in say, Affirmative Action, and
cast your lot with the side of the issues that appeals to your
sense of truth and justice.

Blaming the Media

In Habermas's semi-historical worldview, the public sphere,
which once gave everyday people a place to fairly and effectively advance their collective interests, slowly died out, leaving a civil society capable of little more than serving petty,
partisan interests. At this point Habermas and Klosterman
appear to be most at odds. Whereas Klosterman has made a
career of studying the hidden and not so hidden virtues of
American popular culture, Habermas takes a stance far more
common amongst the intelligentsia. He blames the media.
More specifically, Habermas bemoans the way in which for-
profit, mass media has replaced sites of more efficient and honest public discourse. The depth, creativity and submerged
meanings that Klosterman finds in even the most banal examples of American popular culture are, for Habermas and his

influential academic protégés, mere by-products of a centuries-long cultural deterioration. If the French salon was the peak of Western communicative discourse, the "don't drink and drive" episode of *Saved by the Bell* that Klosterman devotes a full chapter to may well by its deepest, if most fun, valley.

The problem, according to Habermas, begins with the way in which the public and private spheres were re-blurred in the industrial and post-industrial eras, setting the stage for crassly commercial modes of public debate and, eventually, media production. Corporations and governments mix their interests to the point where you can't tell them apart. Congress is inundated with corporate lobbyists. Groups of citizens have no choice but to act in kind, putting together admirable but unmistakably advocacy-oriented groups like the NAACP, GLAD, and ACLU in order defend their own interests. When they argue, it has very little to do with truth. It's sort of like the exchange between Julia and Vance in *Downtown Owl*, where Klosterman tells you both what each character says as well as the kind of creepy, totally selfish thing that they are really trying to get across. When companies or interest groups talk in the public sphere they try to sound ethical and kind, but just like Julia, they're mostly trying to screw whoever they're talking to.

And this, Habermas argues, is just the beginning. It's not just the mind-set with which groups and individuals enter debates that limits the success of the public sphere. It is also the means by which they are able to do it. Salons and literary journals were crafted, according to Habermas, for the specific purpose of fostering real, rational debates. Discussions were informed not simply by the momentary interests of the masses, but also by an understanding that certain topics must be grappled with for the public good. This is not, of course, the case with the vast majority of major contemporary Western media. The texts that Klosterman engages with, by and large, exist for a single purpose: to make people money. Time travel movies, the NBA, and Britney Spears are commercial products with aesthetic or political attributes that may well be overwhelmed by the interests of their financial backers. At the very least, they wouldn't exist if they couldn't turn a profit; the shareholders wouldn't stand for it. And certainly this phenomenon is not exclusive to the realm of entertainment media. Cable news stations, ostensibly places with ample time for debates on real

issues, work hard to brand themselves to appeal to niche view-
erships, combining the interests of their corporate advertisers
with those of specific target audiences to create a sphere in
which rational argumentation is at best a tertiary concern.
Essentially, Habermas contends that our newer forms of argument and cultural expression—the newspaper, television,
mass-produced literature—let motivations like money, fame,
and political advocacy get in the way of the fully rational
debates we ought to be having. With every moment of our dis-
cursive experiences seemingly sponsored and targeted
towards specific goals, there simply is no public sphere that
exists even as a meek substitute for the mythical European
past he celebrates.

On the surface, Chuck Klosterman's work seems to represent a mad celebration of Habermas's dreary vision.
Klosterman is most certainly a commercial entity, having
worked for mass-media giants like ESPN. His books, high-
priced retail items in their own right, make the case for further
consumption of media and the interest-group driven advertis-
ing that underwrites the production of popular culture. Many
would argue that Klosterman's very celebrity image and public
persona serve as an advertisement for the crass, commercial
elements of American life. Seeing the respect and admiration
conferred upon a pop-culture devotee such as Klosterman gives
people an excuse to feel okay about their lack of real engagement in the world of public affairs. While apparently more con-
scientious media critics bemoan the demise of investigative
journalism, Klosterman tells us that Billy Joel's music cuts to
the heart of the human condition. He thus absolves us of our
pop culture crimes and makes us feel okay about deleting *Meet
the Press* from our DVR so as to squeeze in another episode of
Jersey Shore. Habermas could not possibly be in favor of such
a move.

Saving Democracy through Pop Culture

To this accusation Klosterman would likely plead guilty,
although he clearly doesn't see it as much of a crime. In fact,
Klosterman actively crusades against the notion of a guilty
pleasure, arguing publicly on the podcast *Contexts* that guilty
pleasures ought not to be thought of as such at all. Klosterman

makes the simple but rational case that aesthetic judgments such as "guilty pleasures" are not only pretentious, they also don't represent the way we truly engage culture. Innocence and guilt simply don't reflect the honest experience of watching movies or listening to music, they reflect the way want people to think about our taste in movies and music. In making this claim Klosterman makes an argument that I believe moves him in a direction that Habermasians ought to embrace. During his appearance on *Contexts*, a free podcast devoted to long-form interviews, Klosterman contends that the sort of criticism that leads one to castigate certain works as "guilty pleasures" attempts to replace individual enjoyment with a top-down system in which the trends embraced by taste makers at a given cultural moment take precedence over one's own experiences.

Although he does not go so far as to embrace Habermas's idea that a "public sphere of letters" ought to employ rational discourse in order to discover the truth about cultural artifacts, he does remark that his unique brand of criticism aims to give people new ways to think about popular culture, not to sway their opinions. For example, Klosterman says that if a mainstream critic likes the way that Fleetwood Mac's album *Rumors* sounds, he'll just conjure up an argument for the social relevance of its lyrics in order to make their instinctual reactions to the work seem intellectually justified. This accusation quite neatly parallels that of the Habermasian critic, who claims that the arguments of the combatants in the contemporary public sphere are driven by personal motivation, not the real truth of the matter. Ideally, for the supporter of Habermas, Klosterman would engage with culture in order to determine its essence and meaning for all of society as the eighteenth-century literary journals supposedly did.

However, coming from a post-modern perspective in which such absolute truths are taken as highly suspicious, Klosterman does the next best thing. He uses rational argumentation in order both to entertain and to provide a template for readers who want to think through the culture around them while avoiding the commercially friendly thumbs up/thumbs down forms of criticism that are so pervasive. Maybe arguing that *When Harry Met Sally* makes us all yearn for "fake love" isn't what Habermas had in mind, but it does evoke a level of rational engagement with culture far deeper than most popular writing and far, far more accessible than what generally comes from our university professors.

And whereas new media forms play a role in the demise of the public sphere in the Habermasian account, new technologies are actually providing Klosterman with a platform to reverse this process. Klosterman's discussion of the problems with contemporary cultural criticism took place in a form rarely seen in popular media over the last few decades: the long-form interview. *Contexts*, the program on which the debate was featured, is available free via iTunes. During the program public figures are allotted up to two hours, commercial free, to discuss contemporary topics. As a result the time and sponsor-driven considerations of most popular media are absent. This is crucial, as Habermas's notion of the public sphere requires lots and lots of time.

If you use Habermas's preferred dialogue method of intellectual discovery, nothing comes fast or easy. One could easily argue that the single greatest detrimental effect that modern media has had on the public sphere is the way in which financial interests perpetually shorten the amount of time in which individuals are allowed to make their point. Sound bites become shorter each year and political slogans have been reduced to single words— Hope, Change, Strategery, Lock Box, and so on. Rational arguments simply can't take place at such speeds. Podcasts such as *Contexts*, however, shake off this trend. By giving their guests more time to speak and allowing someone like Klosterman the ability to logically discuss engaging topics in full, this new media form has the potential to fill a similar role to that of the literary journals that Habermas celebrates.

The Message in the Medium

This improved form of public discussion is even found in the realm of commercial podcasting as evidenced by Klosterman's extremely popular appearances on ESPN's *The B.S. Report* podcast, such as the Lebron James episode. The *Report* is an undoubtedly commercial affair, featuring guests promoting new movies and interviews brought to you by the Subway Fresh Take hotline. However, just like the commerce-free

Contexts podcast, *The B.S. Report* is a truly long-form interview program, with discussions of sports and popular culture that can exceed two hours in duration. Such a situation is simply unthinkable anywhere else in the ESPN media universe, where *Sportscenter* feature stories are often no more than three minutes long.

However, Marshall McLuhan was wrong, the medium is not the message. It takes a figure such as Klosterman to bring out the potential of Simmons's platform. Whereas most *B.S. Report*s have a pleasant, trivial feel to them, Klosterman's episodes inevitably dig deeply into issues that, while perhaps not the sort of thing Habermas would discuss over a pint, nonetheless provide fodder for substantive discourse. For example, on the March 5th, 2010, episode, Simmons remarked that he believes the hip-hop and R&B artists don't belong in the Rock'n'Roll Hall of Fame. In most commercial contexts such a comment would go unchecked, as there would be little time or motivation for a major corporate entity like ESPN to engage with such a question. However, given his approach to popular culture and the freedom of the podcasting medium, Klosterman called out Simmons on his statement, asking him to justify it and going on to assess the racial elements of aesthetic criticism in American music.

It was a rational, in-depth conversation that was both fun and available to Simmons's millions of devoted fans. While many people might disagree with Klosterman's take on the racial implications of music criticism, the podcast modeled a discussion about a crucial American issue in a forum that draws the attention of a wide swath of the American public. No, the hardcore Habermasian is not likely to declare *The B.S. Report* the modern-day equivalent of the French salon, but Klosterman's work in the medium of podcasting nonetheless provides a counterbalance to the prevailing narrative in which the mediated public sphere gets worse with each passing day.

So is Chuck going to save American democracy one fake review of *Chinese Democracy* at a time? No, probably not. But personally, I think he's helping, not hurting. Sure, there will be those who read him, fall in love and decide to devote their lives to getting to the bottom of *Full House* as opposed to investigating government corruption or fighting for social justice. But if they write like Chuck and get us thinking about our culture in a way that recognizes how meaningful the seemingly small things can be and, along the way, teach us a little bit about rational thought, that's fine by me. Personally, I believe that no matter what we do, the next generation of top American thinkers is pretty likely to have honed its debate skills through arguments about reality TV with a few drinks in them after their freshman poly-sci midterms. And trust me, if you happen to end up at table next to them in the bar, you'll be happy they're doing their Chuck impersonations, not their Jürgens.

10

Football, Fútbol, and Chuck

BENJAMIN LISLE

I spend an inordinate amount of time trying to deduce the nature of existence by watching football games.

—CHUCK KLOSTERMAN

I spend an ordinate amount of time trying to induce the very human artifice of culture by watching football games. Like Chuck Klosterman, I love sports. I am certainly one of Klosterman's sporting sixty percent—that group of his readers possessing "a near-expert understanding of sports," as opposed to the other forty percent with "no interest whatsoever" (*Eating the Dinosaur*, p. 148).

Like many people, my relationship with sports has been one of the most persistent and enduring associations of my life; it stretches back to my very earliest memories, costumed in crimson corduroys, perched on the blowy upper deck in Norman, Oklahoma. Rife with passion, though somewhat short on eroticism, my relationship with sports has been deeply emotional, psychological, and, at times, intellectual. When Chuck Klosterman forces himself on my sports, fondling them with his shabby interpretations, violating them and then (and then!) boasting about it in print, something must be done.

Why should I—or you—care about how Chuck Klosterman interprets sports? Sports are meaningful. They are a major mode of cultural expression, a practice through which millions of people gather to play and watch every day. Sport has been a space where ideals are staged, challenged, and inverted. Sport has been where we work out what it means to be "manly" or what becomes a "lady." It has been a lens through which we examine race and contemplate how it intersects with socioeconomic class and biology. Sport has been a socializing agent, where we've educated children and lazy half-wit foreigners about American virtues of hard work, competition, and co-operation. And demonstrated their opposites. Chuck Klosterman presumably doesn't watch Kent State play Eastern Michigan in football to recalibrate his sense of proper masculinity. But certainly watching Kent State play Eastern Michigan recalibrates Chuck Klosterman's sense of proper masculinity.

Klosterman's interpretations of sport—particularly the two footballs, soccer and American gridiron—are interesting both because they are idiosyncratic and because they are representative. They are stamped with his characteristic markings: hyperbole, digression, and inventiveness among them. But they also channel mainstream American sporting discourse. Klosterman's exegesis of the footballs is a good sample of a certain prominent American sports ideology.

The meaning of a sport like football—like any cultural text—is unstable. It shifts and evolves, depending on (among other things) who is interpreting, when they're interpreting, and how the game is played and watched at that moment. Chuck Klosterman is not only an armchair quarterback, but an armchair anthropologist as well. His interpretations of sporting cultural practices—like mine—aren't definitive. They are contestable.

Chuck Klosterman and the '86 Celtics

How do we interpret sport? The ideas of Hans-George Gadamer in *Truth and Method* give us a way to consider how things are interpreted. According to Gadamer's theory of interpretation, Chuck Klosterman's subjectivity—his thoughts, his concerns, his sense of himself, his *prejudices*—come about through his experiences and conversations with the world around him and its people, past and present. I'll call this "culture," using a broad conception of that word. Culture is the human world we live in and how we think about that world.

When Klosterman comes across something he needs to understand—something he must *interpret*—the basis for that interpretation is his culture. He inherited culture, but he also constructs and channels it, continuously, contributing to shared cultures. So, when Chuck encounters a "text" (in the broad sense of that word)—let's say, the 1986 Boston Celtics— he brings to bear preconceptions and prejudices born from culture as channeled through Chuck. He interprets the 1986 Boston Celtics armed with these cultural beliefs and tendencies, regarding, for example, basketball history, racial politics, and moustache semiotics.

Klosterman can't make the 1986 Boston Celtics mean anything he likes. The text, the Celtics, can resist certain interpretations. They can't (for example) truthfully be read as an expression of gay liberation—because any self-respecting, self-critical interpreter remotely savvy to the text and its historical moment wouldn't read them that way. In fact, the Celtics can challenge Chuck's preconceptions, altering his cultural orientation. They can convince him that he should, in fact, prefer a sexual position that resembles Danny Ainge's jumper to Jamaal Wilkes's (*Sex, Drugs, and Cocoa Puffs*, p. 105).

And so, reader and text, Klosterman and the Celtics, are in dialogue. This dialogue isn't historically fixed and frozen, but fluid and continuous. Interpretations aren't stable, because interpreters and the objects of interpretation change. Danny Ainge's jumper may have expressed a certain sexual position when Klosterman wrote the essay "33." After seeing Ainge in a suit for the last few years, Chuck's interpretation of that jumper's sexuality has shifted, if just ever so slightly.

Soccer Resists Klosterman

Klosterman provides readers a lovely example of a sport resisting an interpretation in his essay on soccer, "George Will vs. Nick Hornby," from *Sex, Drugs, and Cocoa Puffs*. When Klosterman sees soccer, he tells the reader, he is reminded of "my guys"—"a collection of scrappy, rag-tag, mostly unremarkable fourth- and fifth-graders I governed when I was sixteen years old" (p. 89). His experience as youth coach of "my guys" was a confounding one for the young governor who, on his job application, listed Bob Knight and George Orwell as his role models (not Orwell the socialist, presumably, but Orwell as stand-in for Orwellianism).

The problem was this: whereas young Klosterman wanted to shape these ten- and eleven-year olds into, as he put it, "a war machine" (pp. 90–91), the mothers of Wyndmere, North Dakota quite predictably and understandably weren't keen on seeing their children turned into Klosterman's sporting Hitler Youth. Or, as he saw it, "They wanted to watch their kids play a game where their perfect little angels could not fuck up, and that would somehow make themselves feel better about being parents" (pp. 94–95).

This little-league coaching experience dictates Klosterman's understanding of soccer. This experience establishes his set of interpretive prejudices and compels him to conclude:

> Real Sports aren't for everyone. And don't accuse me of being the Ugly American for degrading soccer. That has nothing to do with it. It's not xenophobic to hate soccer; it's socially reprehensible to support it. To say you love soccer is to say you believe in enforced equality more than you believe in the value of competition and the capacity of the human spirit. (p. 95)

Ouch. He doesn't stop there. "It should surprise no one," he writes, "that Benito Mussolini loved being photographed with Italian soccer stars during the 1930s; they were undoubtedly kindred spirits." Really limbered up, Klosterman makes his big exit: "Every time I pull up behind a Ford Aerostar with a '#1 Soccer Mom' bumper sticker, I feel like I'm marching in the wake of the Khmer Rouge" (p .95).

I can appreciate the tyranny of the minivan and won't begrudge a man a taste of that sweet hyperbole—particularly if he's trying to sell a few books. But an author needs to recognize that when a text says "no," it means "no." His argument is this:

1. **Soccer is an anti-sport, an exercise in "enforced equality" in the best traditions of militaristic, totalitarian regimes.**

2. **The youth sports leagues of Wyndmere, North Dakota illustrate this point because mothers there resist the totalitarian militarization of their ten-year olds.**

Klosterman's thinly sublimated attraction to *Il Duce* seems to cloud his logic. He extracts an interpretation of an entire sport from a minute sliver of that sport's form and practice—in this case, the culture of its youth leagues in rural North Dakota. This becomes even more problematic when we consider that "my guys" were a little-league *baseball* team.

Yes, Chuck Klosterman's interpretation of soccer is built on his experience as a youth baseball coach. He first tries to barge his way through this inconvenient truth, writing, "And even though I happened to be coaching the game of baseball that summer, this was the experience that galvanized my hatred for the game of soccer" (p. 90). Of course. Perhaps worried that some readers might actually be paying attention, he later revisits this potential pitfall, explaining, "Now, perhaps you're curious as to how my ill-fated experience as a baseball coach has anything to do with my maniacal distaste for soccer; on the surface, probably nothing. But in that larger, deeper, 'what-does-it-all-mean?' kind of way, the connection is clear. What those . . . mothers wanted me to do was turn baseball into soccer" (p. 94).

Hold on a minute: who's turning baseball into soccer here?

Given the dynamism of meaning—its inherent instability born of shifting subjectivities, intersubjectives, and historical contexts—I hesitate to brand an interpretation "wrong." But certainly an identifying characteristic of an inaccurate, erroneous, untruthful interpretation is a willful intellectual neglect on the part of the reader. There may not be definitive, objective truths, but surely there are definitive, objective falsities. Klosterman isn't engaging this text in dialogue at all; instead he whacks away at a soccer straw man constructed by boilerplate red-blooded American sports discourse—soccer is Marxist, soccer is socialist, soccer is fascist, soccer is for pussies. Klosterman unwittingly provides a lovely example of soccer as viewed through one half of the culture wars. But that certainly doesn't make it a plausible interpretation. The text is not having it.

Klosterman, Football, and the Thwarted Dialogue

Klosterman's reading of the other football, American gridiron football—most fully realized in the essay, "Football," from

Eating the Dinosaur—is certainly more compelling than his interpretation of soccer (though that, in itself, isn't an endorsement). For starters, he actually knows something about football, which facilitates more of a dialogue with his object of interpretation. He also considers the game's shifting historical contours—an examination that is central to his interpretation.

What is football? What does it mean? Klosterman concludes that the game satisfies a fundamental need that he and others possess; its popularity emanates from its "interesting contradiction." He writes that football

> feels like a conservative game. It appeals to a conservative mind-set and a reactionary media and it promotes conservative values. But in tangible practicality, football is the most progressive game we have— it constantly innovates, it immediately embraces every new technology, and almost all the important thinking about the game is liberal. *(Eating the Dinosaur*, pp. 127–28)

Football seems conservative, but it's really liberal: an intriguing argument. Klosterman believes that the onus is on him to define the game's "liberality" rather than its "conservatism"— the latter largely goes without saying. And certainly, the game is shot through and encrusted with all sorts of conservative virtues—ideological and iconographic. Football is thoroughly patriarchal, defined by hyper-masculine warriors at the center and hyper-sexualized eye candy on the fringes. Much of the sport's energy—particularly at the high school and college level—emanates from its traditions, its local alliances and rivalries, its cultural initiations handed down from one generation to the next.

But then, a reader can't really be certain what Klosterman means when he terms something "conservative." When he calls football "a conservative idiom" compared to baseball, ("A Brilliant Idea!"), I wonder if there's some other cultural practice named "baseball" of which I'm unaware. Surely he's not referring to the sport without a clock, the sport that begins with the planting and ends with the harvest, the sport that still sometimes stages games in the middle of a weekday. The one with wood bats. The one that Klosterman claimed, in a different essay, "sells itself as some kind of timeless, historical pastime that acts as the bridge to a better era of American life"

(*Eating the Dinosaur*, p. 153). To call football a "conservative idiom" in relation to the original American team sport demands the question: more conservative how?

Sorting out what "conservative" means should be the easy part. What about "liberal"? Klosterman seems to interchangeably use "liberal," "progressive," "freethinking," and "innovative." He claims that gridiron football's liberality is expressed through the tactical innovations that appear on our television screens every few years or decades—offensive plays like the read option or defensive shifts between three- and four-man fronts. He uses the rise of the "read option"—a particular play in which the quarterback "reads" the weak side defensive end before determining his course of action—as a prime example of football's inherent progressiveness. Inherent, that is, but unexpected, given the game's conservative veneer. The read option is remarkable, Klosterman argues, because it is essentially a strategic flash-in-the-pan, illustrating how liberal, progressive, and innovative the game is. "It's still new," he writes, adding, "It didn't really exist in the 1970s and '80s, and when I first saw it employed in the late '90s, it seemed like an idiotic innovation" (p. 141). Here's how Klosterman describes the seemingly innovative read option:

> the quarterback . . . 'reads' the weakside defensive end. If the defensive player attacks upfield, the quarterback keeps the ball and runs it himself. . . . If the defensive end 'stays home' . . . the QB hands the ball to the running back moving in the opposite direction. Basically, the read option is just the quarterback making a choice based on the circumstance. (*Eating the Dinosaur*, p. 149)

The play sounds deliciously simple—a simplicity that strains Klosterman's claim for its being an innovation. Klosterman's description sounds a lot like sportswriter Arthur Daley's account of the "keep-or-give option play" in 1954. The quarterback, Daley explains, "takes the snapback... holds the ball . . . and looks the end squarely in the eye. . . . If the end lunges in at him, he flicks outside to a halfback. If the end veers wide to cover the halfback, the quarterback keeps the ball. No matter what he does, the end is dead." This "fashionable" offense, run out of the Split-T formation, was being used in the mid-1950s to great effect by Bud Wilkinson at Oklahoma, Jim Tatum at

Maryland, and Frank Leahy at Notre Dame. It was an offense so pervasive that the *Times* ran another story in 1955 ("Football Hard Work for Fans, Too") that explained to readers what they were watching on television and hearing on the radio every weekend. The key to the offense, the writer instructed, was the quarterback "keep option," wherein "the quarterback retains the ball until the defensive end commits himself."

Whoa, Nellie! The forward-thinking modernity of the read option suddenly seems an exercise in postmodern nostalgia—a fashionable repackaging of the option plays run out of the Split-T in the 1950s, the Veer-T in the 1960s, and the Wishbone in the 1970s and 1980s. New England Patriots head coach Bill Belichick (quoted by Tim Layden in "Old Is New Is Old") said of Klosterman's supposedly innovative option plays run out of the spread offense, "Call it whatever you want, but it's single wing football." The "single wing" Belichick refers to was indeed a major football innovation . . . in the early 1900s when hatched by the legendary Pop Warner. We might pretend that the contemporary read option is dramatically different from these earlier—and constantly present—tactical maneuvers. We might grant Klosterman his timeline, under which the read option didn't exist twenty-five years ago and was a play of "mild desperation" in the late 1990s. But even then, an inquiring reader must ask herself: "If football is so innovative, why did it take twenty-five or even just ten years for an effective play to become popular?"

My primary mission here, however, is not to challenge Klosterman's nebulous conceptions of the liberal and the conservative, but instead to examine what the read option means to him—for that is where we start to decode what he really sees when he watches football. For Klosterman, the read option is not particularly interesting as it is executed. Its importance, instead, is symbolic. The read option "is symbolic of something unrelated to the practice of football; it's symbolic of the nature of football and how that idea is misinterpreted because of its iconography" (*Eating the Dinosaur*, p. 128). Football's conservative iconography thus runs at odds with the game's actual "nature." In fact, it conceals it, causing people to "misinterpret" the game.

In this configuration, the game's "nature" is revealed through its tactics and, by extension, its strategies. Play-calling is football's essence. This is an interesting claim, for it pushes to the margins many elements of the sport that most people would consider also essential to its character—the brute physicality, the blinding speed, the acrobatic elegance, the tailgating and stadium fan cultures, the cheerleaders, the girlfriends, the parents, the jumbotrons, the patriotic fly-bys, the John Maddens, the uniforms, even just the actual execution of the plays on the field. In fact, according to Klosterman these things that seem so central to the game are deceptions, part of the "iconography" of "misinterpretation."

This reductive assessment constrains the game of football to a series of tactical and strategic adjustments. To understand this, the reader only need skim the essay. Klosterman writes about the read option. He writes about the impact of forward passing. He walks the reader through some of the game's more recent innovative coaches. (This final move comes after a profoundly disingenuous assessment of how the game is packaged; Klosterman claims that the NFL "only uses football" to sell its sport, unlike its major-league competitors, as if it's not one of the most patriotically bombastic artifacts in American cultural history.) This is a telling presentation, almost wholly devoid of actual players (Brett Favre, Klosterman's totem of football conservatism, makes a cameo appearance). Klosterman makes a fetish of football play-calling, and thus, a fetish of the football coach.

The Fetish of the Intellectual Tyrant

Klosterman's essay on soccer is, of course, not about soccer at all. Or even baseball. It's really about the tension between a coach and players. It's a conflict fueled by Klosterman's desire to be the Whitey Herzog of Wyndmere. In the midst of his description of the "my guys" episode, he detours to explain his coaching philosophy and motivations:

> To be honest, I was merely coaching these kids the way I had wanted to be coached when I was in fourth grade. I was a pretty fucking insane ten-year-old. I was the kind of kid who hated authority—but sports coaches were always an inexplicable exception. For whatever the reason, a coach could tell me anything and I'd just stand there and listen; he could degrade me or question my intelligence or sit me

on the bench to prove a point that had absolutely nothing to do with what I did, and I always assumed it was completely valid. I never cared that much about winning on an emotional level, but winning always made sense to me intellectually; it seemed like the logical thing to want. Mostly, I just wanted the process of winning to be complicated. I was fascinated by anything that made sports more cerebral and less physical. (*Sex, Drugs, and Cocoa Puffs*, p. 91)

Klosterman here moves effortlessly from the figure of the coach-as-tyrant to the intellectual complexity of sport (seated, as it is, in the figure of the coach-as-cerebral-complicator). By suggestion, he fuses together these two coaching identities, the tyrant and the philosopher.

Authoritarianism and intellectualism: two virtues that most people would much more likely ascribe to Marxists, communists, and socialists than flag-waving, proto-American sports nationalists (or Americans in general). These are two virtues that Klosterman seems to ascribe to soccer: it is, after all, the sport of Mussolini and the Khmer Rouge. And yet, authoritarianism and intellectualism are those qualities that Klosterman seems to most value in American sports, as suggested in his essays on the two different forms of football. How could this be? How could soccer be "inherently un-American" while football—the sport whose "nature" is expressed through the tactical innovations hatched by the intellectual lording over a managed bureaucracy—be somehow essentially American?

Considering the roots of football might help Klosterman work his way out of this wet paper sack. In "Football," he makes much ado about the addition of the forward pass to the gridiron game. For those who used and faced it, the forward pass expanded the spatial dimensions of the playing field in a practical sense, most famously with Notre Dame's upset of Army in 1913. Many believe that this period marks the beginning of the modern game of gridiron football because it is when football started to resemble the game we know today. But if we want to unpack the game's fundamental modernity—the game as an expression of a modern, organized, rationalized worldview—we should step back a bit further.

Football as soccer and football on the gridiron both emanated from roughly the same game, practiced under different sets of unstable rules—those that emphasized kicking and those that allowed handling. Walter Camp, the "Father of American football," played the central role in codifying the gridiron version in distinction to its soccer and rugby cousins from the 1870s through the 1890s. He oversaw the game's transformation into a modern sport—modern in the sense that it acquired a set of accepted rules, codified by organizations, which allowed it to be played competitively by strangers. Under the steerage of Camp, football became a symbol of not only manliness—important in a period when people widely fretted over the manliness of its urbanized men (particularly effete university men)—but also corporate organization.

Camp, who also managed a New Haven clock factory, was fascinated by Frederick Winslow Taylor's "time-and-motion" theories of scientific management that revolutionized American industry. He recreated football as a bureaucracy; in fact, football's closest analogue wasn't war, but the expanding bureaucracies of the late 1800s. For Camp, football was a way to develop young men—a vehicle for forming characteristics that would assure success in a newly incorporated America. Football, he theorized, would teach men to become useful cogs in larger machines. In *The Book of Football*, he wrote:

> The object must be to use each man to the full extent of his capacity without exhausting any. To do this scientifically involves placing men in such position in the field that each may perform the work for which he is best fitted, and yet not be forced to do any of the work toward which his qualifications and training do not point. (Oriard, *Reading Football,* pp. 44–45)

It's not quite Marx's "From each according to his ability, to each according to his needs." But it does idealize submission to a managed hierarchy, like one a young man might face when he left Yale and entered the workforce as an aspiring manager, several rungs down the bureaucratic ladder. And it most definitely was not association football.

Association football, or soccer, was and is a much less rationalized sport. The dynamism of the game—its free-flowing play—put the impetus on players rather than coaches. This was what Camp cast his game against. Everything about gridiron football was managed; for example, the rugby scrum was separated into alternating possessions, the field was divided into intervals (resembling a "gridiron"), the play was split into "fairs" (now known as "downs"), and individual plays were scripted. Camp replaced spontaneity with control and predictability. Atop it all sat the intellectual tyrant, the puppet master pulling the strings.

Now just because this is what Camp was trying to do—and succeeded in doing formally on the field—doesn't mean that this is the meaning, essence, or "nature" of football. As cultural historian Michael Oriard argues in his excellent study of early football and the media, *Reading Football*, the media often worked against Camps' ideals and goals. Camp thought the sport inculcated modern corporate values, subordination to the group, industrial time discipline, hierarchy, and specialization. The media, instead, celebrated individuals and sensationalized violence, stoking spectators' desire for a more open-ended, dramatic form of play than Camp envisioned. This desire would contribute to the institution of the forward pass.

But the mutability of meaning—at any moment and across time—doesn't change the fact that Camp wrote his values into the genetic code of the game. Watch the two footballs today. Football is hyper-rationalized, spatially and temporally; all of its players play particular, specialized roles and set out, over-and-over again, to execute pre-scripted actions dictated by a cabal of managers. Its organizational structure is vertical and compartmentalized. Soccer's continuous, non-linear action and the players' relatively interchangeable skill sets reflect a horizontal structure. Does this horizontality signify "enforced equality," as Klosterman claims (*Sex, Drugs, and Cocoa Puffs*, p. 95)? Hardly, for the power of the tyrant—that necessary power of enforcement—is diminished. This is a horizontality that combines the athletic expression of individuals working in combination for collective imperatives, loosely steered by the strategic vision of a marginalized leader. Sounds rather American. Or, at least, it sounds rather like Americans like to think of themselves.

What does Chuck Klosterman see when he watches football? He sees something he understands. It's something ordered and Taylorized—a series of specimens in separate Petri dishes. It is *rationalized* and controlled, easily broken down and assessed. Its power structures are clear. The game of football reveals itself to the reader.

The game of soccer doesn't. Its tactics and strategies are more mysterious to the American raised on the discrete episodes of options and quick slants. Soccer is fluid and messy—often more exasperating, but also more often transcendent, than its gridiron cousin. In it, Chuck Klosterman thinks he sees dictators and shackled souls, yearning but unable to breathe free. But what he would see, if he listened to the text, is the game that Walter Camp, the proto-modern bureaucrat, couldn't manage.

11
Media Ecologist without a Cause

KEVIN BROOKS

Chuck Klosterman is more than a music critic or a sports talking head; he is a media ecologist. From *Fargo Rock City* to *Eating the Dinosaur*, he offers extended philosophical investigations into the ways in which media—not just music, but television, radio, 'zines, the Internet, "new media," clothing, food, hair, sports, and occasionally politics—work together to significantly shape (or at least massage) our sense of identity, our sense of being, and our relationship to the world, without us generally knowing or realizing what is going on.

A media ecologist is a philosopher with an eye turned towards big-picture analyses of the history and philosophy of technology and media (hence "ecologist"), rather than a philosopher working on small, focused philosophical problems, or a media critic reviewing and evaluating cultural products. Klosterman has been and often seems like a critic because he eats Cap'n Crunch and media content for breakfast, but at the end of the day, he is in fact frying the bigger fish for dinner.

Chuck is using his analysis of heavy metal, Britney Spears, U2, *Saved by the Bell*, and laugh tracks to try to understand the social, psychological, and ontological effects of media on individuals and culture. Klosterman's clearest ties to the media ecology tradition manifest themselves through his consistent riffing, borrowing, and remixing of the language and approach of media ecology's leading figure, Marshall McLuhan (1911–1980), an influence Klosterman has yet to acknowledge in print.

You Owe McLuhan Everything, Duuuude!

Klosterman is a kind of Marshall McLuhan for the twenty-first century for a few legitimate reasons and some random coincidences.

1. McLuhan proved that a dude from nowhere—Winnipeg Manitoba Canada, about three hundred miles north of Wyndmere, North Dakota—could be the world's premier media wonk, paving the way for Klosterman.

2. McLuhan broke almost all the ground on academic analyses of popular culture and media, starting with sixty short essays (*The Mechanical Bride*, 1950) on everything from newspapers to Superman to sports and Coca-Cola, followed by twenty-six chapters on media as diverse as bicycles, clocks, and television in *Understanding Media* (1964). McLuhan's analyses, however, weren't very academic, so in a way, Klosterman has comes full-circle in paying his unacknowledged debt to McLuhan, hammering out elaborate quasi-academic, organically philosophical analyses with occasional sources cited—something McLuhan rarely bothered with. McLuhan got people to take media seriously, and his disciples, like Klosterman, went nuts!

3. Woody Allen had the good sense to give McLuhan a cameo in *Annie Hall*, undoubtedly prompting the writers of *The OC* to give Klosterman a similar (though less embodied) cameo in one of their episodes.

4. Klosterman's key concepts, his vocabulary, and his analytical style seem to owe McLuhan almost everything (as I will elaborate below), but he has yet to come clean and acknowledge any debt. I'm writing, Mr. Klosterman, to collect on this debt.

McLuhan, in breaking all this ground, didn't have to worry about whether he was providing socially valuable knowledge beyond "understanding media"—that was enough. Klosterman carries on this important project; he brings to it a fresh and foul-mouthed perspective, and he is willing to pay close attention to all sorts of mass media products that would choke, like a rock star's vomit, most critics and philosophers. But unfortunately, Klosterman doesn't even want to claim this little bit of importance for his work. He prefers to just wanna have fun: "All my criticism is autobiography. I have no interest in persuading (or dissuading) readers from liking anything" (ESPN). And of course, he is famously not feeling guilty about not doing anything to save the world, let alone the bell ("Not Guilty," *Fargo Rock City*, pp. 259–263).

But that attitude is just wrong, and Klosterman knows it—he even hints that he knows he could do more to make himself useful. So, in the tradition of the great American pragmatic philosopher Richard Rorty, who didn't believe it was possible to really convince people with arguments so much as humor, I'd like to "josh" Klosterman out of his complacency, and get him to use what Rorty calls "light-hearted aestheticism" for good, instead of indifference. I'd like him to become a media ecologist *with* a cause.

Chuck Klosterman: 85% Media Ecologist

But first the praise, because Klosterman is doing some good in the world, in spite of his lack of intention. Klosterman was helping the world understand media and the much-neglected phenomenon of heavy metal as early as "Dec, 12, 1985." This chapter from *Fargo Rock City* is a quintessential media ecologist's attempt to understand why a few kids who listened to heavy metal end up killing themselves, while most, like Klosterman, just put a blow-drier to their head. The underlying message of metal, Klosterman argues, is "get noticed." Killing yourself is one way to do that; big hair is a more reasonable option.

But Klosterman doesn't just hop from point A to point B in this serpentine chapter. He wanders through an analysis of Rush as Christian Rock band—perception is reality, Klosterman argues—and then he provides deft analysis of the media ecology of the 1980s and early 1990s. He points out that metal, unlike punk or late 1960s psychedelic, was available on mainstream, album-oriented, FM radio: media source #1 for getting some attention. The Eighties were also what Klosterman calls "The Golden Age of Periodicals" (*Fargo Rock City*, p. 51)—*Hit Parader*, *Circus*, *Kerrang!*, and *Metal Edge* provided real coverage of the metal scene, not just teen idol posters. These magazines made it to rural North Dakota when and where media source #3—MTV—couldn't always penetrate. But Klosterman offers his sharpest media ecology insight when he says, "You did not have to see MTV to be affected by it: You only had to know it was out there. One way or another, the images would all slip into everyone's collective unconscious" (p. 52). What better way to be noticed than to penetrate someone's unconscious? What better way to do media ecology analysis than notice the convergence of various media forms, resulting in a spike of popularity for a particular musical genre (hair metal) at a particular time, and even in a particular place (rural America)?

Near the end of "Dec. 12, 1985," Klosterman offers up a twisted variation of McLuhan's global village: "With the proliferation of media, the need for attention became paramount. All of America was now a singular club scene. You could see a band perform through videos, and you could effectively "hang out" with the guys in the group by reading magazine articles" (*Fargo Rock City*, p. 56). The "singular club scene" will resonate with most readers interested in media as "the global village" writ small, but Klosterman, perhaps unknowingly, also grasps McLuhan's belief that communication at the speed of light is largely "haptic," is largely about "keeping in touch," or "hanging out" because, as Klosterman acknowledged earlier in the chapter, the "interviews were often horrible and the information often fabricated" (p. 51).

This kind of analysis permeates *Fargo Rock City*; Klosterman's media ecology approach makes *Fargo Rock City* required reading, not only for understanding heavy metal but for understanding media. When I recommend *Fargo Rock City* to people, they frequently say, "I don't like heavy metal." I don't know anyone who hates heavy metal more than I do, but Klosterman's analysis makes sense of why this senseless genre was so popular, why it flourished in the Eighties but has chugged along consistently since then, an example of what McLuhan would call the "figure-ground" effect. Heavy metal accomplished its goal of gaining great attention and notice, (*the figure*), then it slipped back into *the ground* or environment of culture and media, still prevalent but not so noticeable. The Guitar Hero/Rock Band driven metal revival makes perfect media ecology sense as it connects some teens and parents through a new medium, retrieving the older media form, re-packaged as a game, but also widely available in new formats (CDs and MP3s) for easy consumption and distribution.

Klosterman has drawn (consciously or unconsciously, I don't know—does it matter?) on other McLuhan concepts throughout his career, clarifying that he is not a critic but a media ecologist interested in tackling big-picture questions through investigations of single artists, athletes, performers, and other curious people. In "Bending Spoons With Britney," we get to see him working at the question, "What is her cultural significance?" and more generally at the question of how a particular type of celebrity functions for various audiences. Klosterman doesn't explain McLuhan's concepts of "hot and cool media," but his answer to these questions is that Britney is a medium in and of herself, and a cool medium at that, despite the many hot pictures of her that appeared alongside Klosterman's original article. "Hot" to McLuhan means "high definition" or "well-defined;" cool means "low definition" or "minimally defined." So when Klosterman notes her lack of definition, he is mixing in some McLuhan:

> She is truly all things to all people: a twelve-year old girl thinks she is a hero, that girl's older brother thinks she is a stripper, that older brother's girlfriend thinks she is an example of why women hate themselves, that girlfriend's father secretly wishes his twelve-year daughter would invite Britney over for a slumber party. As long as Spears never overtly says "This is who I am," everyone gets to inject their own meaning. Subconsciously, we all get to rebrand Britney Spears. (*Chuck Klosterman IV*, p. 18)

Klosterman acknowledges that understanding Britney Spears is only important if you care about understanding popular culture, but of course we should want to understand popular culture. It is a multi-billion dollar a year industry; it occupies our time, our attention, our energy, our money. We need to understand how media work, especially as we move through an era in which the tools of production are increasingly available to individual citizens, not just the media giants. So those of us who care about media owe Klosterman a debt of gratitude for pushing media ecology into realms most academics and philosophers don't want to tread—heavy metal, Britney Spears, and *Saved by the Bell*, to name a few—and for making the analysis so much more entertaining and insightful than the product itself. For this work, I have credited Klosterman with being eighty-five percent of a media ecologist; with just a little philosophical refresher and a tiny commitment to something other than himself and popular culture, he can (and should) become fully formed.

The Other 15%

As Klosterman continues to "probe," as McLuhan liked to say, more diverse topics and media, he fortifies his core media ecologist values. *Eating the Dinosaur* includes his best media ecology essays yet (about the NFL channel and laugh tracks), and his most sustained reflection on technology in general, worked out through his response to the Unabomber's manifesto, *Industrial Society and Its Future*. Klosterman's response, however, re-iterates his obsession with authenticity and his apparent belief that there might be some self and some world outside or beyond technology and media. No one-hundred-percent-card-carrying media ecologist believes this.

Klosterman uses this essay to admit that he hates technology but it is of great importance to his life (so far so good), that the Unabomber's critique of the dehumanizing effects of media is not so crazy (agreed), and that we have never been less human than we are now (whoa—hold on a minute!), but we like it (okay).

> We are living in a manner that is unnatural. We are latently enslaved by our own ingenuity, and we have unknowingly constructed a simulated world. The benefits of technology are easy to point out (medicine, transportation, the ability to send and receive text messages during Michael Jackson's televised funeral), but they do not compensate for the overall loss of humanity that is its inevitable consequence. As a species, we have never been less human that we are right now. (*Eating the Dinosaur*, p. 228)

I might appear to be splitting hairs as I pick apart this paragraph, because there is no doubt that as a species we are more removed from the natural world than we used to be. We are undoubtedly more dependent upon technology. I can even live with "enslaved" by technology—that was certainly McLuhan's language and concern. And we do indeed live in a more elaborately simulated world.

But all of these qualities are just part of being human.

Maybe we have gone too far, as Klosterman suggests, but maybe we haven't gone far enough, as a futurist like Ray Kurzweil argues in *The Singularity Is Near: When Humans Transcend Biology*. Kurzweil thinks technology will enable him (and perhaps a few believers) to live forever. Klosterman has staked out his simplistic position that we are somehow less human because of our technology, instead of recognizing that we have always been, and will continue to be, tool-using animals.

Klosterman is even further out of line, however, when he writes about the "the overall loss of humanity that is [technology's] inevitable consequence" (p. 228). McLuhan was very clear in *The Medium Is the Massage* and other works that "There is absolutely no inevitability as long as there is a willingness to contemplate what is happening" (p. 25). The whole point of being a media ecologist is to understand the media, which in turn will enable our species to make better choices about which media and technologies to embrace or shun, or even better yet, to understand the positive potential as well as the negative implications of any media. Klosterman, in this crucial paragraph, seems to believe that we are enslaved by our technology and that we might as well stop worrying and learn to love the text message. He has also suggested that we can dream of a future war against the machines—we can optimistically imagine that we won't lose ("Robots," *Chuck Klosterman IV* p. 292).

This paragraph by Klosterman, and this essay on the Unabomber, is just one more example of Klosterman's obsession with authenticity. He is usually worried about whether celebrities and their products are authentic or not, but in this essay, he is actually wondering if any of us can ever really be authentic, ever really be human, in our media saturated world. I would really like Klosterman to give up this obsession, because media ecologists have more or less dealt with and dismissed the problem. We are tool-using, symbol–(including media)–using animals, and there is no world outside our tools and symbols that we can get to or inhabit in order to become fully human (again?). The annoying thing about Klosterman is that he actually understands this, but he won't give up on the dream, and that is what makes him a media ecologist without a cause.

While he might desire this natural, unmediated world, he knows that he's pretty much trapped in the heavily mediated existence he currently inhabits: "I aspire to think of myself as an analog person, but I am not. I have been converted to digital without the remastering, and the fidelity is appealing" (*Eating the Dinosaur*, p. 229). This acceptance of his digital existence should have enabled him to stop obsessing about authenticity and ontology, and allowed him to focus more on politics and ethics, as any self-respecting philosopher and media ecologist who read and absorbed Richard Rorty's *Philosophy and the Mirror of Nature* (1979) was able to do. But Klosterman hasn't been able to do that, even though he frequently acknowledges that he probably should. Until Klosterman can make these changes—give up ontology and metaphysics, take on politics and ethics—he will remain only eighty-five percent of a media ecologist.

Everyone Is Guilty of All the Good They Haven't Done—Really

Klosterman knows that the mass culture crappola he writes about is worse than trivial in relation to real human problems. He writes, "Compared to the depletion of the ozone layer or the war in Liberia, I concede that the existence of Britney Spears is light-years beyond trivial. But if you are remotely interested in the cylinders that drive pop culture, it's hard to underestimate her significance" (*Chuck Klosterman IV*, p. 14). Klosterman uses the same syntactical and logical structure in "'Ha ha,' he said. 'Ha ha'" when he writes about laugh tracks in television. "These are not real problems (like climate change or African genocide), because those issues are complex and multifaceted; . . . these [non problems] are things that make me feel completely alone in the world because I cannot fathom how the overwhelming majority of people ignores them entirely" (*Eating the Dinosaur*, p. 162). Klosterman is clever enough, and not incorrect, to say that Britney Spears and laugh tracks matter—he does an exceedingly good job of explaining their importance. But why does he so consistently compare the importance of his insignificant (yet oh-so-significant) topics to the really massive, really important, issues of the last fifteen years?

The reason, I wildly speculate, has a lot to do with being from a German Catholic family in North Dakota. Media is not the only powerful institution in our lives; family, religion, community, and place are pretty significant too. To be from North Dakota, regardless of one's ethnic heritage, instills a need to be useful; add to that a little German stoicism, a touch of Catholic guilt, and I suspect that Klosterman knows that he could turn his substantial interpretive powers to more weighty issues. He has admitted as much: "if I spent as much time analyzing al Qaeda as I've spent deconstructing Toby Keith's video for 'Whiskey Girl,' we probably would have won the war on terrorism last April" (*Chuck Klosterman IV*, p. 263). Nothing that we know about him would suggest that he is in fact remotely interested in climate change, Liberia, or Rwanda, except for the fact that he keeps bringing these topics up before he launches into the massively trivial stuff he really cares about.

So, I am going to call his bluff and ask him to turn his powers—philosophical and linguistic—towards one of these issues. I am not going to ask him to become Bono, and actually do something that might reduce global poverty. I'd be satisfied if he would think about and write about the media ecology that keeps so many people watching *Saved by the Bell* re-runs or the NFL channel, at the expense of paying attention to the mounting tensions in Sudan that might result in a return to war after a mere five-year respite from one of the longest and bloodiest civil wars in Africa. Or I'd love to see him tackle the inverse problem: why is it that our haptic technologies, the ones that made the head banging crowd feel they were hanging out with Def Leppard when they read *Kerrang!*, cannot make us feel similarly close to the displaced people of Darfur?

McLuhan made a bit of an attempt to apply his interpretive powers to global problems when he wrote *War and Peace in the Global Village* during the height of the Vietnam War, but he barely referenced the war and probably spent too much time talking about the historical significance of the stirrup—brilliant stuff, but a little confusing, and a little too far from the issue at hand. Klosterman, you owe McLuhan everything (even if you didn't realize it), so at least try to finish this battle for your figurative father, okay?

Susan Moeller's *Compassion Fatigue* is probably a better media ecology model than *War and Peace in the Global Village*, as she documents the way that many global crises of 1991 resulted in news agencies unable to "sell" another crisis to their audience. Somalia's, Sudan's and Ethiopia's internal battles, mixed with famine and disease, were indistinguishable to the average American news consumer, and the news agencies of the time were content not to sift through the differences. There is nothing funny about *Compassion Fatigue* and its subject matter, but I think turning his attention to real global problems will give Klosterman a nice challenge. I want him to be smart, funny, and philosophical, but I want to see him tackle an issue or two of substance. He knows what the issues are—he keeps listing them at the start of his essays—so why won't he take them on?

Klosterman might be more comfortable revisiting Bono after all these years, or turning his probing mind to the substantial global work done by Angelina Jolie, but in doing so, I really, really hope he doesn't ask "Is she for real?" and "Is this kind of work authentic?"

If Klosterman decides to take on the more pressing issues he hints at, I will certainly not be wondering: "Is he testing his audience the way Garth Brooks tested his audience with Chris Gaines?" "Is Klosterman just trying to be Nicholas Kristoff, or does he see himself as the George Clooney-type?"

I'll be saying loud and clear, "Way to go, Chuck! You make the Peace Garden State proud!" And I'll be pounding my gavel and saying "No longer guilty!"

Jack and Jane pseudo-rationalism?

HYPERthetical Response #4

Jack and Jane pseudorationalism

GEORGE A. REISCH

In *Chuck Klosterman IV*, Chuck offers a hypothetical question to his readers. Jane breaks up with her boyfriend, Jack, because he ended up watching a woman masturbate in his apartment. Jack never touched her or kissed her, but during a late night drunken and flirtatious conversation, he indulged this woman's "bizarre sexual quark" (p. 272). Chuck wants to know whose side you would take, Jack's or Jane's.

Chuck's hypothetical about Jack and Jane (CKIV, 271) points to a classic philosophical trap. Otto Neurath, one of the greatest philosophers that you've never heard of (because, in fact, most philosophers have barely heard of him) called it "pseudorationalism."

The "rationalism" part is just what Chuck's hypothetical gets into—the reasons and rational framework we appeal to when we try to specify exactly why something is wrong, such as cheating on your spouse or partner. The rationalist presumes that this framework is real and objective. If they just think about it right, everyone can see it and understand it.

The "pseudo" part is the trap. Because rationalism fails. Often. Big time. It clearly succeeds in logic, in mathematics, and other symbolic languages that we humans have created because those languages *are* the rational definitions and rules we've put into them. But when the goal is to understand things like nature, people, and ethics, we're not in this logical Kansas anymore. The hope that matters can be captured and analyzed in some rational system is bound to fail because so many things

177

we care about exist outside of our imaginations, definitions, and rules.

Nancy Cartwright, the philosopher (not the voice of Bart Simpson) who happens to be a big fan of Otto (the philosopher, not Bart's bus driver) wrote a book called *How the Laws of Physics Lie*. They lie because laws of physics are mathematical relationships, like F = *ma*, that describe how physical objects behave only when they are connected to busloads of qualifications and caveats that the laws themselves *don't* mention. Relationships and events in nature—involving temperature, atmospheric conditions, motions, chemical compositions, radiation levels, gravity, friction, and so on—are in fact always more complicated than textbook stories about perfect objects moving on "frictionless" planes in the absence of all interfering forces or conditions. The world in which the laws of physics *don't* lie is the world of our imaginations, not the world of nature itself.

That's okay because we know the laws lie and we know, or can usually figure out, how they lie. Science can deal with it. But *human* relationships are more complicated than physics or chemistry. With people involved, rationalism almost automatically becomes pseudorationalism because human phenomena and relationships are so varied and complex. That's why there's no agreement about whether what Jack did was so bad. That's why, even among those who agree that Jane was right to dump him, "everyone uses a slightly different, weirdly personal argument to explain what makes it so bad" (*Chuck Klosterman IV*, p. 272).

Ethically, we're all pseudorationalists. We read the story against the backdrop of our own personal values and experiences and try to fit the story, as we've interpreted it, into neat and clean definitions of ethical behavior. We each interpret the story at least a little bit differently, and then suppose, falsely, that each of us accepts the same rational definitions of ethical behavior. Finding that ten or twenty people agree precisely about Jack and Jane is like finding ten or twenty that agree about whether *The Exorcist* is more scary than *Alien*, or whether *Chinese Democracy* is better than *Abbey Road*. We know that's impossible, but we still try to convince each other that our take on Jack and Jane is the *right* one.

The crucial thing is whether Jack and Jane themselves are pseudorationalist. If they are, that's bad—not bad philosophy (which they probably don't care about) but bad for them and their relationship. If Jane honestly believes that she has to dump Jack only because he violated some cosmic rule that says *when in a committed relationship thou shalt not watch thy neighbor masturbate* then she's a pseudorationalist. It's not that she's dumping him for a bad reason, it's that she's dumping him for a reason that really isn't a reason. Outside Jane's imagination, there is no such objective, rational law. As Chuck points out, "watching someone masturbate" is too vague to support a law or a policy—what about pornography? Madonna on the 1984 MTV music video awards? Baboons at the zoo? Is Jack forbidden from watching porn, Madonna, or going to the zoo?

Well those are *different*, the pseudorationalist will reply, and concoct qualifications and exceptions in a vain attempt to prop up their rational ethical architecture. "Baboon's aren't people," they'll say. Yes, but they are distantly related to us and everyone has a cousin or two who seems inhuman, at least in some respects. So it would be okay to watch them masturbate? "Madonna didn't actually masturbate," they'll say. But what if Jane didn't actually masturbate in front of Jack but just went through all the motions and pretended to? This is the thing about pseudorationalism. Whenever you try to get to the bottom of something, you always spend more time defending your pseudorationalism instead of figuring out what really matters.

There may be good reasons for Jane to dump Jack. They're just not "rational" or objective. She doesn't need to rely on some cosmic moral rule to dump him if the incident shakes her faith in his commitment, confirms doubts she's been having about her happiness in the relationship, or if she believes he did it to hurt her, or *whatever it may be*. We don't actually know the reasons why Jane did what she did, but if she's not pseudorationalistic about it, I think she did what she had to do. It was as right as things get in a non-pseudorationalist world.

But if she's a pseudorationalist, it may not have been right. Suppose she dumped Jack in 2005 not because of her honest, personal reasons but instead because of some know-it-all friend convinced her to accept the commandment: *When in a committed relationship thou shalt not watch thy neighbor mas-*

turbate. Then, in 2006, depressed about the breakup, she enrolled in a grad program at NYU to try to make a change in her life. In 2007 she read Nancy Cartwright and Otto Neurath and in 2008 decided that she no longer buys into pseudorationalistic ways of thinking. Then she realizes . . .

BOOK V

Downtown Owl
of Minerva

12
How Chuck Got Chicks

LUKE DICK

"Put this next to the title page," says the clerk exhaustively, tiny eyes peering over the rims of his Buddy Holly glasses. I can't tell if he's bespectacled from some natural vision deficiency or of the need to be ironically dorky. He hands me a yellow sticky with my name, handwritten in all caps: *LUKE DICK*. The lack of serifs always seems to make my moniker more startling than normal.

I fumble through my new copy of *Killing Yourself to Live* to find the title page (viii, if you care) and wonder why the fuck it would matter which page Klosterman signs. The two hundred or so people in front of me at the Barnes and Noble in Union Square seem to share something in common, besides a liking for CK and a need to prove to their friends that, indeed, Klosterman has physically touched their book. I'm not quite in the mood to ponder it just yet.

I let the aroma of overpriced coffee carry me through the line at a zombie's pace, wondering if it's at all desperate for a grown-ass man to be waiting for a culture critic to sharpie something impersonal for me. Actually, I wonder just *how* desperate it is. The line is filled with plenty of beautiful women, and here I am waiting for an autograph, listening to Boston's "Rock'n'Roll Band" (probably Chuck's mix) through a PA at an ironically high volume for the literature section. I'm reminded of being a ten-year-old, waiting on Brian Bosworth ("The Boz") to sign my football jersey, secretly hoping that the two-time Butkis Award-winning linebacker would notice I was donning his trade-marked haircut. The University of Oklahoma linebacker's professional career was short-lived and controversial. Thank God he is immortalized in *Stone Cold*, amongst other action thrillers. I still regard him as the Axl Rose of football and am awaiting his swan song.

Even though I haven't gone so far as to emulate Klosterman's hairdo, every minute in the line is somehow emasculating, and by the end of it, I am feeling ten and lost again. Listening to the fans in front of me ask Chuck questions on politics, sports, and the future, gives the impression that he's some kind of oracle. How did Klosterman do it? How did writing about rock stars make him a rock star, cool kids hanging on his every word? AND, how did Chuck get three to four hundred suckers like me to line-up on a weeknight to listen to a journalist? Despite his occasional self-deprecation, he's an empowered dude, with plenty to show for his work. I want to know why, where, and how he came by this power.

The Mystery of Generating Cocoa Puffs

Now, if I were looking to historically detail the rise of Chuck, I could trace his career, from Fargo to Akron, Akron to NYC, charting his time and highlighting the progression of his essays, but these would be only superfluous details to his empowerment. Better to look at the nature and spirit of his writing.

I found *Sex, Drugs, and Cocoa Puffs* on a Barnes and Noble shelf as an undergraduate. I couldn't resist the title and bought it, almost sight unseen. When telling my Okie friend about going to see Chuck at a signing, he answered with a bizarrely southern joke about *Sex, Drugs, and Cocoa Puffs* in his most radical drawl: "If you talk to ol' Chuck, tell him I li'kat book about fuckin' 'n' Fruity Pebbles." Kudos, Scribner. You picked a winner.

I can't remember if I ever had the balls to pass it off as "research" in an academic setting, but I couldn't deny that Chuck Klosterman was onto *something*, whatever that something may be. Besides, it read a hell of a lot easier than Heidegger. There are plenty of pop culture journalists critical of Klosterman, but I would dance on Lester Bangs's grave arguing that CK is the most insightful rock critic I've ever read, especially when he talks about Led Zeppelin. Of course,

Klosterman's supremacy is debatable, as is everything associated with art and art critique. I actually spent a few hours reading the one and two-star reviews (criticisms) of Chuck's books on Amazon. This experience was actually side-splittingly funny, because most of the people who took it upon themselves to shit-talk the man seemed to invoke their own inner-Klosterman to do so. That is, I was reading *inspired* insults. Klosterman-inspired.

Negative criticisms are a dime a dozen. So are shitty bands. These two entities feed off each other in a self-perpetuating pop culture cesspool. Regardless of how funny this can be (and it can be very funny), it's really no more valuable than listening to the wittiest kid in class hurl insults at the fattest kid. The interplay is utterly forgettable when it comes right down to it. Klosterman is unique in that he has more to offer than snarky jabs at average bands.

At his best, Klosterman gives both extraordinary and mundane pop culture reflective credence. He is inspired, and it shows in his writing. Inspiration is mysterious, a neglected and worthy philosophical topic. The initial spontaneity required to spark a quality creative effort as a song or as an essay is perhaps something other-worldly—or at least inexplicable. Where does an idea come from? Most everyone who has a television experiences Pamela Anderson and Lady Gaga, yet Klosterman is the one cranking out sentence after sentence. How does he come by his ideas? Given that they both seem to read and watch the same things, why is it Klosterman who is writing the books and not, say, my sister? There is real talent and creativity at work in his ability to draw meaning out of even in the most ephemeral pop happenings. The effects of his writing are magnetic.

B-*Ion*-ic Spectator

How is it that *anyone* ever "comes up" with an idea? Klosterman has had more than his fair share of inspiration for his essays: Billy Joel = cool for being uncool . . . Gaga = famous for being famous . . . Reality TV = the confusion of reality with what is supposed to be reality. . . . He has distinguished himself from the vast majority of critics in that he actually has some aesthetic ideas and makes cultural connections in his writing rather than simply throwing around some adjectives.

So, what's the process? Perhaps he is eating his Cocoa Puffs, or maybe he's in the middle of ordering his cheeseburger when—BAM—somehow a conscious connection is made between his passive absorption of all things pop and his inclination to ascribe meaning to the world. Then, he sits down, writes, is inspired more, writes . . . and, *voilà*: a new pop essay. Maybe General Mills' cereal recipe is the incendiary, igniting the flame of inspiration. Or perhaps the secret to creative spontaneity lies in perfectly melted American cheese. Doubt it. Plato has a theory about this phenomenon.

Plato's pop culture dialogues read about as easy as Shakespeare to a high school stoner, which is to say, considerably easier than most other philosophers' works. Plato's greatest hits are more voluminous and have lasted longer than any pop culture icon, save Homer or Sophocles, whom Plato would consider emotional sellouts. Longevity has to count for something in pop culture, right? Just to give us some perspective: the Beatles have fifty years under their belt and still sell gobs of records. Plato has been on the scene roughly 2,400 years, and his work still commands a dollar. Not to mention that his body of work addresses pretty much any real issue of human importance for both thinking *and* non-thinking types.

Plato discusses the notion of inspiration in his dialogue entitled *Ion*. The dialogue is a conversation between Socrates and a rhapsode named "Ion." In ancient Greece, rhapsodes were something like the tribute bands of our times. Instead of playing G N' R's "Use Your Illusion" (I and II) from beginning to end, rhapsodes would travel town-to-town, performing epics from the great poets. There were even popular contests for the best rhapsode at various festivals. Granted, this sounds like as much fun as a medieval fair, but that was a different time and place. Don't be surprised if in two thousand years years our brand of popular culture is obsolete. As much as I love Gaga, I doubt trapezoidal hair and giant great Danes will be all the rage in the year 4000. Fame, as well as fame monsters, are ephemeral.

Ion was the Homer tribute band, perhaps performing as a one-man-band under the name "Homer Alone." Often performing the *Odyssey* in one sitting, Ion would pull all-nighters, provided the wine. Ion only had eyes for Homer, and his passion for the stage and narration ended with Homeric epics. As Plato puts it, when addressed or asked to discuss any other poet, Ion "went to sleep," so to speak. Perhaps this is what you all are doing now, since I have switched subjects to something un-Klosterman. I realize it was probably Klosterman's name and not Plato's that prompted you to buy this book. But bear with me.

Plato's explanation of Ion's passion for Homer is that Ion is actually experiencing indirect, maddened possession. This "possession" is a chain reaction, beginning with the splendor of the divine muses. The muse inspires a poet like Homer, working him into a frenetic stupor until he has created a poem. This mysterious creative genesis finally results in a piece of art the artist or poet perhaps doesn't even understand. If you've ever actually made a piece of art, you might be able to relate to the obsessive behaviors that result from the act of inspiration and creation. The artist or poet works on their piece to get it "just right," not knowing precisely how to define what "just right" is. After listening to an artist's mission statement, you'll often be bored to tears and left rolling your eyes at their inability to articulate anything remotely accurate about their art.

Plato estimates that a muse sets off a chain reaction, directing inspiration to a poet or artist. The poet, in turn, channels the inspiration into the creation of a poem or epic, inspiring rhapsodes, actors, and eventually spectators. The chain of inspiration goes something like this:

Muse → Poet → Art → Rhapsode → Actor → Spectator

This step-wise relationship of aesthetic experience, Plato likens to a magnet. The muses are the magnets, full of force and vitality, drawing in the poets and causing inspiration in them. The poet's art, in turn, attracts the rhapsode, the actor, and eventually the spectator. The assumption is that the farther away from the muse one gets in any given piece of art, the less the magnetic force. That is, listening to G N' R perform *Appetite for Destruction* is much more compelling than listening to a local tribute band's rendition of the same, because they were the ones originally inspired. Still, even a great tribute band can be pretty powerful and draw a crowd of spectators.

I imagine that most of us are spectators, as there are many more people watching movies than writing or acting in them, many more music enthusiasts than songwriters or performers. As spectators, we are several levels away from the intensity of that initial inspiration, in Plato's estimation. That's not to say that experiencing the effects of the muse is dull for a spectator, by any means. How many movies have made you cry? How many concerts have compelled you to sing at the top of your lungs? We're all spectators to some degree, and the effects of the arts on us are powerful. Klosterman got his start by being an inspired spectator, reviewing records and writing about pop culture. Hundreds of ideas and essays later, he's a bestselling author, and holds court at the front of Barnes and Noble, signing autographs.

I want to know if he's really inspired, or if he's just a spectator like I am. That is, does Chuck get to love up the muses or just a few bookish types? If Plato is any reliable guide, my guess is that before *Downtown Owl,* he probably only got to second base with the muse, Thalia. *Downtown Owl* was the first time he'd gotten to smoke the post-coital cigarette with her. But they were both drunk at the time, and since then, it has been hard to tell if their romp was just a one night stand brought on by good beer, good jokes, and a good juke box. All we know is that in the morning, she was gone. No note. No number. The muses don't have cell phones or Facebook accounts. They're those mysterious and enigmatic chicks you just hope to run into on a lucky night.

Chuck's Power Chord

If Klosterman isn't regularly knocking boots with the muses, how is he selling so many books? Other than *Downtown Owl,* he's only given us his own articulate musings—neither philosophy nor gifts of the muses, according to Plato. Yet CK has gained power by hawking words. If he's generally just another spectator by Plato's lights, then how does he command such a crowd? Why wouldn't the crowd simply go directly to the artist, rather than listening to a critic? I've noticed a trend in Klosterman's facial hair. Perhaps his success and empowerment are directly proportionate to his beard. If so, it's probably best if we seek the answers to questions of empowerment from the man who donned the most wicked moustache of all, Friedrich Nietzsche. Stylistically, I would liken Nietzsche to the love child of Tom Waits, Captain Beefheart, and Ted Nugent: Brilliantly abrasive, intellectually austere, and frequently cocky. His records are equal parts compelling, rocking, and irritating . . . be warned.

Nietzsche, like so many philosophers, sold far more books post mortem. Much of his philosophy concerns notions of power and how it has been acquired and interchanged throughout the history of mankind. Even morality can be attributed to a long and complex power struggle, according to Nietzsche. At the very heart of nature is the imperative to live and survive. As humans, we're bound by this imperative, which impels us to procure food and shelter and to procreate by any means necessary. For many animals, hunting and mating territories are delineated and maintained by physical power. If one animal encroaches upon another's territory, there is some form of physical challenge, eventually decided by the more cunning and powerful animal. Physical power is the main currency of the animal world. Just spend one Saturday watching PBS's *Nature*; there is plenty of evidence to suggest that our history as humans embodies this struggle for power, albeit on a more sophisticated and bloodier level. Pull up Google Maps, and rest assured blood was shed for just about every boundary drawn. Google boasts Maps, Books, Images, and Videos, but there is no Google Morality. Nietzsche is certain that the lines delineating morality and human artifice were drawn by power struggles.

The life of one organism requires the death of another. I have to kill to live, whether it's a cow or a stalk of ripe broccoli I choose to eat. This brutality exists for all living things. Granted, the lettuce doesn't run from us when we pick and eat it, but it has a natural impetus to survive. Anything with cells does. Nietzsche claims that modern moral values, such as altruism, meekness, humility, spiritual goods, are unnatural. It was once the case that the warrior class ruled, enforcing their own values, which included valor, pride and strength. Every ancient empire was built in this manner, valuing and perpetuating the warrior's ideal of power. The history of human civilization is an espousal of raw, brutish power, in which conquest, enslavement, and building empires on the back of the vanquished foe is the penultimate goal. Nietzsche deemed the warrior class's notions of morality the "master morality." The warriors became the masters through physically and strategically overpowering the weak and procuring shelter, stability, and civilization through acts of force. Over the past two thousand years, however, Nietzsche estimates that the slaves and their notions of morality have cunningly taken over.

The concept and practice of mercy, for instance, did not resonate with the Spartans, who practiced infanticide if a newborn should be deemed physically unfit. This is obviously harsh by our standards, but there is no doubt that such hardened hearts created powerful armies. Given that the greatest empires of all time have done so much warring to create "civilization," it's amazing that more peacefully intellectual values ever came to pass.

Meekness, altruism, and love of one's neighbor are what Nietzsche considers slave moralities. Nietzsche's estimation is that the weaker classes propagated their own value system in order to counteract the fact they lacked the physical strength to overcome the warrior class. The priestly castes overthrew the warrior class slyly and with intellectual rigor. Mercy, forgiveness, and altruism are all characteristics that the priestly class touted as "noble" and "good" precisely because these traits were advantageous to their own futures. Through the intellect, the slave classes were able to change the moral landscape, shifting moral impetus away from physical prowess. As Nietzsche sees it, the history of Christianity and its values is a history of the slaves finding a cunning way to rule their masters and the civilizations that had been built by brute warrior strength. It's hard to argue with Nietzsche. After all, we don't send lawyers and priests to fight wars. They only come in after the dirty work has been done.

So, how has Klosterman come by his power? By Nietzsche's estimation, Chuck has cunningly taken it from the artists. After they've made their art, the critic focuses all his wit and wile into an attempt to exhibit his own intellectual prowess. Somewhere along the way, Klosterman found a way to uniquely articulate an artistic opinion. Our continued support of Klosterman is partly because we're either amused by his opinions or we share in the opinion with him . . . or both. If we share his opinion before reading, it's probably the case that he articulates our own opinions far better than we can ourselves. He gives a litmus of reasons to love or hate a band. In some ways he's philosophic about his opinions in that he provides reasons for believing a certain aesthetic.

As Klosterman fans, we identify with his sentiments, and we laugh at them. He's so adept at what he does, we're willing to pay to read his spectating. With his talents, he can explain and re-create the initial artistic inspirations through his commentary. He manipulates words in a way that explains the significance of a pop event, like a song, band, or athlete. Chuck's power chord is the G—the people's chord. He's in good company in G—he shares it with both "Sweet Home Alabama" and Don McClain's "American Pie." Chuck's whole career depends upon the art that the artists make. We're the lowly spectators, and we would prefer to possess the power of artists, but agreeing with critics is the best we can do.

Art occupies a more primary place than art criticism. Without art, there is no *Sex, Drugs, and Cocoa Puffs*. Deep down we know this is where Chuck stands in the scheme of art experience. I think Chuck knows it, too. Klosterman hovers around this subject in his Lloyd Dobler essay, albeit in a sexual context, when he says that Woody Allen made it possible for nerdy intelligent guys to score with women who are actually out of their league. See "This Is Emo" in *Sex, Drugs, and Cocoa Puffs*. I'll argue that Sartre was way ahead of Woody Allen's game. Sartre preceded Allen, was far uglier, and was a master of seduction. Even without the aid of motion pictures, Sartre seemed to be doing fine with the ladies.

Art and sport (and the artists and athletes themselves) occupy a more powerful rank than commentary that critics apply to them. This is why both Wilt Chamberlain and Mick Jagger (and probably any other NBA basketball player or rock star) will have more notches on their bed post than Klosterman. One's ability to attract mates is just another manifestation of power. It is infinitely more powerful in the Nietzschean sense to be on the court, or on the stage, than to be intellectualizing and typing away in one's La-Z-Boy. But even typing away and intellectualizing can get you three to four hundred fans (half of those being women) on a Tuesday night in New York, if you're Klosterman.

I watched VH1's *Behind the Music* on the Red Hot Chili Peppers. The band had just played a concert in tighty whiteys. Some female fans had made their way backstage after the concert, only to find a lone roadie. The roadie tells them the band's gone, but that they left one piece of Chili Pepper paraphernalia: Flea's sweaty stage underwear. In an act of frenzied inspiration (Plato might say), one of the girls takes the drenched draws above her head, wringing out the sweat in her mouth so she could "have a piece of Flea inside of her." Lovely. Now, this incident probably indicates a whole host of pathologies that I haven't the time to go into, but I would say with confidence that this type of thing only happens to artists. Rest assured, this will never, ever happen to Chuck Klosterman, because he's a critic and not a rock star; critique of art will never be as inspiring as art itself. Klosterman's underwear are safe. Just ask Nietzsche. He spent a good deal of time courting Cosima Wagner, who was married to the great composer, Richard Wagner. Nietzsche even tried composing music for Cosima. Sorry, Friedrich, I'd be surprised if any composer in history could have written a piece of music that could have stolen or even impressed Wagner's wife. Nietzsche's moustache was so gargantuan that it was most definitely a haven for all kinds of leftovers, which is an insurmountable hygienic foible to overcome in courtship.

Artists may become artists and athletes become athletes because it's the only way they can gain any power. That is, all sport and art could be primarily motivated (consciously or subconsciously) by the possibility of empowerment (and the choice of mate).

Stay Alive

I'm on the podium now, only three people between me and Klosterman. It's too late to bow out, and by now, I've discerned that it might be good for Luke Dick to be emasculated a bit. Maybe these Nietzschean notions of power are a bit too brutal. After all, a Spartan warrior had a life expectancy of around forty. I'd prefer to stick around Earth a bit longer than that. I'm all for the slaves making laws and taking over civilization after the killing is done, so long as it means a more comfortable existence where I don't fear for my life on a daily basis. I listen as the fellow in front of me puts in a quarter and asks The Klosterman if NYC is better off without LeBron, while formulating what I'm going to say.

I often find it difficult to talk to people who I find even remotely famous, especially if I like their work. After all, I know so much about them, and they know nothing about me. In the worst cases, you try to find some way to set yourself apart from other fans by saying something, like, "I REALLLY like your work. I mean, your critique of Billy Joel was absolutely brilliant." In the end, you end up feeling like another sycophant. Well, I'm at the front of the line. Fuck it, here goes:

> **LUKE:** Hey, Chuck. Dig your books. I'm writing an essay about you for a book called *Chuck Klosterman and Philosophy*.
>
> **CHUCK:** What's your essay about?
>
> **LUKE:** Nietzsche and Wagner and the social role of the critic . . . blah, blah, blah . . .
>
> **CHUCK:** Oh, yeah. Nietzsche and Wagner kinda had their interesting back-and-forth.
>
> **LUKE:** Yup.
>
> *Awkward pause. Chuck hands book to Luke and blinks a few times.*
>
> **LUKE:** Welp, thanks.
>
> *Luke walks out to the exit music of Journey, wondering if a literary device was worth the trouble.*

Nietzsche is right about one thing—there is some aspect of power to all of our interactions. Unlike Nietzsche, I'm quite sure that I prefer the slave's world to the master's. Nietzsche might call it a weakness, but I like the idea of getting old and not fearing the effects of warrior conquests. Weird, right? Most sane people with a spouse or a kid would agree.

I'm sure there's plenty of art and writing that's at least partially motivated by the sheer joy of creating it, rather than any power that comes from it. Klosterman's writing is a good example. Chuck is much more endearing when he's back to being sixteen and in love with a song. Great works of art are similar. I'm sure Picasso loved the fame (and the women) his art brought him, but I'm also sure that he loved to get lost in it and enjoy the creative process. On the other hand, I know that everyday I wake up, I'm out in the world trying to procure my place in it, attempting to distinguish and empower myself. This is the case with most people to some degree. It is absolutely the case with Klosterman. Power is how we stay alive. We make a buck and buy groceries, pay rent, and live to fight another day. If we are strong enough, creative enough, or cunning enough to find some way to really get ahead, we've empowered ourselves further than most other human beings. Chuck has sold plenty of books, but even he's still fighting. With every line I write, I'm enjoying the process, but I'm also trying to make a living.

As I walk out of Barnes and Noble, I crack the pages of my new book to page viii. Right there, in large, un-serifed typeset reads the name:

CHUCK KLOSTERMAN

The pecking order of power is ever-so-clear. Here I am, writing an essay for a book that only exists because of Klosterman's work. It's pretty clear who has the upper hand. I have many more lines to write before I can sleep easy, knowing rent is paid. I'll be taking the train home to a five-story walkup flat. Chuck's probably taking a cab home to an elevator building. Klosterman's name at the front of the book is both a reminder of my status in the world as an unknown, as well as a good, Nietzschean voice of encouragement. Beneath his name, in much smaller, un-serifed sharpie scribbles, it reads: "To Luke: Stay Alive!" Indeed.

13
Writing Poetry about Pushpin

JOHN R. FITZPATRICK

Either Chuck Klosterman grabs you or he doesn't. When I read the following passage in *Sex, Drugs, and Cocoa Puffs*, it certainly captured me. After telling us he never expects to be in love, he offers this reason:

> It appears that countless women born between the years of 1965 and 1978 are in love with John Cusack. I cannot fathom how he isn't the number-one box-office star in America, because every straight girl I know would sell her soul to share a milkshake with that motherfucker. For upwardly mobile women in their twenties and thirties, John Cusack is the neo-Elvis . . . And these upwardly mobile women are not alone. We all convince ourselves of things like this . . . We will both measure our relationship against the prospect of fake love. (p. 2)

This concept of fake love strikes me as a tool that could allow us to better inform ourselves on a whole host of issues. Klosterman is using it for the purpose of showing how characters in movies are more appealing than real people. First dates would be easy, if we could stop time and contemplate our next moves like characters in the movies, puppeteered by screenwriters, do. Screenwriters take months to provide John Cusack's characters with brilliant repartee. The idea is that women are not falling in love with the actual John Cusack, but rather with some character.

As Klosterman explains:

They don't love John Cusack. They love Lloyd Dobler. When they see Mr. Cusack, they are still seeing the optimistic, charmingly loquacious teenager he played in *Say Anything*, a movie that came out more than a decade ago. That's the guy they think he is; when Cusack played Eddie Thomas in *America's Sweethearts* or the sensitive hit man in *Grosse Pointe Blank*, all his female fans knew he was only acting . . . but they assume when the camera stopped rolling, he went back to his genuine self . . . which was someone like Lloyd Dobler . . . which was, in fact, someone who *is* Lloyd Dobler, and someone who continues to have a storybook romance with Diane Court (or with Ione Skye, depending on how you look at it). And these upwardly mobile women are not alone. We all convince ourselves of things like this. (p.2)

But this also explains what's wrong with male performances in porn and male characters in romance novels; real people cannot be expected to meet the needs of others as these mediums depict. Few women have or want Pamela Anderson's augmented breasts or platinum blond hair; few men have a Brad Pitt allure, which women are unable to resist.

We can apply this insight to other media too. Reality and TV reality are not the same thing. And, as Klosterman's discussions of media illustrate, Reality TV is often less real than fictional films or TV dramas. Klosterman finds that *Saved by the Bell* and *Roadhouse* work by using fiction to present useful archetypes; *The Real World* works by presenting non-actors who can easily be flattened into a limited number of representative personality types, the Puck, the Pedro, and others. But if we measure ourselves against reality as represented by either TV and movie fiction or reality TV, we come up short. Real men cannot rock the Tommy Lee look without looking like disingenuous copies; Real women are not incarnations of an insatiable Pamela Anderson, although sadly some try to be.

Chuck Klosterman, in his low culture manifesto *Sex, Drugs, and Cocoa Puffs*, tells us early in the preface that while he believes that high culture philosophy could well be a source of enlightenment, he would rather spend his time exploring low culture. He is unequivocal in this declaration. The "elite thinkers" spend oodles of time looking at great philosophers, well regarded classical musicians, and the great books of literature.

These intellectuals have little interest in exploring what everyday people are spending their time consuming. This seems odd, to Klosterman, because what the many find of value, should be of interest to the intellectuals. After all, if some intellectuals are interested in policy in a democracy, then understanding what the many believe should be of great importance. Similarly, intellectuals who respect the values of pluralism and diversity should welcome Klosterman's rigorous attempt to explicate, evaluate, and examine low culture. If it is a liberal truism that no one has a monopoly on truth and if intellectuals believe that both the elite few and the not-so-elite many can benefit from exposure to those supposedly great philosophers that make up the Western Canon, why would it seem strange if a serious examination of popular culture would yield fruitful results?

Klosterman's work is a tribute to the idea that pop culture can produce intellectual fruits healthier than Chuck's Fruity Pebbles. And I tend to accept this idea too. As Aristotle argued over two thousand years ago, we might well begin our inquiry by looking at the opinions of the wise or the many, and then try to find if the many have any important contribution to make. However, while Aristotle is willing to consider the opinions of the many, ultimately he would suggest that this project is on a hopeless track.

Cocoa Puffs, the Meaning of Life, and Some Things Aristotle Thinks Are True

The relationship between pleasure, happiness, and the meaning of life has been part of Western Philosophy since its inception in Ancient Greece. Aristotle's *Nicomachean Ethics* is an attempt to find the form of happiness that is most conducive to a complete human life. Aristotle arguably finds some usefulness in crude pleasure and low culture telling us that the philosopher Anacharsis is correct in asserting that "we must rest, and play is a form of rest" (Book X, Section 6). However, ultimately Aristotle thinks a successful human life cannot be simply one of amusement.

Klosterman would hardly disagree. After all Klosterman is married, holds down a job, and has published several books. Klosterman is hardly some mindless seeker of pleasure. He is hardly a crack addict, even if he makes it clear that he is not opposed to the recreational use of alcohol and drugs, documenting periods in his life where his drug and alcohol use seem excessive.

And at times these episodes seem more than excessive. At one point in *Killing Yourself to Live* he discusses "Midwestern Power Drinking." He tells us that folks in the other parts of the country don't match this: "people in the Midwest drink differently from everywhere else." These are not "recreational drinkers," but rather they "stay focused," "work fast," and "swallow constantly" (*Killing Yourself to Live*, p. 160). In my mid-twenties I had a good friend from Iowa, and he was definitely a Midwestern Power Drinker. A night out with my Hawkeye pal Robert often ended in a worship service to the porcelain goddess.

In *Fargo Rock City* Klosterman tells us that heavy drug and alcohol users value their substance of choice for two main reasons. The first is rather mundane—they like getting "fucked up." The other reason is more interesting:

> It's not just fun to be high; it's fun to smoke pot. Its fun to score dope and put ice cubes in the bong and put on boring reggae records and talk with other stoners about idiotic stoner topics. It's fun to browse through liquor stores and mix drinks on the coffee table and tell memorable puke stories. There is an appeal to the Abuse Lifestyle that exists outside the product. (*Fargo Rock City*, p. 61)

In *Chuck Klosterman IV* Chuck tells us that while he is skeptical about the concept of "guilty pleasures," he finds it pleasurable to "snort cocaine in public bathrooms," which always makes you feel guilty. Drinking "more than five glasses of vodka before (or during) work" is also a technically guilty pleasure, according to Chuck (pp. 277–78).

But for Aristotle, a happy life must be centered on the elevated pleasure of high culture philosophical contemplation. Chuck is skeptical of this position, and his attack on the concept of a guilty pleasure, in the non-technical sense, demonstrates this. Chuck thinks people who consume popular culture, from *Saved by the Bell* re-runs to *Real World* episodes, call these activities guilty pleasures as if they would be curing cancer or just reading *War and Peace* if they did not give in to these supposedly guilty pleasures. But Klosterman's beef aside, most Americans do not use the term "happiness" as Aristotle intended. Cocoa-Puff-munching, pornography-watching, heavy-metal-listening Americans tend to equate happiness with pleasure, guilt-inducing or not. Aristotle is not opposed to pleasure, but a complete life is much more than this. It's a life of human flourishing. A life of Aristotelian happiness is a life "well lived" or a life of "deep satisfaction." We might think of this as a "successful life," but one where success is not only equated with material wealth. Having a successful life is not simply getting rich.

Surely, Klosterman would have no objections at this point. Chuck does not just nosh sugar cereal daily; instead he reflects on the subliminal premises of sugar cereal ads and their relationship to our cultural concept of coolness and exclusivity. Perhaps it's pleasurable to eat Cocoa Puffs, but maybe it's part of a flourishing life to think about the iconography of consumer products in an intelligent way. I say Klosterman is no mindless lover of pleasure. He lives *some* sort of intellectual life. However, Aristotle argues that a happy life has much more intellectual rigor than Chuck is willing to exert—the guy suspects that he secretly hates reading, for crying out loud.

Aristotle tells us that "the human activity that is most akin to the gods' activity will more than any others, have the character of happiness" (Book X, Section 8). Klosterman's obsession with tribute bands such as Paradise City probably doesn't mirror the activity of the gods, but I don't know the activity of the gods with any certainty. If it turns out that the gods have little interest in rock'n'roll, they may well have less interest in Guns N' Roses, and even less interest in a sophisticated (or pseudo-sophisticated?) examination of the importance of a Guns N' Roses tribute band. It would be hard to see an Aristotelian defense of devoting yourself to being a copycat of low culture, let alone elevating them to heights of cultural achievement.

After all, if Aristotle would find listening to the music of heavy metal bands a waste of time, devoting your efforts to an analysis of tribute heavy metal bands would seem like a an insane waste of time. Aristotle's teacher Plato thought that all art was third removed from truth. Art imitated things in the material world, which imitated their true form, which was eternal, pure, and changeless. There is a. the beautiful itself, the form or idea of beauty, b. the beautiful entities we find in the world such as beautiful celebrities like Pamela and beautiful North Dakota farms which participate in the form of beauty, and c. artistic depictions of nature that are copies of the beautiful entities. Paradise City actually imitates the imitation of the imitation, copies the copy of the copy. How sad.

Play Pinball or Write Poetry? Cocoa Puffs or Vegan Casserole?

This argument about the relationship between pleasure and happiness touches on one of its most interesting debates in the history of ethics—between John Stuart Mill and Jeremy Bentham. Both men believed in hedonism, which is the view that the good life is devoted to pleasure. Bentham thought that all things being equal, more pleasure is better than less, that what we wanted in life was a greater quantity of pleasure. When Bentham finds quantities of pleasure to be equal, he tells us that poetry is not superior to pushpin. (Pushpin is the nineteenth-century equivalent of pinball).

Klosterman tells us that the rock critics love country acts like Uncle Tupelo and Lucinda Williams. But for every rock critic and hipster who loves alternative country, there are a thousand Wal-Mart customers buying Toby Keith. Keith "seems like a troglodyte," writes about fake cowboys, but Klosterman finds him to have genuine "middle-class importance." He writes with great clarity about a "completely imaginary . . . nineteenth-century Lone Ranger fantasy." But fake cowboys are the cowboys America fantasizes about; nobody would want to be a real cowboy (*Sex, Drugs, and Cocoa Puffs*, pp. 175–76).

All this makes Keith's work look phony, and his popularity then becomes somewhat troubling. But Klosterman is hunting different game. Chuck rejects the concept of "guilty pleasure" as a needless category. For Klosterman and Bentham, there are only pleasures—watching *Saved by the Bell* and reading Tolstoy's *Anna Karenina*—and one is no guiltier than the other. On this matter Bentham writes in *An Introduction to the principles of Morals and Legislation*:

Nature has placed mankind under the governance of two sovereign masters, pain and pleasure. It is for them alone to point out what we ought to do, as well as to determine what we shall do. . . . They govern us in all that we do, in all that we say, in all that we think . . . (Chapter 1, paragraph 1).

There are times when Klosterman seems to echo this viewpoint. The episodes of drug and alcohol abuse reinforce it, as do the tribute bands, and the reverential treatment of heavy metal music. But I am inclined to think that this is not the end of the story.

Eating Peaches and Being Happy

The story I've heard about the naming of the Allman Brothers Band album, "Eat a Peach," released after the death of Duane Allman is very dark. Supposedly Allman, riding his motorcycle, died in a collision with a peach truck. Klosterman, in *Killing Yourself to Live*, thinks finding the exact location of this accident is important; thinking about this death is important. But is this worth doing? One way of evaluating this question is through the moral philosophy of utilitarianism. Both Bentham and his friend's son John Stuart Mill, were utilitarians.

Do the ends justify the means? The utilitarian answers yes; right actions are those that tend to promote happiness, produce the greatest good for the greatest number. What utilitarians disagree about is how to evaluate the ends. Bentham and Mill have a serious disagreement. Evaluating whether Klosterman's writing has value might not involve determining which of these philosophers is correct, but it may be crucial in order to decide how important Klosterman is. Is examining the lives of dead rock stars as Klosterman does in *Killing Yourself to Live* mere sensationalism, or is it telling us something about the human condition that might help in the pursuit of a life of happiness? Does this examination merely titillate us, or does it tell us something of value?

Brooks and Twain, Dylan and Phair, and John Stuart Mill

Bentham would find Klosterman's work of value even if it is mere sensationalism and titillation, since these give pleasure. But can we place Klosterman's work on a higher plane than this? I believe that the utilitarianism of John Stuart Mill may very well allow us to do so. Mill suggests that there must be both qualitative as well as quantitative elements to happiness. He tells us he would rather be "a human being dissatisfied than a pig satisfied, better to be a Socrates dissatisfied than a fool satisfied," thus rejecting Bentham's *quantitative* hedonism in favor of a more Aristotelian definition of happiness, which places emphasis on the *quality* of the pleasures we seek.

One way to read Klosterman's manifesto, *Sex, Drugs, and Cocoa Puffs*, would be to find him one-upping Bentham; all things being equal, pushpin is superior to poetry. But this strikes me as really wrong. He writes about what the listeners of Garth Brooks and Shania Twain find satisfying about their music, why he thinks these artists have been so successful, but at various times he tells us that his actual preferences are quite different. In *Sex, Drugs, and Cocoa Puffs* he tells us that he regularly listens to Bob Dylan and Liz Phair, artists that high culture music critics react as *favorably* to as they react *negatively* to Brooks and Twain.

But why the *contemplative* life of low culture? Perhaps Mill can help us answer this. Mill argues that opinions can be true, partially true, or false. True opinions we will refuse to censor, because ultimately the truth is useful to us. Partially true opinions we allow because we want to dig out the truth they contain. But why allow false opinions? Mill argues in Chapter II of *On Liberty*:

> . . . even if the received opinion be not only true, but the whole truth; unless it is suffered to be, and actually is, vigorously and earnestly contested, it will, by most of those who receive it, be held in the manner of a prejudice, with little comprehension or feeling of its rational grounds. And not only this, but . . . the meaning of the doctrine itself will be in danger of being lost, or enfeebled, and deprived of its vital effect on the character and conduct: the dogma becoming a mere formal profession, inefficacious for good, but cumbering the ground, and preventing the growth of any real and heartfelt conviction, from reason or personal experience. (paragraphs 42–44).

Thus we must allow purely false ideas to circulate. Mill's explanation is that without allowing our truths to be debated, we are in danger of reducing our truths to mere prejudices and dogma. A major part of the utility of true ideas lies not simply in understanding *that* they are true but *why* they are true. What censorship does is prevent one from engaging opposing viewpoints in a free marketplace of ideas, and Mill finds that it is only in such an environment that actual understanding occurs. Once again, understanding why ideas are true or false can be as or more useful than understanding that ideas are true or false.

Low culture is inferior to high culture in the amount of truth that it contains about the human condition, but high culture is not perfectly true, and low culture is not devoid of truth. Klosterman's insight is that low culture contains elements of truth that would be tough to discern through a study of high culture. What truths Klosterman believes we can learn from watching Pamela and Tommy Lee fornicate in public can be explicated through high culture, but might very well go unnoticed there. In any case, Mill and Klosterman would argue that without some analysis of low culture, the truths of high culture would not be knowledge for us. Their value would be reduced to mere dogma.

Chuck Klosterman IV is divided into the three sections: Things that Are True, Things that Might Be True, and Something that Isn't True at All. And the book has an oddly Millian feel to it. Defending McDonalds against the food police in "The Amazing McNuggets Diet" offers an unpleasant politically incorrect truth—eating junk food in moderation is unlikely to destroy your health. Strangely, eating only Chicken McNuggets for a week, if not done on a regular basis might be good for your health. Klosterman tells us that in a week he consumed as many as 280 McNuggets or forty a day, and that he gained a pound. I looked this up the calorie information at McDonalds' website and they report that a ten piece Chicken McNuggets has 460 calories; thus forty McNuggets have 1,840 calories. Most adult men would loose weight on 1,840 calories a day (the average American male consumes 2,800 calories a day). My guess is that Chuck really *lost* weight, but the 4,000 milligrams of sodium in forty Chicken McNuggets resulted in significant water retention. This is an unusual Atkins diet, but my understanding of this is that low carbohydrate diets work, though living this way over years would be really unhealthy. But spending a week doing this is harmless.

Similarly, discussing things that might be true, may well lead to interesting discoveries. But even things that aren't true can be useful, if we learn some truth by working our way through their details.

The Not So Amazing McDonalds Diet

In the chapter after "The Amazing McNuggets Diet" Klosterman tells us about seeing Morgan Spurlock's well received documentary "Super Size Me," and having a chance to discuss the film in Klosterman's aapartment with Spurlock and his vegan chef fiancée, now wife, Alexandra Jamieson. Spurlock purportedly spent thirty days buying all his food and beverages at McDonalds, averaging about five thousand calories a day. The 6' 2", 185-pound Spurlock gained 24.5 pounds and had serious medical consequences including liver damage. In an early scene, we see Spurlock at his weigh-in wearing bikini briefs, and he looks like one fit dude. He has large biceps, a narrow waste, and a large chest. To realize how well conditioned Spurlock is consider Steve Nash, the world class athlete who plays point guard for the NBA Phoenix Suns point—who by the way is not a communist, but then again, neither is Spurlock. Nash is 6' 3" and weighs 178 pounds. My own assessment is that these guys are both very fit; Nash is seriously cut, but Spurlock has larger arms and a more pronounced chest to waste V. As the Willie Dixon blues standard goes, Spurlock the actor is "built for comfort" (on the eyes) but not—as Nash the point guard is—"built for speed, but he got everything that a good [vegan chef] need[s]."

Klosterman has his doubts about this documentary. After all, he ate McNuggetts for a week and may have improved his health; in Spurlock's documentary we find him puking out the window of his car on day three. There is an element here that either might be true, or might not be true at all.

I certainly don't believe that three days of junk food would have me puking out of car windows. I often travel and eat inappropriately at restaurants for a few days, but I have never puked out of the window of my car as a result. Klosterman's skepticism is entirely justified. My own guess is that if Spurlock had actually done what he claimed to have done and exercised as he had done in the past, he would have gained a few pounds, but suffered little health damage. This is what his doctors predicted. Spurlock could lose weight during thirty days at McDonalds, if he wanted to. Supersize the zero calorie coffee, or unsweetened iced tea, or diet coke and save a thousand plus calories a day. Pick the chicken or fish over the beef; Filet-O-Fish = 380 calories, Angus Mushroom and Swiss = 780 calories. After all, anyone heard of Jared "Subway" Fogle? He lost two hundred pounds on a fast food diet. Klosterman smelled a rat, but didn't bother to follow it through to conclusion. But he did smell the rat! And my intuitions are that this is a particularly stinky rat.

But notice how this examination of the amazing McNuggets diet and a subsequent celebrity interview has high culture implications. Is the fast food industry a major villain in American health or merely a convenient target? Given our current difficulties in providing affordable health care, this is not a trivial issue. Given the costs to human freedom and ultimately human happiness that significant regulation of the food industry would entail, the issue is a serious one indeed. This highlights Mill's point made earlier. It is only through a rigorous free market of ideas that we can discover new truths, and there is no reason to assume that an examination of low culture cannot provide some.

Ultimately this is the point of all of Klosterman's work. Maybe Garth Brooks and Pamela Anderson have something positive to teach us. Maybe they don't. But learning why they don't would be a positive thing to know. If no one is willing to give a critical high-culture examination to low culture, whatever truth is there to be discovered is unlikely to be exposed by a low-culture examination. The only way to know that poetry is more valuable than pushpin, is to give pushpin the same quality of examination that poetry gets, and compare the results. So, there is much to be said for Klosterman's high-culture examination of low culture.

14

Are You Sure That's What You Want?

DANIEL R. MISTICH AND
RYAN P. MCCULLOUGH

> We all want things. We all need things. We all want to need things,
> and we all need to want them. This is not double-talk; this is truth.
>
> —CHUCK KLOSTERMAN, *Chuck Klosterman IV*, p. 283

The relationship between glam rock and hair metal is like the relationship between philosophy and psychoanalysis. Without glam rock, hair metal would never exist. David Bowie had to dress up as Ziggy Stardust before Tommy Lee could go on stage wearing a jock strap with suspenders. We also had to have a fundamental understanding about how we know what we know (philosophy) before we could begin to analyze others and ourselves (psychoanalysis). Psychoanalysts like Sigmund Freud had to cover Plato and other Greek philosophers just like Quiet Riot had to cover Slade's "Cum on Feel the Noize."

Chuck Klosterman's writings increase our knowledge about ourselves and the way we think. Why? His analysis of pop culture and his own personal relationships reflect major philosophical themes regarding the nature of desire. These themes help us understand his writings and make them even more enjoyable. Van Halen's "Eruption" is far more interesting to listen to if you know something about classical music. In the same way, Chuck Klosterman's work is far more interesting if you know about philosophical and psychoanalytic treatments of desire.

Klosterman articulates an understanding of desire rooted in philosophical-psychoanalytical traditions in three ways:

1. He recognizes the inability to fulfill desire.

2. He identifies how our desire either brings or fails to deliver certain social recognitions.

3. He acknowledges that pop culture informs the fantasies that frame our desires.

I Can't Get (or Give) No Satisfaction:

You can't always get what you want. Seriously. You can't get what you want. Okay, we ripped those lines from Mick Jagger, but he ripped off every African-American blues musician who came before him, so our crime isn't as grave. The point ought to be well taken, though. If you've read "This is Emo" in *Sex, Drugs, and Cocoa Puffs,* you'll see that Chuck Klosterman is definitely picking up what the Stones are putting down. In that essay, Klosterman reflects on an important position taken by many philosophers and psychoanalysts—the fulfillment of desire is either impossible or not recommended.

From its very beginnings, the Western philosophical tradition has posed questions related to what we want and why we want it. Understanding desire is central to theorizing our human existence. Heraclitus, a pre-Internet and pre-Socratic thinker, whose works have remained in fragmentary form (sort of like Dylan's basement tape recordings with The Band), argued that "it is hard to contend against one's heart's desire; for whatever it wishes to have it buys at the cost of soul" (*The Beginning of All Wisdom*, p. 37).

Plato, arguably the most important figure in all of philosophy, also noted that desire is inherent in the very structure of our souls. In his account, desire's a good thing, as long as its aim is for something good. The situation gets ugly when desire takes over and we wind up wanting what we don't really need and not what's best for us.

Klosterman opens "This Is Emo" with a masterstroke: "No woman will ever satisfy me. I know that now, and I would never try to deny it. But this is actually okay, because I will never satisfy a woman, either" (*Sex, Drugs, and Cocoa Puffs*, p. 1). From the getgo, it's clear that Klosterman is painfully aware that sometimes things just don't go our way. If we read closely, though, we see that Klosterman adds a bit of a twist to Mick

Jagger's nugget of wisdom. Certainly, you can't always get what you want, but you can't even help someone else get what they want. This sucks for you, but it also sucks for the rest of us. While we almost certainly agree with Chuck that "fake love is a very powerful thing," what is most interesting to us (and probably to other psychoanalysts and philosophers of desire) is his suggestion that, well, he *can't get no satisfaction*. If you think long enough about Klosterman's point (and trust us, we have), it's easy to see that this suggestion is more than just a simple observation about the inability to have stable relationships in our media-saturated world.

But it gets worse.

Although we think that Klosterman is disappointed (*unsatisfied*, perhaps?) that unfulfillment is our lot, Slovenian philosopher-psychoanalyst-obvious winner of any grizzly bear look-alike contest (we're serious, Google that shit), Slavoj Žižek, makes it clear that desire isn't *supposed* to be fulfilled. Owing a debt to the French psychoanalyst-philosopher Jacques Lacan, Žižek suggests that the "realization of desire does not consist in its being 'fulfilled', 'fully satisfied', it coincides rather with the reproduction of desire as such, with its circular movement" (*Looking Awry*, p. 7). Put in a way that is hopefully less confusing, we have a fundamental *desire to desire*, and, consequently, the fulfillment of our desire could lead to tragic results. For instance, George Lucas had a desire to improve the marketability of *Star Wars* merchandise during the Christmas shopping season. He tried to fulfill those desires by creating *The Stars Wars Holiday Special*. If you have seen a bootleg video of this thing, you know the results were tragic. Really, REALLY tragic.

In "This Is Emo," Klosterman wanted nothing more than to spend a weekend with a woman he liked at the Waldorf Astoria. His visions of "romantic love" included fun weekends spent in New York City at expensive hotels. However, Chuck quickly found these romantic visions difficult to fulfill because the woman he wanted to spend time with would have rather gone to see Coldplay than be with him. He ended up alone. He didn't get what he wanted. He was not satisfied. Why? Because he *wanted* satisfaction. He, or anyone else for that matter, cannot achieve happiness. According to Chuck, if we frame happiness as a "romantic weekend" or "romantic love," we will not get it.

But it gets worse.

On the surface, Žižek's point and Klosterman's experiences are disheartening. Unfortunately for those of us who think we ought to get what we want every now and then, Žižek isn't the only one to come to the conclusion that we're better off having our desires go unsatisfied. Famed American philosopher Judith Butler concurs with Žižek on this point. Butler writes:

> Lacan infamously cautioned, "Do not cede upon your desire." This is an ambiguous claim, since he does not say that your desire should or must be satisfied. He only says that desire should not be stopped. Indeed, sometimes satisfaction is the very means by which one cedes upon desire, the means by which one turns against it, arranging for its quick death. (*Giving an Account of Oneself,* p. 43)

In other words, being unsatisfied by our desires is, well, sort of good for us. To have our desires fulfilled would be for desire to be foreclosed permanently. Instead, those from the Lacanian tradition would insist (as we think the Klosterman of "This is Emo" also would) that we simply accept what Butler has previously called "psychoanalytic inevitability of dissatisfaction," or, as she puts it even more poetically, "the necessary nausea of appetite" (*Subjects of Desire,* p. 15, p. 2). In this way, we might read "This is Emo" as a text that articulates a pseudo-Lacanian perspective on desire: we can't ever really get what we want. As Sean Homer writes, we have "the constant sense . . . that something is lacking or missing from our lives. We are always searching for fulfillment, for knowledge, for possessions, for love, and whenever we achieve these goals, there is always something more that we desire" (*Jacques Lacan,* p. 87). Sorry, Mick, it's even worse than you thought.

But it gets better?

We know this all sounds like a bummer. We could read the closing lines of "This Is Emo," ("I want fake love. But that's all I want, and that's why I can't have it."), get depressed, and then slit our wrists (and THAT would be emo) (p. 10). It might seem as though all is lost. It might seem as though we're continually chasing the unattainable. HOWEVER, and this is a big however, we could re-read this closing line while remembering that being unsatisfied is a good thing. That it is good to have desire. That being fulfilled closes us off to opportunities that are still out there. If we can read "This is Emo" with a certain degree of optimism, we can realize that it's okay to not always get what we want. Although Klosterman certainly laments this inevitability throughout his essay, it's clear that he understands the point that satisfaction isn't all it's cracked up to be.

I Want You to Want Me

Robin Zander seems really annoying. Not only does he want you to want him, but he also needs you to need him. He's really asking a lot of you. But here's the thing: We are all like the dead sexy Cheap Trick front man. We ALL want someone to want us. We ALL need someone to need us. This need for *recognition* is a major topic in psychoanalysis and western philosophy as it is in Klosterman's writings. Consequently, we would want, need, love, and beg for you to join us in our exploration of this philosophical position that is both interesting and relevant to our understanding of ourselves. (As far as we know, there's no *Cheap Trick and Philosophy*, so there's no need to bother).

Yes, Robin Zander is annoying, but he is only 7% as annoying as Billy Joel. In "Every Dog Must Have His Day, Every Drunk Must Have His Drink" (*Sex, Drugs, and Cocoa Puffs*) and "The Stranger" (*Chuck Klosterman IV*), Chuck presents Billy Joel as a quasi-tragic figure, a pop music Charlie Brown who is eternally asking the question, "Why is everybody picking on me?" Obviously, Billy Joel really isn't *that* tragic by most standards. He is insanely wealthy and famous, and he has bagged some really good looking women. Most people (read: heterosexual men) would trade lives with Billy Joel in a heartbeat. However, he is tragic according to Klosterman in one very important way. (Well, it's important in that it can help us make an argument): He wants rock critics to want him, but clearly, that ain't happening.

Klosterman makes it painfully clear that most rock critics and historians of the genre will never consider Billy Joel to be "among rock music's pantheon of greats" (*Chuck Klosterman IV*, p. 168). But this is what Billy Joel craves. Given Klosterman's interpretation, Billy Joel's classical album could really be read as a boring version of the Cheap Trick hit. In Joel's case, however, he wasn't seeking the affection of a woman. He was seeking the affection of the people that write the history of pop music. He wants those opinion leaders to view him as an important, talented, and significant figure within the genre. He openly laments *Rolling Stone* not liking him. This is why Billy Joel is the positively tragic color of "burnt orange" (p. 168). He really wants to be *recognized* as cool or important, but he has not (nor will he ever) receive that recognition.

All of this talk about Billy Joel might have you wondering what the hell it has to do with desire from the western philosophical tradition. Well, the Russian-born philosopher Alexander Kojève would say that it has *everything* to do with it. As Kojève writes,

> Desire is human only if the one desires, not the body, but the Desire of the other; if he wants "to possess" or "to assimilate" the Desire taken as Desire—that is to say, if he wants to be "desired" or "loved," or, rather, "recognized" in his human value, in his reality as a human individual. (*Introduction to the Reading of Hegel*, p. 6)

Desire might traditionally be thought of as being related to carnal appetites for sex. However, much like other philosophers who carefully considered desire in the twentieth century, Kojève "ain't talkin' about love," as David Lee Roth might put it. Desire can manifest itself in the *desire for recognition*, and, a reading of Klosterman's work from a psychoanalytic perspective would suggest that Billy Joel embodies our desire for recognition.

Thanks to Chuck, Billy Joel gives us more than just a crappy history lesson ("We Didn't Start the Fire"). He gives a lesson about the seemingly fundamental need for recognition. In other words, we become recognized through desire and our desire is a desire for recognition. As Butler explains, desire is always directed: "Desire is *intentional* in that it is always desire *of* or *for* a given object or Other, but it is also *reflexive* in the sense that desire is a modality in which the subject is both discovered and enhanced" (*Subjects of Desire*, p. 25).

The desire to be recognized is not just a problem for Billy Joel; this is a problem for you, us, and anyone wearing a giant Motörhead patch on back of a denim jacket. Klosterman acknowledges this desire as universal by analyzing, of all things, cereal boxes, in "The Lady or the Tiger":

The desire to be cool is—ultimately—the desire to be rescued. It's the desire to be pulled from the unwashed masses of society. It's the desire to be advanced beyond the faceless humanoid robots who will die unheralded deaths and never truly matter, mostly because they all lived the same pedestrian life. Without the spoils of exclusionary coolness, we're just cogs in the struggle. (*Sex, Drugs, and Cocoa Puffs*, p. 123)

Obviously, Klosterman argues that we're all searching for that coolness, but we believe that you could easily replace the word "cool" with the word "recognized." Coolness (read: recognition) makes us unique, and separates us from the other guy or gal. If we aren't cool, we aren't being singled out for recognition. "But if we can just find that one cool thing that no one else has . . . we can be better than ourselves" (p. 124).

Chuck also takes aim at this problem when he confronts his own issues with potential mates in *Killing Yourself to Live*. Take, for example, Chuck's discussion of Diane, one of three women involved in his life during the writing of his book about death and rock'n'roll:

Diane's inability to love me makes me love her more. Without a doubt not loving me is the most alluring thing Diane (or any woman) can do. Nothing makes me love Diane as much as her constant rejection of my heartfelt advances. This is compounded by Diane's own insecurities; the fact that she can reject me time after time after time is what she finds most endearing. She knows I will never give up. She could hate me and I would love her anyway. (p. 27)

Although Chuck later admits that he is "not psychologically flawless" because the reader discovers that his relationship (or lack thereof) with Diane is as complicated as any episode from the fourth season of *Lost*, this passage highlights a few key points relevant to our philosophical discussion at hand. First, we might re-emphasize our earlier point that desire (and especially Chuck's desire for Diane's love) remains fundamentally unfulfilled or unsatisfied. As the passage shows (and the rest of the book reminds us), Chuck's love for Diane is hardly reciprocated, which only makes him want her more.

But second, and perhaps most important here, Chuck doesn't simply want Diane (not to mention Lenore or Quincy, his other objects of desire in *Killing Yourself to Live*). Chuck wants Diane *to want him*. His desire is really a desire to be recognized as her boyfriend, and this is particularly evident when Chuck gives Diane three weeks to decide whether or not she loves him. Chuck's ultimatum is really just another way of expressing how, above all, he desires her recognition as her boyfriend.

We think that the desire to be cool (in the case of Joel) and the desire to be loved by another person (in the case of Chuck and Diane) are one in the same: they are both the desire to be recognized. We may not always achieve this goal, but we tend to agree with one of Kojève's major conclusions related to desire: "all Desire is desire for a value" (*Introduction to the Reading of Hegel*, p. 6).

It's All Part of My Rock'n'Roll Fantasy

The quality of the sources that have inspired our section headers has significantly decreased, hasn't it? We started with the Stones, and everyone knows they are bitchin.' We then moved to Cheap Trick, and if you are reading this book, I am sure you would agree with us that "Surrender" is an amazing song. But now we have scraped the bottom of the creative barrel. We are referencing, ugh, Bad Company, a British "supergroup" which has never really done anything super.

ANYWAY, we'll start this section with yet another analogy, but this time it will come in SAT style.

Fantasy : Desire

A. Wilco : Radiohead

B. Cinderella : Ratt

C. The Stooges : The Clash

D. Bruce Springsteen : Tom Petty

If you're confused by the question, don't worry. A return to Sigmund Freud should make the answer pretty clear. He theorized that a happy person never fantasizes, only "unsatisfied" individuals have fantasies. Fantasies are the result of a wish that has not been satisfied or fulfilled, and the fantasies are created to fulfill that wish. For Freud, we create fantasies to correct the world around us. We use fantasy to fill voids in our lives. This need to fantasize stems from our childhood, as Freud states:

> As people grow up, then, they cease to play, and they seem to give up the yield of pleasure which they gained from playing. But whoever understands the human mind knows that hardly anything is harder for a man than to give up a pleasure which he has once experienced. Actually we can never give anything up; we only exchange one thing for another. What appears to be a renunciation is really the formation of a substitute or surrogate. In the same way, the growing child, when he stops playing, gives up nothing but the link with real objects; instead of *playing*, he knows *phantasies* . ("Creative Writers and Day-Dreaming," *The Freud Reader*, pp. 437–38)

Freud noted frequently that we go through several changes in the transition from childhood to adulthood, but one of his more important points is that fantasy is a central part of our lives.

For many psychoanalysts and philosophers of desire, fantasy is that which makes desire possible. If fantasy makes desire possible, then the answer to the analogy that we posed must be C. The proto-punk Stooges made a band like The Clash possible. Iggy Pop (or at that time, Iggy Stooge) needed "danger little stranger," before The Clash could "have a riot of their own." Without The Stooges, The Clash would never have happened, and without fantasy, desire would never have happened. We hope this exercise was instructive, even though Chuck Klosterman finds punk rock utterly ridiculous.

As Sean Homer writes, "unconscious desires are manifested through fantasy. Fantasy is an imagined scene in which the subject is a protagonist, and always represents the fulfillment of a wish. Fantasies are never a purely private affair but circulate in the public domain through such media as film, literature, and television" (*Jacques Lacan,* p. 85). Or, in Žižek's words, "What the fantasy stages is not a scene in which our desire is fulfilled, fully satisfied, but on the contrary, a scene that realizes, stages, the desire as such" (*Looking Awry,* p. 6). We need fantasy in order to have desires, regardless of whether or not those desires are actually fulfilled in our "real" lives. As we've already mentioned, these desires often remain unsatisfied, but it's important to stress here that a fantasy might be thought as a condition for the possibility of desire itself.

Although we would agree with these basic claims about the role of fantasy and desire, we might also add that Klosterman is keenly aware not only of the sometimes public character of fantasies, but that fantasies are to an extent *determined and produced* by popular culture and its circulation. He contends that the production of fantasies occurs in two very important ways: 1. Our romantic appetites, and 2. our sexual appetites. With regard to the first way in which fantasies are produced, consider Klosterman's observations about John Cusack's character in the movie *Say Anything*, Lloyd Dobler and the British band Coldplay, also from "This is Emo." Addressing this issue in "This is Emo," Klosterman writes:

> Pundits are always blaming TV for making people stupid, movies for desensitizing the world to violence, and rock music for making kids take drugs and kill themselves. These things should be the least of our worries. The main problem with mass media is that it makes it impossible to fall in love with any acumen of normalcy (*Sex, Drugs, and Cocoa Puffs,* p. 4)

In this passage (and throughout the essay), Chuck suggests that the mass media is somewhat responsible for the conception of love that most of us operate with. The media projects (sometimes literally on a screen) a version of love that structures our desire for it. Klosterman perhaps says it best when he writes that the "mass media causes sexual misdirection: It prompts us to *need* something deeper than what we *want*" (*Sex, Drugs, and Cocoa Puffs,* p. 6).

Chuck also muses on the importance of the production and circulation of fantasies in his essay on pornography from *Sex, Drugs, and Cocoa Puffs,* in which he gives a few shout-outs to Sigmund Freud and Carl Jung, two icons of the psychoanalytic tradition. As Chuck writes, "Porn sites are the window into the modern soul; they're glimpses into the twisted minds of a faceless society" (p. 112). But Internet porn doesn't just function as a mirror that reflects our earlier established desires. Instead, porn helps constitute our desires. According to Chuck, porn even functions to change "the way people think about their own existence" (pp. 115–16). These sexual fantasies reflected on the web structure our desires.

Chuck doesn't just have vitriolic hatred for the media-saturated world that we now live in. Klosterman also admits that the same system that created these entities also make it possible for him to have any relationship at all. "Woody Allen changed everything," Chuck writes, "Woody Allen made it acceptable for beautiful women to sleep with nerdy, bespectacled goofballs; all we need to do is fabricate the illusion of intellectual humor, and we somehow have a chance" (*Sex, Drugs, and Cocoa Puffs,* p. 5). Instead of simply hating the media-generated fantasies that are produced by popular culture, Klosterman finds their nature mutually detrimental and beneficial.

This Is a Tribute

When we read Chuck, we experience several "ah-ha" moments; moments when we feel as though Chuck is peering into our soul. His writings speak to us in a way that elucidates our common experiences and identifies why we feel or think in a certain way. We think (and we hope that you think this as well) this is a by-product of his works reflecting major philosophical themes concerning the nature of human desire. More specifically, Chuck points us to the important relations between desire, satisfaction, recognition, and fantasy, whittling down philosophical traditions of Freud, Lacan, Žižek, Butler, and Kojève to their very core, in a way accessible to the masses.

Remember the joke we made earlier about the Rolling Stones ripping off African-American blues artists? This does not mean we dislike the Rolling Stones. On the contrary, we love the Stones. Yes, they should have hung it up in 1982, but we love the Stones. The Stones are great because they stole from great artists and made the African-American blues tradition accessible to white kids.

Just like the Stones, the work of Chuck Klosterman has the potential to be transcendent, and this is significant given the speed at which our culture moves. Even though he might be elaborating on a genre of music (emo) that might be a mere footnote in the history of pop music, his work will stand the test of time because his writing reflects philosophical conceptions of desire, which is an innate part of the human psyche. This is why the work he produces will last, and this is why we will keep reading his stuff.

But if he writes the equivalent of *Steel Wheels*, then we're out.

My literate cat?

My literate cat

MELISSA VOSEN

For reasons that cannot be explained, cats can suddenly read at a twelfth-grade level. They can't talk and they can't write, but they can read silently and understand the text. Many cats love this new skill, because they now have something to do all day while they lay around the house; however, a few cats become depressed, because reading forces them to realize the limitations of their existence (not to mention the utter frustration of being unable to express themselves). This being the case, do you think the average cat would enjoy *Garfield*, or would cats find this cartoon to be an insulting caricature?

— *Sex, Drugs, and Cocoa Puffs*, p. 131

I know what most of you are thinking. Garfield is a lazy, sarcastic cat that is best known for his rotund physique and his love of lasagna. Of course cats would be offended and find this to be an insulting caricature of their species, right? Wrong.

While Klosterman suggests that some cats become depressed as a result of their new found skill, I argue that being able to read the comic strip *Garfield* would provide a sense of hope for these furry felines. Garfield, in many ways, becomes an archetypal image, a hero, and I believe the comic strip would reaffirm their sense of purpose. Without Garfield, the strip becomes much darker. Without Garfield, it is obvious how lonely and self-loathing the main human character, Jon Arbuckle, is. There is a reason the strip is named after the fat tabby—he is the glue that holds Arbuckle together.

I believe *Garfield* would give these cats a new perspective on life. It is clear after reading the strip without Garfield how important Garfield is to Jon. With the endorsement of Jim Davis, the creator of *Garfield*, Dan Walsh published a book filled with Garfield comics—without Garfield. (You can buy it on Amazon if you are interested or check out Walsh's website, http://garfieldminusgarfield.net/).

After reading only a few of these strips, a reader can easily see the existential crisis Jon is in. If the cats aren't able to see how Garfield is the only thing stopping Jon from having a complete breakdown, they should at least be able to appreciate that Garfield's life is far less depressing than Jon's. And whether we like to admit it or not, we all find some relief knowing we do not suffer from the ailments of others—particularly, often taboo, mental conditions.

Garfield is clearly the glue that holds this family together. I think cats would find comfort in this. Their life is not meaningless, and *Garfield* should provide great comfort in the fact that life could always be worse. They could be Jon Arbuckle. The comic also proves what cats have been trying to prove for so long—they are, indeed, smarter than dogs.

Canines, on the other hand, might find great offense to Jon's dog, Odie. He is often portrayed as unintelligent and outwitted by the clever, and far superior, Garfield. Really, what is there for cats not to like?

BOOK VI

Eating the Philosoraptor

15
Puritan Dinosaurs

SETH VANNATTA

When I was twelve, I went to a Christian camp in rural Missouri. My two best friends were going, and the brochure advertised this giant blob in the pool that you would jump on and get launched off of by others. My friends and the blob were the highlights of the camp, for sure. The mantra of the camp combined the seemingly innocuous ideal "I'm Third" (God first, Others second, Self third) with other more Draconian measures, which included three football practices a day in the July heat, followed by a devotional session, "Devo," which took place late at night in our dark cabins and involved answering questions about our devotion to Christ with a flashlight pointed in our faces.

The camp also had an obsession with competition, which seemed to be in tension—if not outright contradiction—with its ideal of "I'm Third." We would chant, "Cooooompetition, competition, compete-ti-ti-ti-ti-tion," making huge Cs with our arms. The campers also played a game, called Gestapo, named after a thuggish instrument of Nazi policy enforcement, in which the young adult, mostly reformed drug addict and born-again counselors—dressed in black and wielding some sort of weapon made out of athletic socks—would whack at or tackle the twelve year-old campers in the dark. Gestapo was sort of like capture the flag meets hell week for fraternity pledges. Did I mention the camp's name proudly donned the initials KKK? My trauma not withstanding, even at twelve I questioned its central mission of "I'm Third." How was it that we were to put God first and others second?

Chuck Klosterman's riffing on the popular culture of born-again Christianity helps us answer that question. Chuck writes, "There is something undeniably attractive about becoming a born-again Christian" (*Sex, Drugs, and Cocoa Puffs*, p. 234). For the born-again Christian, represented by the premises of the *Left Behind* series of novels and certain Victory Television Network cable programs, there are no gray areas between right and wrong, true and false, or saved and damned. The human quest for certainty in an otherwise precarious world is an intense drive, and the born-again mindset is "attractive" in part because they are certain of their certainty.

Who are these folks? The born-again are, according to Chuck, a "bizarre subculture of 'good people,'" most of whom Chuck has never met (p. 228). The born again know "the way" and "the truth," and the road from the former to the latter is an all-important, take-no-detours, direct path to the Promised Land. The premise of the *Left Behind* novels is, if you are not with us, you are against us, and you'll get "left behind." But the born again are charged with a mission, the only important issue of their lives, which is to save others—point a flashlight in their face and get them to accept Jesus Christ as their personal savior. The born-again do not bother with nuanced arguments concerning the ethics of the death penalty or the social consequences of outlawing abortion. They have only one mission: convert others or risk going their way, which I'm told is awfully hot and humid.

Klosterman even writes about Steven, a character on the Victory Television Network, whose sole "temptation" is *not* to evangelize others. As Chuck notes, Steven "is not frayed by the desire to go down on his girlfriend or the desire to get drunk and feel cool" (*Killing Yourself to Live*, p. 99). Rather, his temptation is to avoid and ignore his classmates at his school, the sinners and unsaved, who presumably *do* go down on their girlfriends while being drunk and feeling cool.

Me and God

Klosterman points out that the *Left Behind* series is based solely on Paul's New Testament Letters and the Book of Revelation. This is important. And if we figure out why it's important, the philosophical issue at hand will disclose itself.

The philosophy of born-again Christianity is kind of like the theology of the old Puritans who inhabited Boston before Klosterman's Celtics ever donned Kelly green tank-tops there. In a way, Puritans are like dinosaurs—they're extinct. But I think Klosterman has pointed out a few dinosaurs roaming among us in the *Left Behind* Series. And I think a few of them were my camp counselors in Missouri back in 1986.

So allow me to give a stripped down version of Puritanism. Puritanism was a specific strand of the Protestant Reformation in general, which really got going when Martin Luther posted those *Ninety-Five Theses* on a church in to-be Germany. For Luther's theological argument, the go-to text of the Bible was Paul's letters, especially his letter to the Romans. In these letters he explained several of the forthcoming theological tenets. The Puritan strand of Reformation theology rested on the premise that we, as humans, are all fallen and sinful in an original way. Klosterman unknowingly tells us he agrees. He writes:

> Any grammar school teacher will tell you that "kids can be cruel" on the playground; the average third-grader will gleefully walk up to a six-year-old with hydrocephalus and ask, "What's wrong with you, Big Head?" And that third-grader knows what he's doing is evil. He knows it's hurtful. Little boys torture cats and cute little girls humiliate fat little girls, and they know it's wrong. They do it *because* it's wrong. Sometimes I think children are the worst people alive. (*Sex, Drugs, and Cocoa Puffs*, p. 236)

Klosterman is not buying into the idea that children are innocent. To Chuck and the Puritans, sin is original.

According to the Puritans, our path to righteousness is not of our own making. We cannot work our way into heaven by, say, buying indulgences or being nice. We've gotta *believe* our way into heaven and *accept* it as a gift from the Big Man. (This was a point Paul made in a letter to the Romans describing Abraham's faith and his righteousness.) Chuck notes that this is the case with the born-agains, too. To be saved, you just need to *accept* the *belief* that Jesus is your personal savior. By the way, I think I'm saved because of this, although I'm not sure what the rules are if you sign the dotted line under duress. I mean, does it count if, during Devo, you accept the one-line ticket to salvation when you're twelve, while you're really tired from doing "man-eaters" on the football field all day, it's dark, and you're facing a flash light held by a college student who might as well be a Guantanamo Bay interrogator?

I think I'm saved on a technicality, but that's okay. Chuck reminds us that "for most exclusivist born-again groups, the technicalities are everything; the technicalities are what save you" (p. 236). The philosophers who waste their time with arguments for the existence of God or who devote their careers to Biblical hermeneutics are lost, wandering in the desert. As Klosterman tells us, "there's no sophisticated reason for believing in anything supernatural, so it really comes down to believing you're right. This is another example of how born agains are cool—you'd think they'd be humble, but they've got to be amazingly cocksure" (p. 238).

For this Puritanical *qua* born-again mentality, we don't need no stinkin' clergy. The clergy is no longer a necessary medium through which the ordinary folks received the sacraments necessary for salvation. Our access to the Truth as God, is no longer mediated through sacramental ritual, symbolic mystery, and older communal forms of institutional religious practice. Instead, as John Calvin put it, "every man was his own priest." Now, through scripture and direct revelation we have an unmediated access to the Truth as God. The Reformation democratized and radically individualized the Christian religion, taking it out of the hands of the Big Bad Catholic Church. According to the Puritans, it's just about God and me.

The task of the Puritan layperson was to hear the calling of God, and heed its call. According to the Puritans God called each of us to fulfill our vocations and use our natural talents in service of God. The calling of the born-again, as represented by the *Left Behind* Series and the VTN is clear. Spread the word . . . or else. Our friend, Steven, on the Victory Television Network knew this. In fact, he even evangelized to a drug dealer who blew him away with a hand gun. Klosterman interpreted this to be a shockingly novel plot twist bordering on a complete paradigm shift in television screenwriting. Steven left the drug dealer behind, and Steven's death was just a fast-track to heaven. The folks left behind in the *Left Behind* series were learning the truth of the end times the hard way when their saved neighbors disappeared during the instantaneous rapture. For those interested, the end times and the tribulation therein are covered in the mystifying, scary, and—as Chuck tells us—"most fucked-up part of the Bible," the book of Revelation (*Sex, Drugs, and Cocoa Puffs*, p. 229).

Sportsmen Love God—Does God Love Sports?

Perhaps there was nothing strange about the Christian camp's obsession with competition. As Klosterman reminds us, "a mind-numbing percentage of pro-athletes are obsessed with God . . . as many as 40 percent of NFL players consider themselves 'born-again'" (p. 230). Klosterman finds this odd because the media usually covers the more sinful side of NFL players' off time—instances of cocaine-use and wife-beating, not to mention dog-murdering and sexual harassment, with or without sexting. Klosterman mentions lots of sports-religion overlap including the famous Catholic quarterback, Roger Staubach, and the super-bowl winning zealot, Kurt Warner. The list could go on to mention that Notre Dame has a mural of "Touchdown Jesus" overlooking the blessed end zone of their football field. The Nazarene looks as if he is signaling six points, but lately fans have wondered if God favors their opponents.

Klosterman has almost been persuaded to believe that God does divinely intervene in football careers. First, Kurt Warner's career went from grocery bagger to NFL MVP by becoming born again. But his careerism and his Christianity taken together just remind us that Warner is a Puritan dinosaur who threw a mean deep ball while wearing gloves. See, the Puritans took Luther's logic about salvation to an extreme. You cannot work your way into heaven, as we are justified by our faith, not our actions. Second, not everyone is saved. Third, God is omniscient, not to mention all the other omnis.

And if we put these together, we conclude that God has knowingly elected those who are predestined to be saved. The problem is that if only God knows who is saved and who will be left behind come rapture time and we cannot do anything to change his mind, then what are we to do in the meantime? Do we "snort cocaine off of Cuban prostitute's thighs and murder our ex-girlfriends," bet on dog-fighting, and grope our message therapists, or do we act as if our actions matter in the divine equation? (p. 230)

Understanding how we learn that we are of the few elected to be saved concerns the way that the grace of God works in the human heart. According to Calvin, the grace of God, his freely chosen gift, causes us to abhor sin. Sin, especially those of the body, can be avoided by eschewing the leisure time during which we usually go astray. To prevent the temptations of the flesh and the sins of the body from taking hold of us, we must fulfill our calling and do the work which we are called to do by God. If the results of our work are earthly success, say, multi-million dollar NFL contracts, and we do not fall into the sins of spending prodigally, then we will accumulate, and such wealth can be a legitimate sign of our chosen status. Get rich, and get saved. Amen. Touchdown.

Klosterman has almost been persuaded to believe that God does divinely intervene in individual football games. As he watched Warner playing in Super Bowl XXXVI, Klosterman witnessed a play so unnecessary and stupid, reversing the momentum of the game, that he, for a time, thought God might love football (and care about the outcome), after all. Warner, whose team was down 3–17, fumbled on his way into the end zone, and the ball was picked up by a Patriots player and run back ninety-nine yards for a touchdown. But the score was overturned because of a defensive holding call on the weak side of the play. Klosterman took this, temporarily, to be a sign that Warner was truly favored by Yahweh. However, the Patriots ending up winning the game, and Klosterman's two-quarter faith was shaken. The next morning, hearing a Patriots wide receiver praising God on the *700 Club*, Klosterman realized that "with competitive spirituality, it's always a push" (p. 231). I guess this means that God gets the juice, the spiritual ten-percent tithe of the combatants.

My question about whether or not God loves sports causes me to recall my unrepressed memory of chanting "competition" at the camp outside Branson, Missouri, surely God's country. We were convinced that something monumentally important hinged on whether the Rangers or the Wranglers won an accumulation of victories during the week-long series of competitions. While the ultimate trophy of the camp was the "I'm Third Award," there was only *first* and *second*, winner and loser, in the Ranger-Wrangler warfare. Here, we learned the virtues of sport, among them aggressiveness, courage, and perseverance. During the competition, we ignored any notions of "the first shall be last, and the last shall be first," that were Jesus's pep talks. We were not concerned with altruism, gentleness, or humility on that battle field. The sports competitions were zero-sum games with a winner and a loser, and we fought to vanquish our foes. We celebrated the values of valor, pride, and force. These were the warrior's values. Shall we call them pagan virtues, the very virtues Jesus's radical morality undermined and were meant to undo?

What was the relationship between being proselytized by these two antithetical sets of virtues, strength and meekness, pride and humility, and the antinomies of our directives, "compete," and "be third?" Needless to say, they confused me. Perhaps we can combine the Puritan, born-again mentality with the competitive vigor of sports, which is modeled on warfare and has its origins in games of war and training of warriors. Perhaps winning is a sign of our work ethic and our foregoing of the sins that come from slothful leisure. Maybe dogging it on wind-sprints and skipping reps in the weight room is tantamount to over-snacking, getting wasted, or paying for sex? If this is the case, then the winners triumph because the grace of God works in them, causing them to abhor the sinful temptation to be lazy. Those with the Truth of God on their side might deserve the victory after all.

On Board with the Lord

The ultimate battle here is not between the Rangers and the Wranglers or even between the Rams and the Patriots. It's between truth and peace. You see, my confusion at age twelve was about how we were supposed to win the "I'm Third Award," besides pouring juice into others' glasses before our own during meals. I knew we had to put others before ourselves (except during competitions), but I was unclear how to put God before others. How was I to pour God's juice before my friends' juice?

I think the philosophical meaning of the "I'm Third" dictum is: *sacrifice peace in service of truth*. This part of the "I'm Third" equation means that we should forego the preservation of our relationships if those with whom we are in potential relationships do not have the truth. If they do not get on board with the Lord, then we must convince them to do so or to or leave them behind. Recall that Klosterman tells us that "once you've crossed over, you do not even have to be nice" (*Sex, Drugs, and Cocoa Puffs*, p. 238). The pilot, Rayford Steele, from the *Left Behind* series figured this out, too. Klosterman writes, "The main psychological hurdle" Steele must overcome "is the fact that he's not an obtrusive jackass, which *Left Behind* says we all need to become. '*Here I am, worried about offending people,*' Rayford thinks to himself at the beginning of Chapter 19. '*I am liable to "not offend" my own daughter right into hell.*' The stakes are too high to concern oneself with manners" (*Sex, Drugs, and Cocoa Puffs*, p. 235).

The relationship between the immediate access to the Truth as God by the born-again Christian roaming around as a Puritan dinosaur is all about this relationship between truth and peace. According to Puritan ideology, truth trumps peace. Truth is what we must fight for (by eschewing good manners and being an "obtrusive jackass") at the cost of peace. Way back in 1675, Native Americans attacked the Puritan settlement in Massachusetts, and the Puritan community convened to discuss their actions which had provoked such evils. That God had punished them for their transgressions by lifting the veil of protection was taken as a given. The Puritans were convinced that they had lost their way with God and so he had stopped protecting them. What had the Puritans done wrong? They enumerated their sins including: men wearing their hair too long, women wearing it in immodest ways, such as curling it, citizens were wearing prideful apparel and strange new fashions, people were leaving church early, the children were disorderly during church, and of course people were getting drunk. Nowhere in this list was any mention of transgressions against the Natives, who actually attacked the Puritans. Peace with their neighbors was not the issue. The matter at hand was getting right with God individually.

We see this Puritanism today in born-again theology. In an interview with Jerry Falwell, Pat Robertson placed the blame for the attacks of September 11th, 2011 on the American Civil Liberties Union, the homosexual community, and the feminists. Their secularization of America, according to Robertson, caused God to lift the veil of protection. Nowhere in Robertson's remarks on 9/11 did he ask if we had transgressed against the Saudis who attacked us. This Puritan political idea, still pervasive today, falls back on the idea that truth, the truth of God and our unmediated access to it, trumps peace. According to this mode of thought, not only is God's punishment of our sins a disruption of peace, but the ways a community might achieve peace with those who would otherwise attack us are not live options if those folks contravene the truth of God.

This way of thinking treats truth as existing antecedent to a community's attempts to live peacefully. The truth is out there, and it plays by rules not of our own making. Klosterman sees that this might be the case. He writes:

> Regardless of what kind of god you believe in—a loving god, a vengeful god, a capricious god, a snooty beret-wearing French god, whatever—one has to assume that you can't get penalized for doing the things you believe to be truly righteous and just. Certainly, this creates some pretty glaring problems: Hitler may have thought he was serving God (or something vaguely similar). I'm certain Osama bin Laden was *positive* he was serving God. It's not hard to fathom that all of those maniacs were certain that what they were doing was right. Meanwhile, I *constantly* do things that I *know* are wrong: they're not on the same scale as incinerating Jews or blowing up skyscrapers, but my motivations might be worse. I have looked directly into the eyes of a woman I loved and told her lies for no reason, except that those lies would allow me to continue having sex with another woman I cared about less. This act did not kill 20 million Russian peasants, but it might be more "diabolical" in a literal sense. If I died and found out I was going to hell and Stalin was in heaven, I would note the irony, but I really couldn't complain. I don't make the fucking rules (*Sex, Drugs, and Cocoa Puffs*, p. 239).

The Puritans didn't make the rules either, but they thought the rules included not letting women curl their hair, regardless of how diabolical curly hair is. Klosterman cops to not knowing the ultimate truth. He does not see any evidence for or against any religious or secular version of the truth. So he sees the born-again version as "unlikely, but still plausible" (p. 228). Our neighbors might disappear sometime soon, and their disappearance will be good news for them (because they're saved) and bad news for those left behind.

Klosterman writes about what he finds interesting, if not downright odd, and I think he finds the *Left Behind* series and its born-again premises fascinating and strange. But does Klosterman have a conception of truth amenable to making the claims of end-time prophesiers plausible? His conception of truth is not monolithic or well-defined. Ordinarily, Klosterman uses truth in a colloquial sense, meaning that things we say correspond to the way things are. But in his interview with Errol Morris in *Chuck Klosterman IV*, the conversation touches upon the difference between what we say being true by *corresponding* to some outer reality and truth as a matter of narrative consistency. If truth is a matter of narrative consistency, then truth is a matter of the *coherence* among our personal narratives, including what we say and what we do. I thought that the camp in Missouri told an incoherent narrative, sending mixed messages about which virtue to embody, and therefore their narrative was not true, according to this latter theory. Speaking of truth . . . this chapter will not mention Tim Tebow, and this sentence is not true.

Truth as an Achievement of Peace

The Puritan articulation of the road to salvation and the resultant stance on the relationship between truth and peace are pervasive in American moral and political culture and discourse. The political premise that America was founded as a Christian nation, while not untrue with respect to the New England settlement, leads to the conclusion that we need to serve the truth of Christian faith at the cost of the peace of the community. According to this line of thinking, the community does not determine truth as a function of its attempts to live peacefully together and with its neighbors. Those in the community who have not signed on the divine dotted line should be left behind along with the potential of living peacefully with them. For the born-again Christian, peace gets "left behind" by truth.

While Puritanism is one of the strongest strands of philosophy running through our national discourse and culture, pragmatism has been called the quintessentially American philosophy. The pragmatists thought that truth was an achievement, an outcome of inquiry. The pragmatists thought that when our habits of action are disrupted, we fall into doubt, and we begin to inquire. If our inquiry is successful, then we fix a belief, and we are no longer in doubt, because for the pragmatists beliefs are habits of action. That is, because the whole of the meaning of a concept is found in its effects, according to the pragmatists, the meaning of a belief is found in our habits of acting on it. Inquiry occurs in a communal setting and our communities are part of the test for how doubts are settled and beliefs are fixed. The idea of truth, here, is that truth is the outcome of a community's inquiry, and lots of people in the community want to get along. The truth of the matter is the good for the community. Truth is an achievement and an outcome, not a fixed reality waiting to be revealed.

Thinking with the born-agains, we have immediate access to truth. As Becky Fischer, a children's evangelical teacher featured in *Jesus Camp*, said, "Excuse me, . . . we have the truth." She's certain of her certainty, and the community of secularists who might serve as tests to that claim do not play a role in her assurance of having truth on her side. Thinking with the pragmatists, our access to true belief is always tested against a community's needs and interests. If the community's interests involve peaceful living, then the moral and political inquiry will be in service of peace. If the end the community wants to achieve through its political inquiry is peace, then the true outcome of that indefinite inquiry will be peace. If we think of truth as the product of inquiry, not as something antecedent to it to which we have immediate access, then we converge truth and peace, where the born-agains are willing to have peace by "left behind" by truth.

If we think with the pragmatists, the only way to conceive of serving God first and others second is to think God another particular, outside the web of human relationships, to whom we, as individuals, might have a personal and particular relationship, one more important than ours with others. Only this type of particular God can be first in line of three. Only God as a particular (or three particulars in one) can have such a causal relationship to careers and games of NFL zealots, to Native American attacks on Puritan settlements, and to passenger planes flying into skyscrapers. Perhaps we could conceive of God, not as some specific third Dude outside the web of human relationship but rather *as* the web of human relationships, as the ground and condition for the possibility of those relationships being moral and peaceful. If we do, God's truth emerges as a product of our attempts to live peacefully with one another. Putting God first would mean including others in our inquiries about how we should live. It would mean trying to achieve the truth of God, instead of just signing on the dotted line of salvation under duress at Devo, trying to get everyone else to do the same, and then leaving them behind if they refuse.

Klosterman ends his chapter on the popular culture of end-times, born-again Christianity reflecting on the fact that he was raised Catholic. As a Catholic, not much of his religious education was founded on the Puritan premises of direct access to God or of justification by faith alone. However, the Puritan dinosaurs in our culture are difficult to evade. So is the quest for certainty in and of itself that born again Christians think they have achieved. Reflecting on the very different version of dogmatism his Catholicism offered him, Klosterman is thankful. If those nuns he grew up with were right, if they have access to the truth, then he's still got a fighting chance. He tells us he's "angling for purgatory, and . . . angling hard" (p. 243).

As for me, I prefer the pragmatic line on truth to the Puritans' take on truth. But as a pragmatist, I am certain that I am not certain. I could be wrong. If the Puritan dinosaurs are right, and peace will get left behind by truth, well, then I guess I'm the lucky one. I was saved during Devo.[1]

---

[1] I am indebted, once again, to Kenneth Stikkers for his work on Puritan philosophy and the logic of Reformation theology, which I incorporated here.

16
WWCD: What Would Chuck Do?

SYBIL PRIEBE

I might be the only person aware of this, which means I am quite possibly a prophet.

—*Sex, Drugs, and Cocoa Puffs*, p. 24

I am not a benevolent God.
I am the master, and I am the puppet.

—*Sex, Drugs, and Cocoa Puffs*, p. 12

Squint your eyes. See, he looks like Jesus.

Now rub his belly. See, he's practically Buddha!

Chuck's obviously the leader of an unknown, as-of-yet undiscovered religion. How is this possible? Let's back up a bit: if we didn't know what a religion looked like, what *could* it look like? If we didn't know what Jesus looked like for Zeppelin's sake, what *could* HE look like? Besides white and from the 1970s.

Let's peel back the layers like a North Dakotan sunburn: what is the typical layout of a religion? A head honcho, right? A list of rules and regulations to live by, some scripture that could be interpreted a variety of ways, a few inspirational quotes, descriptions of the afterlife, promises of hope through altruistic means, and so forth. If we *could* take this formula and just plug in what we wanted, wouldn't Chuck fit quite perfectly? Maybe too perfectly?

Yes is the answer you were looking for.

Check out this guitar riff:

Afterlife Descriptions. Check.
Rules and Regulations. Check.
Promises of Hope. Check.
Deity. Check.
Inspirational Quotes. Check.
Scripture. Check

Maybe traditional religions have played their last encore, and all that's left are their imitators, like members in a tribute band. Chuck plays the lead now. By doing so, I create a new blasphemous religion with the underlining philosophy of sex, drugs, and stage dives. In order to replace religion's boring items, I'm looking to what Chuck has written as well as how he has written it.

Here's yet another perspective on it: as a teacher (like Buddha and Jesus and other multi-tasking deities), we're given a list of pedagogies to teach with. Just as there are many kinds of religions, there are also varying types of pedagogy. The philosophy that makes the religion or pedagogy unique comes after the formula has been created and mastered.

Why bother to make up this crap called religion? Because a. we can, b. it gives us something to live by and hope with, and c. it makes us superior to others. These very same reasons are reasons Chuck-ites exist.

Like music videos, religion is up to interpretation. And, like music videos, you can show off how superior you are to others with your bling, leather pants, and busty women.

For a lot of purists, that's exactly what's bad about music videos:

> They stop people from creating their own perception of what a piece of music means. By now, even the interpretation of sound has become a socialized process. Without a doubt, the video age is the worst thing that ever happened to teenage creativity. But—at least in the example of 'One'—it's hard to imagine how any kid could come up with anything better. (*Fargo Rock City*, p.110)

Okay, to start out with the blasphemous idea that religions are just formulas or that anyone can create a religion from scratch may not be a good idea, but it's not like Chuck's going to argue with me. This time, with a Chuck-based religion, he's killing himself to live and not necessarily dying for our sins or Ozzy's. Or something like that.

Oh My Chuck!

So, for starters, behind 85% of all organized religion(s) is a "dude." He's viewed as wise and "pure" and, as The Dude in *The Big Lewbowski* demonstrates, he must don facial hair and love liquor. Maybe he writes something or has stuff written about him (see Jesus, Moses, Muhammad, L. Ron Hubbard, etc.). From there, followers interpret what's said in these holy books (see the New Testament, the Torah, Qur'an, various Dianetics texts); this has led to many religions (see Islam, Judiasm, Islam, Scientology, etc.).

Again, what I'm proposing is that there is a parallel between the structure of organized religion and good ol' Chuck Klosterman. He's a dude, he wrote some stuff, and people have attempted to interpret what the hell he means. He's a modern-day Jesus, yet not everyone's signing up for his pub crawl. Why? Because, like organized religion, he has offended people or something along those lines. (Or maybe they are fussy about the rules and regulations.) And, oddly, organization (in *how* he writes) is what links Chuck Klosterman to religion in the first place. The guy is too organized! Well, organized in his own way. You know what I mean.

Once a group of people realize that what they know could be, well, wrong, they can more readily accept how Chuck is a potential deity. Ask yourself: "How do I know what I know?" Well, you do know what you know through what others have told you. And let's be honest, *everyone lies*. But Chuck, unlike other gods and saints and nuns, will admit to this: "Everybody is wrong about everything, just about all the time" (*Sex, Drugs, and Cocoa Puffs*, p.14) because "maybe we're all pretending" (*Killing Yourself to Live*, p. 144). These are not crazy notions. The idea that these organized religions are not absolutely, positively "correct" is as true as what Chuck has said about any music video, band, or singer. That's quite the connection, isn't it?

Followers of organized religion rarely allow that train of thought. Their leader is right. Done. No questions asked. So, fine, let them have their Jesus and Allah and Buddha. If long ago some guy said some things, and people believed him, I sure as hell should be able to drink the holy water of Chuck:

> This does not mean I'm always right and you're always wrong, nor does it mean I subconsciously need other people to feel the same way I do about anything. You don't need to side with the Boston Celtics to be a good person. But you should definitely side with *somebody*. Either you're with us or you're against us, and both of those options is better than living without a soul. (*Sex, Drugs, and Cocoa Puffs*, p. 107).

So if no one is right, no one is wrong. Now that's offensively bad logic. But Chuck fully accepts that, and, therefore, creates the best combination higher powers have ever seen: a blasphemously organized religion!

Oddly enough, it's not as blasphemous as I'd like it to be. It's all that damn organization.

Thanks Be to Chuck

As a former Catholic, and current Chuck-ite, I feel quite qualified to explain the Word of Chuck. Honestly, at first, I was confused by him (as I imagine some were by Jesus). He had opinions and ideas, and they didn't always intersect mathematically like the lines of an e.e. cummings poem. His organization is a bit unorthodox. Perhaps some feel this way when they are introduced to other religions. When I first read up on Buddhism in college, because every fallen Catholic usually takes the dive then when their über-Catholic moms aren't around, I was perplexed that the hardcore Buddhists were strict about being vegetarians and not drinking. Their laws and regulations were crazy; although just like there are bad Catholics, I'm sure there are bad Buddhists.

So, maybe there are bad Chuck followers out there who go behind his back and secretly detest KISS or really like the town of Wahpeton, deemed "as dreadful a community as there is in North America" by Chuck (*Fargo Rock City*, p. 206). Yet I find more people who simply "don't get him" yet all the while finding him "interesting." My friend Cheryl stated that she didn't always agree with him when he wrote for *The Forum*, but she kept reading. Sounds like the *Bible* to me.

What I'm saying is this: If part of the religious formula is to confuse and have strict rules, Chuck as a reference point for a religion isn't that far off the backstage staircase. *Sex, Drugs, and Cocoa Puffs* re-baptized me in a way more bad-ass religion. I became a disciple (or apostle – what's the difference?); I was blessed, telepathically, in holy beer. I'm Matthew, I'm Mark, I'm Luke, and I'm John. And I'm here to convert you.

Say unto Others as Chuck Would Say unto You

Sure, Chuck as a god is a pretty hard thing to wrap one's melon around. Yet, the guy has had some intriguing thoughts; they're practically Yoda-meets-Ghandi catch phrases. Some are even pick-up lines (skip to Commandment #10, boys). If "I say onto you," was Jesus's go-to phrase, "But that's not my point; my point is" is Chuck's.

Chuck has said (about another person), which is a reflection back onto himself, that "he's a potential god who realizes that everyone is either 'overtly or covertly unhappy'" (*Sex, Drugs, and Cocoa Puffs*, p. 4). Yet, he's "not interested in trying to convince anyone that they should (or shouldn't) adore whichever denim-clad icon they choose" (p. 47). To him, a "genius can be a genius by trying to be a genius; a visionary can only have a vision by accident" (*Killing Yourself to Live*, p. 89) and whether your god is a genius or visionary, "you can never really know someone until you've seen them positively enraged" (p. 191). Who gets more enraged than followers of organized religious? Chuck's apostles will fit in nicely alongside other followers of organized religions by virtue of their covert unhappiness, sublimated rancor towards their nemeses, and their general raging against the machine.

Chuck knows that "What they are is more important than what they do" so that is why Jesus, and other gods (James Dean, Kirby Pucket, Marilyn Monroe, Michael Jackson), have to die young. Unless they die before the age of thirty-three, nobody's entire career matters, and we all unconsciously understand this" (*Sex, Drugs, and Cocoa Puffs*, p. 44). Chuck knows what it takes to be a god and to speak like one; he's demonstrated this so far in his writing career.

To add a psychological dimension, and bonus points, to his god-liness, throughout his books, he practically lays out sermons. They're like conference notes we could've found in Jesus's backpack:

As I try to analyze this incongruity, I feel myself swaying between 'overthinking' the answer and 'underthinking' the answer. One moment, the difference seems complicated; the next, it seems completely obvious. The complexity comes from the assertion that men and women think about the world in a fundamentally different way. The simplicity comes from the fact that just about everyone accepts this premise and always has. (*Sex, Drugs, and Cocoa Puffs,* p. 118)

Religious people don't consider that the people we look up to and praise have had self-esteem battles. This is no different for our dear Chuck; he doesn't always feel that his followers have his back. He writes, "This is how I feel all the time. Whenever I try to be ironic, people think I'm serious—but every time I'm actually right about something, everyone assumes I'm crazy. Nobody ever believes me when I'm telling the truth" (*Fargo Rock City*, p. 56). Isn't it like reading a prophet's blog entry?

We all want to be cool, and it's hard for some of us to admit we're not. When I tell people I came from a town that didn't have a single stop-light, I make myself smile, even though I don't know why this is funny (or why it should be embarrassing). When I admit that I spent many nights assuming I would die a virgin, I act like I'm being self-depre-cating, even though I'm mostly being honest. When I remember how confused I was while I drove up and down the empty streets of my snow-packed hometown, I try to be wistful, even though I fucking hated having no one to talk to. (*Fargo Rock City*, p.283)

Living in "God's country," dying a virgin, having no one to talk to? Did Jesus write this?

Trying to encapsulate his thoughts into words so others would understand was, at times, defeating. Yet, "Self-deprecat-ing cleverness has become a virtue" (*Sex, Drugs, and Cocoa Puffs*, p. 6). Many deities most likely felt the same, minus the cleverness, perhaps.

For Those about to Pray, We Salute You

While Chuck spews catch phrases, worthy of being screened onto tees and sold at Walmart, he also teaches us through his scripture. All in all, "we are able to study something that defines who we are; therefore, we are able to study ourselves" (*Sex, Drugs, and Cocoa Puffs*, p. 102). As we dissect Chuck, we dissect ourselves and create a whole new spirituality at the same time.

We can find many of Chuck's comparisons that are substitutions for his own thoughts on religion. In addition to soccer, he's taught us about religion through The Sims, *Seinfeld*, the Pamela Anderson versus Marilyn Monroe comparison, and *The Real World*, just to kick around a few.

In the essay "George Will vs. Nick Hornby," Chuck states that "most children don't love soccer; they simply hate the alternatives more" and isn't that truly a reflection on religion? I mean, most don't love being Catholic or religious, for that matter, they just can't grasp or deal with the opposite. Children are in soccer because, according to Chuck, "it's the only sport where you can't fuck up" (*Sex, Drugs, and Cocoa Puffs*, p. 89). This explains organized religion, and to a certain extent, advertises Chuck's. He's not about fear; he's about domination. Chuck prophesies, "To say you love soccer is to say you believe in enforced equality more than you believe in the value of competition and the capacity of the human spirit" (p. 95).

Organized religions do not necessarily push their followers to be individualistic. This is what is different with Chuck because, honestly, he wants stand-outs. He wants only the good ones to play, and while Catholics will simply not respond when their children ask about other religions, Chuck will tell 'em to go out there—see what they're missing—because he knows they'll return. He's not afraid of competition.

A Chuck-fueled religion is kind of like being "reminded that the unattainable icons of perfection we lust after can never fulfill us like the Platonic allies who have been there all along" (p. 6). Why reach for God when Chuck is on your nightstand? Or in your nightcap?

The Gates of Chuck (or His Take on Religious Places)

Many new followers of any religion ask, "Is there a heaven? Is there a hell? Is there an afterlife?" And, more importantly, what does Chuck feel is the meaning of life? I mean, why didn't someone get that sound clip from Jesus? For Chuck: "We are always dying, all the time. That's what living is; living is dying, little by little. It's a sequenced collection of individualized deaths" (*Killing Yourself to Live*, p. 112). And that works hand-in-hand with his secondary idea that "We're all tourists, sort of. Life is tourism, sort of. As far as I'm concerned, the dinosaurs still hold the lease on this godforsaken rock" (p. 4). His meaning, this cynical explanation, is the reason we should all bow to Commandment #1 (coming soon to a bar near you) more often.

If we're just touring life, then heaven looks fairly similar. Chuck's subconscious take on heaven is that its "incessant noise and an accelerated pace of life decrease anxiety," as well as "neon lights," plentiful movie theaters and establishments open twenty-four-hours. There are people "like you who already reside here" who "will understand you," and he assures us that "things will be great, for sure" (p. 57). So you see, even Chuck's heaven looks pretty damn good.

He's nailed down life and heaven; what about the in-between that Catholicism lays out before us semi-bad people?

> For as long as I can remember, I've had a theory that life on earth is purgatory, because life on earth seems to have all the purgatorial qualities that were once described to me by nuns. It's almost like we're all Bruce Willis in *The Sixth Sense*, but nobody on 'earth' has figured this out yet, even though it will suddenly seem obvious when we get to the end. Sometimes I think that the amount of time you live on earth is just an inverse reflection of how good you were in previous existence; for example, infants to die from SIDS were actually great people when they were alive 'for real,' so they get to go to heaven after a mere five weeks in purgatory. Meanwhile, anyone who Willard Scott ever congratulated for turning 102 was obviously a terrible individual who had many, many previous sins to pay for and had to spend a century in his or her own purgatory (*KYL*, p.24).

Thus far, you have to admit, Chuck's descriptions of heaven and hell, as well as his own version of reincarnation, are more appealing than others.

Our Chuck, Who Art in Essays, Hallowed Be Thy Ink

I require my college students to mimic Chuck's writing style for a particular writing assignment. This means that they need to dissect his wacky style, found in the assigned essays of *Sex, Drugs, and Cocoa Puffs*. They have to break him down. It's tough, and it sometimes requires prayer. Typically, a list of guidelines, about ten items long, is born. Yes, ten items. Coincidence? No way, man. It's called parallelism!

Chuck has been subconsciously creating a list of rules and regulations through his writing style. So, structurally, we plug in the pieces. What we find through writing like him are useful elements in the creation of the Chuck regulations.

Chuck has been subliminally brainwashing the way we think about the world in a new way. This is what Chuckism (read: play on the word Catholicism) looks like when it is scribbled upon some bathroom stall.

Commandment #1: Thou shalt rock

Okay, so this commandment isn't on the list of "Chuck's Writing Style Items," but the underlining theme to his writing, and to his religion, is fun. Students, when mimicking Chuck, have to delve into their fun zones. They have to joke; they have to incorporate humor. Chuck's religion has the same tone. In his essay, "Appetite for Replication," he quotes "Axl" of the Guns N' Roses tribute band, Paradise City, "This is for everybody who told you not to smoke weed or not to drink beer every day. There are just too many people who make life hard." And that's the gist of the Chuck religion; he quoted that Axl-wannabe for a reason.

Possibly the one thing that doesn't connect between Chuck's religion and others is the coolness factor. To emphasize this coolness (and this commandment) further, let's take a moment to get fired up:

> It is time for all of us to embrace our heavy metal past. It is time to admit that we used to rock like hurricanes. It is time to run for the hills and go round and round. It is time for us to *Shout at the Devil*. We've got the right to choose it, there ain't no way we'll lose it, and we're not gonna take it anymore. (*Fargo Rock City*, p. 12)

Commandment #2: Thou shalt swear

They *are* just words, right? The Lord's name in vain? *Eh.* In fact, Chuck probably wishes his name was shorter so one could spout it out in the midst of a rage, akin to Clark Griswold's freak-out moment in *National Lampoon's Christmas Vacation*:

> Hey! If any of you are looking for any last-minute gift ideas for me, I have one. I'd like Frank Shirley, my boss, right here tonight. I want him brought from his happy holiday slumber over there on Melody Lane with all the other rich people and I want him brought right here, with a big ribbon on his head, and I want to look him straight in the eye and I want to tell him what a cheap, lying, no-good, rotten, four-flushing, low-life, snake-licking, dirt-eating, inbred, overstuffed, ignorant, blood-sucking, dog-kissing, brainless, dickless, hopeless, heartless, fat-ass, bug-eyed, stiff-legged, spotty-lipped, worm-headed sack of monkey shit he is! Hallelujah! Holy shit! Where's the Tylenol?

Maybe there's a chance, given the famous "Kelly Clarkson" moment in *40-Year-Old Virgin*? Either way, Chuck is not opposed to the vernacular, so feel free to f-bomb and f-bomb well.

And use big words to confuse too—just like the boring organized religions do. Chuck wouldn't leave you without a sample (in a Pepto-sized cup), like "archetypical." Example: "This is what happens when you don't construct an archetypical persona: If you're popular and melodic and faceless, you seem meaningless" (*Sex, Drugs, and Cocoa Puffs,* p.47).

Commandment #3: Thou shalt name-drop

The Gospel according to Mark? Marky Mark? Mark Jacobs? We've heard all the religious celebrities, and aren't we a bit sick of them? Moses did this, Mary was a virgin, Joseph was a simple carpenter... blahblahblah. Where were the papparazzi back then? If they were around, we might be reading *Enquirer*'s coverage on Moses smoking weed (doesn't that beard give him away?), Mary as a Britney Spears (both have claimed virginity at optimal times—Just sayin'), and Joseph was in the closet. (Evidence: He didn't have sex with Mary). These people have been placed on massive pedestals: "All the academics give props to older academics no one else has ever heard of" (*Sex, Drugs, and Cocoa Puffs,* pp. 222–23); no one can attain their goodness, and why try? Instead, Chuck asks his followers to just name-drop those who YOU know. That's what he's done over and over.

Someone doesn't know the lead-singer's name in KISS? Great, he's the person who told you that Chuck said cheesecake doesn't cause cancer. Your aunt Sylvia gave you some advice about pimple-control? Fabulous! Chuck asks you to name-drop her in your next conversation. When someone spouts off about what the *Bible* says, you tell 'em that verse 13, page 61, of *Killing Yourself to Live* said that that person is just "worried about the possibility of everyone else understand something that they're missing" and then get yourself a gin and tonic.

Commandment #4: Thou shalt not make sense. Be illogical

Most organized religions don't make sense anyway, so he's just following the trend (and you would be too), and trends are important to follow. So, thou shall be random and surreal and abstract in all conversations about religion. Or in any conversation about anything; Chuck will be so proud of you, and it's all about making the "guy with the open fly" happy.

In *Chuck Klosterman IV*, as a more recent oddball example, Chuck has a discussion with Christian Scientist Val Kilmer who is gung-ho on the fact that "an institution cannot be classified as a religion unless God is involved" (p. 43). They are never able to find that definition in any of the dictionaries owned by Kilmer. It doesn't really make sense why Chuck would argue that definition with someone so "religious," but, again, he doesn't make sense. And I mean Val.

While you are out in the world, drinking and not making sense and throwing logic into the cow pasture, spew out some extra arguments to frustrate non-followers further. For a deeper explanation, see this clip from page 70 of *Sex, Drugs, and Cocoa Puffs*:

> The formula is as follows: When discussing any given issue, always do three things. First, make an intellectual concession (this makes the listener feel comfortable). Next, make a completely incomprehensible—but remarkably specific—"cultural accusation" (this makes you insightful). Finally, end the dialogue by interjecting slang lexicon that does not necessarily exist (this makes you contemporary).

I recently tried this out regarding the oil spill in the Gulf: "You are so right on! I mean, just because BP 'plugged' the hole doesn't mean they did so rhetorically or morally, and if they can't figure that out, they won't be the only blind eyes trying to see over the cloudy political terrain." See, even Chuck-ites get step-by-step instructions handed out to them. Do other religions do that?

Perhaps I should clarify that while you are out in the desert of life, without real religion for forty days and whatnot, being a Chuck-ite and not making sense, etc., that doesn't mean you aren't allowed to declare *some* insights about the world. *You* can make sense, if you so desire. Chuck's a hypocrite and allows for leeway when it comes to arguing both sides—especially if you're doing it to confuse followers of other non-fun religions. As Chuck states from behind his beer pyramid, "Now, don't get me wrong: I am not suggesting that the music *made* these people go violently insane. But it's equally as stupid to argue that there's no connection at all" (*Fargo Rock City*, p. 58). Or: "If art is stupid, it can't really be harmful. If it's not stupid, then it can't be dismissed as socially irrelevant" (p. 133). Now, Chuck's illogic here is exemplary. See, the major premises in these two syllogisms are NO stupid things are harmful and NO non-stupid things are socially irrelevant. And there is a missing major premise, which allows him to use the excluded middle at all, which is ALL things are either stupid or not stupid. Now these three missing premises are really bad logic. But that's Chuck.

In your decision to be a part of this religion, be illogical. Don't become a Chuck follower because everyone else is doing it. But do it for the good of mankind. And because there are backstage passes involved. And free keg beer.

Commandment #5: Thou shalt use over-the-top comparisons (and spike your metaphors)

Possibly the most famous comparison is the apples-to-oranges comparison; when it comes to religions, then, Chuck may ponder, in a sermon, if his religion can be compared in that apples-to-oranges way with others. You, as a good follower, would have to disagree. And then quote him: "Apples and oranges aren't that different, really. I mean, they're both fruit. Their weight is extremely similar" (*Sex, Drugs, and Cocoa Puffs*, p. 85) and then compare his religion to an old, rusted Ford truck; the other religions are just unreliable engines in Chinese imports.

Let's say someone tells you directly that Chuck's religion is *not* better than theirs. Well, comparisons are the best way to a. explain yourself, b. have fun, and c. confuse them a wee bit. And maybe you bring in Commandment #7, too. "Following a Chuck commandment is like listening to Ozzy speak. Sign language may be necessary (read: usage of a particular finger)."

Some of Chuck's other hits with comparisons, much like Jesus's miracles with wine or the blind:

- Queensryche is like an Elvis who was never particularly good-looking, but who also never got fat. (*Fargo Rock City*, p. 277)

- Journey was rock's version of the TV show *Dynasty*. (*Sex, Drugs, and Cocoa Puffs*, p. 55)

If Pam Anderson is the new Marilyn Monroe, Chuck's the new God on the street.

Commandment #6: Thou shalt be brash and unapologetic

Once, while running in Chahinkapa Park, I was accosted by two men—Mormons?—and they asked me if I wanted to talk about Jesus. Mid-sweat, mid-breath, and mid-"Pour Some Sugar on Me," I had to decline. That seemed like an extreme measure to me; why wouldn't a runner already be somewhat religious? Running is an acceptable form of suicide. How much closer to God can one be when one is asking for spiritual intervention at every mile? Modern day runners would have made great Medieval monks.

Perhaps the same can be said for those "talking to dinosaurs" near the Porcelain God after a night of drinking.

Speaking of drinking, when it comes to the opinions of others' religions, in common conversations at North Dakotan pubs, feel free to preach if you are preached to. Just make sure to utilize those other commandments, like not making sense or using odd comparisons. This will guarantee that they'll walk away and leave you alone with your scotch or beer or whatever. Need a sampling of some of Chuck's abrasiveness? Here you go: "Another good reason to hate heavy metal is Ted Nugent, or—more accurately—people who are like Ted Nugent. Every time

I go to a big rock show, I see herds of these kind of men, and they always make me wish I had the power to give people polio" (*Fargo Rock City*, p. 229). If confusing them with gibberish or comparisons doesn't work, or hitting them with Queensryche-Elvis comparisons doesn't work, unfortunately you'll have to resort to this. Putting others down isn't nice, but neither is forcing knee problems onto young Catholics.

Essentially, this commandment calls for a much more intellectual version of "You're going to hell."

Commandment #7: Thou shalt relate most things to music or sports

Celtics vs. Lakers isn't far off from Catholics vs. Lutherans, right? I mean, how many people have referred to Joe Mauer as Baby Jesus? People are already implementing this commandment without Chuck's permission (unless they are secret followers). Chuck, himself, refers to Bono as Jesus in *Chuck Klosterman IV* (p. 28) and he claims that "pro basketball is exactly like life" (*Sex, Drugs, and Cocoa Puffs*, p. 96) which is probably why "for at least one decade, God was obsessed with pro basketball" (p. 98). How many of us cross our fingers and toes when that :01 seconds left free throw is being attempted? How many ask God to let the Vikings win during the playoffs, before or after the Favre saga; relating sports to anything, even religion, isn't that far off from what other religious folks do.

People often feel spiritual cranking Enya in their Volkswagens; others feel closer to God when they witness a slam dunk. Chuck's not going to tell you how to worship, where to worship, or who to make into your gods. You wish to do yoga in your Mauer jersey while surrounded by Guns N' Roses? Wonderful! Go forth and constantly relate your religious ponderings to the Minnesota Twins or Lynyrd Skynyrd at will.

Commandment #8: Thou shalt use footnotes

Explained in a different manner, you shall fill-in-the-blanks like Catholics do with supposed "rules" by using footnotes; in Chuck's case, they must be humorous. Catholics once had some no-jeans-in-church rule that somehow fell by the wayside; was Jesus concerned about denim? Doesn't say in Mark, Matthew, Luke, or John, does it? So, rules that are made up by Chuck or his followers are subject to change. *At any time*. In fact, ignore this rule and just use parentheticals at the end of your sentences as I have done.

Commandment #9: Thou shalt be grammatically correct in all blasphemy

Correct spelling, grammar, and punctuation is a must if you are going to be a follower in this religion. Followers of Chuck need never feel "bitchy" when they have to correct someone saying "Anyways." Focus in on the words others use for your illogical ramblings and crazy comparisons because "the one thing nobody wants is sentences, and they certainly don't want paragraphs. People despise paragraphs. Focus groups have proven this" (*Sex, Drugs, and Cocoa Puffs*, p. 214). Those words should include, but are not limited to, f-bombs and their varying parts of speech, big words, sports terminology, as well as the names of unknown bands.

Chuck will probably not look favorably upon those who sprinkle their speech with "like." No Chuck follower will say, "Like, Chuck is a god, because, like . . ." They may get shot on sight. Instead, be articulate. Wear fake glasses. Get your geek on, and show some respect for rock'n'roll. And for God's sake . . . errr, Chuck's sake, don't look like an effing dumbass!

Commandment #10: Thou shalt love frequently

Alright, so this last item, like the first, isn't necessarily linked to the list of items that are the backbone to his writing philosophy, and yet it is one of his most obsessively covered topics (beyond music and sports). Any religion needs to comment on love, since it apparently makes the world go around like a Harlem Globetrotters routine. And it's part of the "sex, drugs, and rock'n'roll" theory that Chuck practically lives by. So, yes, *love*.

The opposite sex is a big deal to Chuck. There will be no rules governing interactions between the sexes here because underneath it all, Chuck is a lover. A lover of too many? Chuck philosophizes, "I can't let go of the past. I can't fall out of love with any of these women. I can only exist in the past and in the future"(*Killing Yourself to Live*, p. 234). Want to love three girls at once and write about them in a book? Go ahead. And Chuck isn't above cheating either, although I think he'd ask his followers to refrain from intentionally trying to crush another man's heart. Well, unless that man is an asshole and his girlfriend is smokin' hot; then, he won't judge. It's important to reflect back, with this commandment, to what he said about Billy Joel in the essay "Every Dog Must Have His Every Day, Every Drunk Must Have His Drink":

> When I hear "Just the Way You Are," it never makes me think about Joel's broken marriage. It makes me think about all the perfectly scribed love letters and drunken e-mails I have written over the past twelve years, and about all the various women who received them. I think about how I told them they changed the way I thought about the universe, and that they made every other woman on the earth unattractive, and that I would love them unconditionally even if we were never together. I hate that those letters exist. But I don't hate them because what I said was false; I hate them because what I said was completely true. My convictions could not have been stronger when I wrote those words, and—for whatever reason—they still faded into nothingness. Three times I have been certain that I could never love anyone else, and I was wrong every time. (*Sex, Drugs, and Cocoa Puffs*, pp. 53–54)

And, a smaller tidbit:

> It immediately dawned on me that we were never going to agree on anything as long as we lived. Our worldviews were so diametrically opposed that we would never share any experience in totality; even if we saw the same film at the same time in the same place, there would be no common ground whatsoever.
> I found this profoundly desirable. (*Killing Yourself to Live*, p. 30)

The intersection of love and religion show through, too, in the same book. "Art and love are the same thing: It's the process of seeing yourself in things that are not you. It's understanding the unreasonable. And although the theory I am proposing is completely unreasonable, it is something I completely understand" (p. 217). A process of seeing yourself in things that are not you; Chuck alludes to another god-like proposition here, although that may not have been his intention to begin with.

And what's something lovers and religious freaks have in common? Chuck tells us: "The worst part of being in love with anyone, which is that people in love can't be reasoned with" (*Killing Yourself to Live*, p. 5).

All Chucks Go to Heaven

I recently wrote as a Facebook status that I didn't need to "be religious." True story. Instead, the status conveyed that because I am a sports fan, I use up all my hope and faith and love on my sports teams. (May Chuck bless them and keep them, all the days of their lives.) Many people "liked" that status, and it wasn't seen as all that blasphemous. I had to frown: Why can we only channel our loyalty into deities we can't see or who make enough to make God jealous? What about the in-between man? The Chuck in us all? The man, or woman, who fucks up and lies about it, but who still inspires us?

Look, Chuck's a god. He has followers. They rock to him, and he gives them hope. They head-bang to his sermons. They rejoice over songs, and quote his lines. Hell, he's there to pray to when you need him. Let us now worship him in our favorite band tees:

Our Chuck
who art back stage
hallowed be thy guitar solo
The beer will come
the ladies be done
in the interview as well as in the den
Give us today our daily F-bomb
and forgive us our screw-ups
as we holler at those
who fucked up against us
Lead us into blasphemy
and deliver much temptations.
For Chuck's is the kingdom
the music and the glory
forever and ever,
Amen.

Conse-
quences of
killing a
clydesdale?

HYPERthetical Response #6

Consequences of killing a clydesdale

JOHN R. FITZPATRICK

Let us assume a fully grown, completely healthy Clydesdale horse has his hooves shackled to the ground while his head is held in place with thick rope. He is conscious and standing upright, but completely immobile. And let us assume that—for some reason—every political prisoner on earth (as cited by Amnesty International) will be released from captivity if you can kick this horse to death in less than twenty minutes. You are allowed to wear steel-toed boots.
Would you attempt to do this?

—*Sex, Drugs, and Cocoa Puffs*, p. 126

Consequentialists believe that you should evaluate the morality of actions by looking at the results. Non-consequentialists believe you must look at the means employed. Asking the question: "Do the ends justify the means?" Consequentialists will answer "yes," and non-consequentialists will answer "no."

When non-consequentialists argue against the merits of consequentialism, they often try to create thought experiments where the consistent consequentialist will agree to do something morally yucky because it will produce good results, and then argues that anyone who would recommend doing something that yucky must be a moral imbecile. And the moral "framing" here is pretty severe. After all, Clydesdales are not as cute and lovable as Pandas, but they have a pretty good warm and cuddly thing going for them. Kick a Clydesdale to death? Only a monster would even consider such a thing, or so the non-consequentialist argues. Since the consequentialists must argue that this is at least morally permissable, and perhaps morally required, there must be something wrong with consequentialism.

But the Devil is in the details, and we have skipped over why the consequentialist must consider doing something that sounds horrific in this kind of scenario. You don't need to be an expert or a historian to realize that many of the folks on Amnesty International's list of political prisoners are in for rough treatment, and some of them are bound to get treatment worse than what we are considering for the horse. As I write this there is a news item circulating on a blog I read about how the body of a fifteen-year-old Syrian boy was found after having been arrested in Syria two months earlier in a protest against the government. Al Jazeera reports that the body was "riddled with bullets, missing an eye, several teeth with a broken neck and leg" <http://english.aljazeera.net/news/middleeast/2011/06/2011696563111657.html>. For many political prisoners in the world today, being beaten to death in twenty minutes would be a blessing.

If this treatment of political prisoners is commonplace, and I believe it is not rare, then there is a distinctly different framing of this ethical dilemma—Would you be willing to do something awful to a horse to prevent something worse from happening to many human beings? And framed this way, I believe only the most extreme animal-rights activists would still say "No."

Of course, Klosterman is a clever guy, and there is a final wrinkle to be ironed out. You can only save the prisoners if you can successfully accomplish this task, and the longer I think about this, the less sure I am that I would be able to do so.

The Somewhat Visible Man

CHUCK KLOSTERMAN

I've spent two hours trying to create a levelheaded opening for this epilogue, but nothing I've pretended to write reflects my feelings about this book in any meaningful or accurate way. As such, I'm just going to skip the manufactured introduction and cut straight to the part that matters.

Here is my problem:

This is a book that's almost entirely about me. It's difficult to accept that notion, but what other conclusion can I draw? The title has my fucking name in it. Even when the various writers attempt to investigate unrelated ideas and seemingly disconnected problems, they've been forced to utilize specific things I've written as a means for reaching whatever point they intend to address. The whole concept is built on that conceit. Yet as I read these essays, almost everything feels unfamiliar and alien (including, oddly, the recontextualized excerpts from my own books). It's like watching a documentary about oneself without recognizing the cast; I suppose it's a little like watching a documentary about someone who looks like me and has the same name, but whom I've never met or spent much time thinking about. Moreover, the writers of this book seem to have anticipated my reaction, which leads me to believe my response is almost comically predictable.

So how am I supposed to react to this?

Certainly, I know how I *should* react: I should be extremely flattered, and I should make a lot of self-depreciating statements about how this whole idea is crazy and perverse and undeserved. And if I did that, I wouldn't be lying: I am extremely flattered by this, and I think the whole concept is nutzo. These are some of the nicest things ever written about me, many of the contributors are clearly better informed about the history of ideas than I am, and being compared to dead geniuses is a wonderful feeling (even when those comparisons are inaccurate). But what good would it do to express those thoughts? No matter how I did it, they'd come across as unoriginal and disingenuous. It's not like this book was some kind of ambush—Seth Vannatta came to me in early 2010 and said it was a project he wanted to pursue, and I said, "Go for it." I've had a long time to think about what this is supposed to mean. I should either strongly defend the existence of this manuscript or openly ridicule it. But I can't do either of those things. And that's not because I don't understand this book; it's because I do.

So that, I guess, is my problem: I understand why this book exists.

This book exists because someone might buy it. More specifically, this book exists because the kind of someone *who never buys books about philosophy* might buy this one, for motives totally unrelated to philosophical inquiry. I'm not authentically famous, but I'm "famous enough." Every person involved with this transaction (both tangibly and intangibly) understands these circumstances. As I skim the assortment of essays in this anthology, I recognize that most of the examples cited come from *Sex, Drugs and Cocoa Puffs*, the least logical, most self-consciously contradictory book I've ever produced. But that book is also (by far) the most popular thing I've ever published, which makes those particular thoughts more valuable to other people. I think about this all the time. If I had known how many people were going to read that book, I could never have written it.

That makes me feel good and bad.

There's a section in this anthology where Sybil Priebe mocks the idea of a religion based around my persona.[1] This is just a metaphor, of course, and not really about me at all. But

---

[1] This is not really accurate, I suppose. This essay—which is pretty funny, actually—is really about the arbitrary orthodoxy of religion, and my name is just the placeholder for whatever people need to believe. But this is a weird thing to hold the place of.

my name is attached, so my perspective is skewed. It seems like a commentary on something I accidentally proposed. And it distracts me, particularly since (a.) no such religion exists, and (b.) no one in the world thinks that it should. It's like she's satirizing an idea that no one has had except herself. But I understand why this happens (or at least I think I do). She's trying to be entertaining, which is totally reasonable. As a commercial writer, it's something I never stop worrying about.[2] I only have three goals when I write anything: to be entertaining, to be interesting, and to be clear. But at the same time, I exclusively enjoy writing about big, unwieldy ideas—nothing else seems worthwhile (to me, unsolvable ideas are always the most intriguing). So this is where a degree of dissonance inevitably derives: I'm trying to write fun, entertaining books about complex ideas, but the ultimate product is typically consumed by individuals who only want ½ of that equation.[3] They either *just* want to be entertained (without having to "examine" anything), or they *only* want to dwell on the ideas (and are thus annoyed by the flippant, comedic techniques that undercut the gravity of the central message).

I suppose this chasm is intentional, although I'd be lying if I claimed to understand why that intent is important to me. I only know that it is.

Someone (possibly Jerry Seinfeld, but probably a lot of people) once argued that comedy is like math proofs: If A = B and B = C, then A = C (and that's the joke, because it never does). I do this all the time, and that makes for flawed philosophy. But that doesn't bother me. I'm not trying to *convince* people how to think or what to feel. Nobody believes me when I say that, but it's true. Why would I want the entire world to think like me? What kind of twisted person wants to impose their personal view of reality onto complete strangers? I'll never understand that impulse. To me, writing is the most specifically personal thing I do. I enjoy the process of arguing, but I have no end

---

[2] Even as I write this epilogue, I find myself worrying that it's not funny enough to publish—despite the fact that there's no reason for there to be any jokes here whatsoever. In fact, some readers would probably prefer there not be.

[3] This dichotomy generally excludes heavy drug users—they always want both.

game in mind; to me, it's just pleasurable and engaging and more worthwhile than making small talk.[4] I want conservative people to perceive me as liberal and I want liberals to perceive me as conservative—that's pretty much the comprehensive template of my political aspirations. I feel the same way about arts criticism: I love KISS and Billy Joel, but why would I care if people who aren't me think they suck? I'm sure they have their reasons.

This is not to say I don't have feelings, because I do. I don't fake love or distaste.[5] I dislike soccer, and I certainly hate the culture *around* soccer (or at least how that culture manifests itself in America). I'm very adept at making fun of it. As a result, I will always be loathed by a certain type of US soccer fan who feels like I consciously attack his (or her) self-identity. They'll never get over it, and they'll always take it personally. They assume my motive for writing a satirical essay about soccer must be the same as whatever their motive would be for seriously advocating its greatness. It becomes the prism for how they interpret everything else I do, and that marginalizes me. But this is not something I can complain about it, because I'm (unconsciously, but also vividly) doing it on purpose.

There's a great moment in Ian MacDonald's book about the Beatles' song catalogue (*Revolution in the Head*) where he mentions how John Lennon accidentally sang the wrong lyrics during the recording of "You've Got to Hide Your Love Away": Instead of going back in the studio to fix the error, Lennon decided to leave the mistake on the album, sardonically saying, "Leave that in, the pseuds will love it." This, obviously, makes Lennon seem cool and laidback and self-aware. But—as

---

[4] In general, I prefer the experience of having *my* mind changed, as opposed to the experience of changing the mind of someone else. And you know what I *really* like? I like discovering authentically new ways to think about classic problems, even if those new ways are insane and temporary and broken.

[5] When I was just starting out as a critic in the '90s, I probably *did* fake these things, at least on occasion. It's normal for critics to amplify their feelings in order to come across as more urgent and intense and engaged, and I still see this quality (all the time) in other writers. But my ability to so easily notice this is why I stopped doing it: To me, there's nothing cheaper and more transparent than fabricated indignation (or, for that matter, fabricated adoration). I feel like readers can see through that immediately.

McDonald later explains—if you consistently create art that's willfully misleading, you can't really complain when someone decides "Helter Skelter" is about a California race war. A great philosopher is supposed to be trustworthy and consistent. That's part of the responsibility. And I'm not a reliable narrator. I'm not even sure how I could be, because I'm not a reliable person.

People ask me a lot of weird questions about my books. However, nobody ever asks me the straightforward question of why I wrote them, perhaps because that question is *so* straightforward that it seems unmanageable (plus, getting an answer would stop the questioner from being able to believe whatever he wants about my motives). But here is my response to that unasked query: I wrote *Fargo Rock City* because it was the book I'd always longed to read, yet couldn't find in stores (also, I wanted to know if writing a book was something I could actually accomplish). I wrote *Sex, Drugs, and Cocoa Puffs* because I believed there were at least ten thousand people in America who wanted to think critically about whatever art happened to shape their life, and I will always believe how you think about that art matters far more than whatever it actually is (also, I was paid $40,000, which was more money than I'd ever seen in my entire life). I wrote *Killing Yourself to Live* because I wanted to write about the things in my life that I loved the most (and also because it happened). I wrote *Downtown Owl* because I wanted to write about people I knew, but who didn't actually exist. I wrote *Eating the Dinosaur* because I believe the media is exponentially changing the experience of being alive, and I wrote *The Visible Man* for the same reason I wrote *Eating the Dinosaur* (and also because I liked the fictional premise and there was no nonfictional way to handle it). I suppose one could argue that all my books are really one big book (released incrementally), and that the theme of this 1,500-page volume is the irresolvable difference between what's defined as "real" and what constitutes "reality." If someone made that assertion, I wouldn't disagree.[6] In fact, I'd be very happy if somebody argued that, although I don't know why. I suspect I'm more self-aware

---

[6] And this point is made quite often throughout this book, which is a big reason I appreciate it. I think my favorite chapter is probably the one on media ecology, much of which I can't contradict (except for the writer's notion that the problem of authenticity has essentially been "solved"—that strikes

than the average person, but I'm certain I have no sense of self. I don't even know if I would enjoy my own books, had someone else written them. And I'll never know the answer to that question. I'll never, ever know.

But that's my problem. Not yours.

---

me as dangerous and totally backwards). Semi-interesting sidenote: Until very recently, my knowledge about Marshall McLuhan was pretty cursory (I remember discussing him during college, but not very often). But then I read a short biography of McLuhan by Douglas Coupland, and I found myself relating to McLuhan in an intense, personal manner. What's really amazing is how often "my" ideas about media precisely mirror things McLuhan had already noted fifty years ago, even though I had never touched most of the books where McLuhan originally made those points. This means that McLuhan's arcane ideas have become so central to our collective understanding of mass media that they can now be absorbed by accident, without even trying. They are now totally normative to anyone who tries to think about media on their own. Could there be a better definition of successful culture writing?

Eighty-Five Percent
True Stories

RANDALL E. AUXIER

Randy Auxier belongs to the twenty-seven percent of college professors who are physically indistinguishable from hobos. He skulks around the campus of Southern Illinois University in Carbondale saying things like "That's an interesting point," and "I'll think about that and get back to you." He is either: 1. not a member of Generation X, or (B) not as smart as he thinks he is, or (iii) neither of those, and (d.) married to a better woman than he deserves. His fantasy is to introduce Chuck Klosterman to each of his cats, someday.

JOHN THOMAS BRITTINGHAM

John Brittingham received an MA in Philosophy from Boston College in 2009 and is a PhD candidate at Southern Illinois University at Carbondale. When he's not taking the disparate elements of mass culture to task with Kierkegaard, Levinas, and Derrida, John works in the area of phenomenology of religion. John also appreciates a decent hipster dance party when the opportunity presents itself. Remember, 15% of the above is not really true.

KEVIN BROOKS

Brooks moved to Fargo about the time Klosterman left; he likes to think of Klosterman as his nemesis, (as opposed to his archenemy). Brooks has since spent the last fourteen years working in the English department at North Dakota State University, occasionally teaching *Fargo Rock City*, regularly teaching about Marshall McLuhan, but never, until now, bringing the two together.

BRUNO ĆURKO

Bruno Ćurko works at the Institute of Philosophy in Zagreb, Croatia, and the philosophy department in Osijek, Croatia. Bruno works with the Philosophy for Children in Association "Petit philosophy" (www.petit-philosophy.com). He is an avid fan of hard, glam, and metal rock music. He has founded two bands, and he intends to return to active playing after the defense of his PhD thesis, which has been known to derail many a music career. He has published papers in philosophy of education, philosophy for children, and Renaissance philosophy, and has written a high-school textbook on ethics. In addition to his other professional services, Bruno has served as secretary of the editor of the philosophical journal, *Metodicki ogledi*, which, rumor has it, Chuck Klosterman subscribes to and reads in Croatian.

LUKE DICK

Confined to a small apartment with no less than six female creatures of varying species (two canines, two felines, one human, one oviraptor), Luke Dick resides in Manhattan, where he is a mercenary philosophy lecturer in just about every borough. Prone to taking strolls through the east village, Dick occasionally catches revelatory glimpses of the pop-culture secrets of the universe: Sebastian Bach is taller than most rock stars and haggles for better cell phone rates in public; James Iha has a distinguished cheese pallet; Jim Gaffigan enjoys McDonalds and Polish sausage. When sequestered to his apartment, Dick spends most of his time on creative endeavors, both of musical and philosophic varieties. He is co-editor of The *Rolling Stones and Philosophy: It's Just a Thought Away* (2012) and composes songs for TV and film (www.lukedick.com).

JOHN R. FITZPATRICK

John Fitzpatrick is a lecturer in philosophy at the University of Tennessee, Chattanooga. He received a PhD in Philosophy from the main branch of the University of Tennessee in Knoxville in 2001. He is the author of *John Stuart Mill's Political Philosophy: Balancing Freedom and the Collective Good* (2006), and *Starting with Mill* (2010). He is a contributor to *House and Philosophy* (2009), and shares with Gregory House a commitment to the virtue of eccentricity, and with Chuck Klosterman a belief in the utility of low culture.

CHAD FLANDERS

Chad Flanders is assistant professor of law at Saint Louis University School of Law. He has a PhD in philosophy from the University of Chicago and a law degree from Yale, so we assume the aggregate cost of his education rivals the aggregate revenue produced by Klosterman's book sales. Chad has written on law and religion, political philosophy, and criminal law. He also writes for the indie music blog inyourspeakers.com. He is grateful to David Svolba for comments and suggestions on his chapter. Some of the best lines are his.

IVANA GREGURIC

Ivana Greguric is a doctoral student in philosophy at the University of Zagreb, Croatia. Currently she is working as research assistant in a project on "Cyborg Ethics." She has published articles on various topics such as philosophy of media, bioethics, philosophy of technology, and philosophy of music. Besides her academic interests in cyborgs, posthumanism, and cybernetics, Ivana is also a songwriter, and performer in the glam rock band Rockstill, whose award winning songs are aired daily on Croatian radio. (She also plays in a tribute band to her own band, which has the exact same members as the original.) She shares with Klosterman her love of glam rock bands such as Guns N' Roses, W.A.S.P. , Metallica, Joe Satriani, and more. She has been known to hang out with current lead guitarist Ron "Bumblefoot" Thal and the rest of Guns N' Roses band after their shows.

BENJAMIN D. LISLE

Benjamin Lisle is a historian of popular culture, the built environment, and sport who teaches American Studies at Colby College. A Celtics man ideologically—though not because he's a closet Republican, as Klosterman would have it—he lives with a woman who would rather watch soccer than gridiron football (because it takes half the time) and Mookie Blaylock (the cat, not the thieving point guard). He thoroughly appreciates Chuck Klosterman's broad intellectual project—to illustrate how popular culture is meaningful and legible. But he can only take Chuck in small doses that inevitably result in shaken fists and imaginary arguments.

DANIEL R. MISTICH

Daniel ("Dan Halen") Mistich is a doctoral student in the Department of Communications Studies at the University of Georgia in Athens, Georgia. Dan received his BA in Communications Studies and Political Science at Marshall University. He later received his MA in Communications Studies and Rhetorical Studies at Syracuse University. In addition to purchasing new frames for his glasses based solely on recommendations from attractive women, Dan pursues research in the areas of contemporary rhetoric and criticism, political theory, and continental philosophy. Although he is far from being the type of KISS fan Chuck is, Dan is at the point in his life where he considers the band "archetypally essential" (especially Ace Frehley's self-titled 1978 solo album).

RYAN P. MCCULLOUGH

Ryan McCullough is an Instructor and Director of Forensics in the Department of Journalism and Communications Studies at West Liberty University in West Liberty, West Virginia. He received his BA in Communications Studies and Political Science and his MA in Communications Studies at Marshall University. His research interests include forensic competition, narrative analysis, media/communication ethics, rhetorical theory and criticism and poverty and Appalachian discourse. Ryan spends entirely too much time on things related to sports: this includes playing NCAA Football by EA Sports. Like Chuck, Ryan makes his team run the option every single play. He also loves sugary cereal and Iron Maiden, even though he is too old to love those things like he once did.

Sybil Priebe
Sybil Priebe is an Assistant Professor of English and Humanities at the North Dakota State College of Science in Wahpeton, North Dakota—twenty-five miles from Chuck's hometown. When she's not teaching, she blogs, reads, listens to classic rock (via 107.9 The Fox), and randomly meets people who know Chuck. She often sees many of the fictional characters from Owl, North Dakota, at the local bar. Rumor has it she put a total beat down on Grendel and Cubby Candy at the same time.

George A. Reisch
George Reisch is the series editor for Open Court's Popular Culture and Philosophy series. He also teaches philosophy and intellectual history at Northwestern's School of Continuing Studies and is writing a book about the Cold War and its impact on our understanding of scientific knowledge. He would take the Brain Pill and, in fact, has taken it already.

Craig Rood
Craig Rood is a graduate student and teacher in the rhetoric and composition program at North Dakota State University. In addition to fake laughs and discussions about the weather, Craig also finds writing in the third person strange—and that is partially why he is interested in Klosterman. He likes Klosterman as much as he does his über-academic colleagues. They're all really intelligent people who are passionate about making sense of culture and life. He's not a fan of 1980s rock, but he finds Klosterman's analysis of pop-culture smart and funny.

Matt Sienkiewicz
Matt Sienkiewicz, whose PhD is from the University of Wisconsin, is a professor at Gettysburg College, as well as an Emmy-nominated screenwriter and documentary filmmaker. His research focuses on the West's investment in Middle Eastern broadcasting initiatives and ethnic representation in American media. His work has been published in *The Journal of Film and Video*, *The Velvet Light Trap*, and

Understanding Community Media. His most recent movie, *Live From Bethlehem*, released by the Media Education Foundation in 2009, has screened worldwide at film festivals from Rhode Island to London. He anticipates his chapter in this volume will earn the same worldwide attention.

SETH VANNATTA

Seth is Assistant Professor of Philosophy and Religious Studies at Morgan State University in Baltimore. He's the author of several book chapters including "The Player Prophet and the Phenomenology of Reading the Ref," in *Soccer and Philosophy: Beautiful Thoughts on the Beautiful Game* (2010) and "The Most Dangerous Rock'n'Roll Band in the World" in *The Rolling Stones and Philosophy: It's Just a Thought Away* (2012). Seth shares with Val Kilmer an unparalleled degree of self-knowledge. By editing this book, he knows what it is like to be Chuck Klosterman better than Chuck himself does.

MELISSA VOSEN

Melissa Vosen is currently working hard to resurrect VH1's short-lived game show *The World Series of Pop Culture*; she hopes to one day go head to head with Klosterman on things that matter most: Guns N' Roses tribute bands, Tom Cruise movies, and serial killer celebrities. When not watching television and listening to music, she teaches first-year composition and visual communication courses at North Dakota State University in Fargo Rock City (the same city in which Klosterman went on his all chicken nugget diet for a week). Rumor has it she once snapped a buck's neck with her bare hands after her brother rifled it from the cab of the family combine.

References

Aristotle. 1958. *Nicomachean Ethics* in *The Pocket Aristotle*. New York: Simon and Schuster, 1958.

Bakhtin, Mikhail. 2002. Carnival and the Carnivalesque. In Storey 200.

Baudrillard, Jean. 1994. *Simulacra and Simulation*. Translated by Sheila Faria Glaser. Ann Arbor: University of Michigan Press, 1994.

———. 1995. *The Gulf War Did Not Take Place*. Translated by Paul Patton. Bloomington: Indiana University Press.

Bentham, Jeremy. 1974. An Introduction to the Principles of Morals and Legislation. In Warnock 1974.

Butler, Judith. 1987. *Subjects of Desire: Hegelian Reflections in Twentieth-Century France*. New York: Columbia University Press.

———. 1999. *Gender Trouble: Feminism and the Subversion of Identity*. New York: Routledge.

———. 2005. *Giving an Account of Oneself*. New York: Fordham University Press.

Camp, Walter. 1910. *The Book of Football*. New York: Century.

Cooper, John M. 1997. *Plato: Complete Works*. Indianapolis: Hackett.

Daley, Arthur. 1954. Sports of the Times: Live and Learn. *New York Times* (30th November).

Dick, Luke, and George A. Reisch, eds. 2012. The *Rolling Stones and Philosophy: It's Just a Thought Away*. Chicago: Open Court.

Eco, Umberto. The Frames of Comic "Freedom". In Sebeok and Erickson 1984.

Freud, Sigmund. 1995. Creative Writers and Day-Dreaming. In Gay 1995.

Gadamer, Hans-Georg. 2004. *Truth and Method*. New York: Continuum.

Gay, Peter, ed. 1995. *The Freud Reader*. New York: Norton.

Habermas, Jürgen. 1987. The Paradigm Shift in Mead and Durkheim: From Purposive Activity to Communicative Action. In *The Theory of Communicative Action. Volume 2. Lifeworld and System: A Critique of Functionalist Reason*. Boston: Beacon Press.

———. 1991. *The Structural Transformation of the Public Sphere*. Cambridge: MIT Press.

Homer, Sean. 2005. *Jacques Lacan*. New York: Routledge.

Kierkegaard, Søren. 1989. *The Concept of Irony*. Princeton: Princeton University Press.

———. 2004. *The Sickness Unto Death*. New York: Penguin.

Klosterman, Chuck. A Brilliant Idea! (For Now). *ESPN.com Page 2* (12th October 2006). http://sports.espn.go.com/espn/page2/story?page=klosterman/061016.

———. 2001. *Fargo Rock City: A Heavy Metal Odyssey in Rural North Dakota* New York: Scribner's.

———. 2003. *Sex, Drugs, and Cocoa Puffs: A Low Culture Manifesto*. New York: Scribner's.

———. 2005. *Killing Yourself to Live: 85% of a True Story*. New York: Scribner's.

———. 2006. *Chuck Klosterman IV: A Decade of Curious People and Dangerous Ideas*. New York: Scribner's.

———. 2008. *Downtown Owl: A Novel*. New York: Scribner's.

———. 2009. *Eating the Dinosaur*, New York: Scribner's.

———. 2010. *HYPERtheticals: 50 Questions for Insane Conversations*. New York: Scribner's, 2010.

———. 2011. *The Visible Man: A Novel*. New York: Scribner's.

Kojève, Alexandre. 1969. *Introduction to the Reading of Hegel: Lectures on the Phenomenology of Spirit*. New York: Basic Books.

Layden, Tim. 2008. Old Is New Is Old. *Sports Illustrated* (1st December).

McLuhan, Marshall. 1964. *Understanding Media: The Extensions of Man*. New York: Signet.

———. 2001 [1968]. *War and Peace in the Global Village*. Corte Madera: Gingko.

———. 2002 [1950]. *The Mechanical Bride: The Folklore of Industrial Man*. Corte Madera: Gingko.

McLuhan, Marshall, and Quentin Fiore. 2001 [1967]. *The Medium Is the Massage*. Corte Madera: Gingko.

Moeller, Susan. 1999. *Compassion Fatigue: How the Media Sell Disease, Famine, War, and Death*. New York: Routledge.

Mill, John Stuart. On Liberty. In Warnock 1974.

New York Times. 1955. Football Hard Work for Fans, Too. *New York Times* (2nd October).

Oriard, Michael. *Reading Football: How the Popular Press Created an American Spectacle*. Durham: University of North Carolina Press, 1993.

Plato. 1997. *Ion* . In Cooper 1997.

———. 1997. *Republic*. In Cooper 1997.

Purdy, Jedediah. 1999. *For Common Things: Irony, Trust, and Commitment in America Today*. New York: Knopf.

Rorty, Richard. 1979. *Philosophy and the Mirror of Nature*. Cambridge: Harvard University Press.

Sartre, Jean-Paul. 2003. *Being and Nothingness: An Essay on Phenomenological Ontology*. Translated by Hazel E. Barnes. New York: Routledge.

Sebeok, Thomas A., and Marcia E. Erickson, eds. 1984. *Carnivale!* Berlin: Mouton.

Sivananda, Sri Swami. 2000. *Philosophy of Dreams*. India: The Divine Life Society, 2000. http://www.dlshq.org.

Stavropoulos, Steven. 2003. *The Beginning of All Wisdom: Timeless Advice from the Ancient Greeks*. Cambridge: Da Capo.

Storey, John, ed. 2002. *Cultural Theory and Popular Culture: A Reader*. Second edition. Athens: University of Georgia Press.

Tyler, Steven. 2011. *Does the Noise in My Head Bother You? A Rock'n'Roll Memoir*. New York: HarperCollins.

Warnock, Mary, ed. 1974. *Utilitarianism and Other Writings*: *John Stuart Mill, Jeremy Bentham, and John Austin*. Harmondsworth: Penguin.

Žižek, Slavoj. *Looking Awry: An Introduction to Jacques Lacan through Popular Culture*. London: The MIT Press, 1992.

Index